A RISING PUBLIC VOICE
WOMEN IN POLITICS WORLDWIDE

A Rising Public Voice
Women in Politics Worldwide

Edited
and with an
Introduction
by Alida Brill

Foreword by
Gertrude Mongella

The Feminist Press
at The City University of New York
New York

Published 1995 by The Feminist Press at The City University of New York
311 East 94 Street, New York, NY 10128
99 98 97 96 95 5 4 3 2 1

Library of Congress Cataloging-in-Publication Data
A rising public voice : women in politics worldwide / edited and with
an introduction by Alida Brill.
    p. cm.
Includes bibliographical references.
ISBN 1-55861-110-X.—ISBN 1-55861-111-8 (alk. paper)
    1. Women in politics.   2 Women in public life.   I. Brill, Alida.
HQ1236.R57   1995
320'.082—dc20   95–13894
                                                                  CIP

The Feminist Press wishes to acknowledge the assistance of the United
Nations Department of Public Information in preparing this publication.
The views expressed are those of the authors and do not necessarily
reflect the position of the United Nations or its Member States.

This publication is made possible, in part, with public funds from the
New York State Council on the Arts. The Feminist Press is also grateful
to Sara Lee Schupf and to the John D. and Catherine T. MacArthur
Foundation, and for a major grant from an anonymous donor.

Cover Art, Design, and Typography by Ascienzo Design
Printed on acid-free paper in the United States of America

For
the endurance and strength
of our grandmothers,
the vision and the patience
of our mothers,
and to the dreams of our daughters,
we dedicate this book.

CONTENTS

List of Tables .... *ix*

Foreword, *Gertrude Mongella* .... *xi*

Acknowledgments .... *xiii*

Introduction, *Alida Brill* *1*

Part One
Reality Politics: Towards a Woman's Global Realpolitik

Not for Want of Trying: Women in Australian and
 New Zealand Politics, 1893-1994, *Janine Haines* 13

The Impact of German Unification on Women: Losses and Gains,
 Hanna Beate Schoepp-Schilling 27

A Conversation with Wu Qing, *Isabel Crook, Lu Dongxiao,
 and Lisa Stearns* 41

Political Women and Women's Politics in India, *Radha Kumar* ... 59

Blaga Dimitrova: A Voice for Change, *Valentina Stoev* 73

The Feminist behind the Spokeswoman: A Candid Talk with
 Hanan Ashwari, *Rabab Hadi* 79

Israeli Women in Two Voices: A Dialogue between Generations,
 Ilana Bet-El and Lilly Rivlin 87

Part Two
Paths to Power: The Political Is Also Personal

From Prison Cell to Parliament, *Thenjiwe Mtintso* 103

Mitsui Mariko: Feminist Assemblywoman, *Emiko Kaya* 119

Portugal: Daring to Be Different, *Maria de Lourdes Pintasilgo* .. 127

Profiles and Portraits
 Carol Moseley Braun 133
 Eugenia Charles 136
 Vigdís Finnbogadóttir 141
 Barbara Jordan 144
 Irina Khakamada 147
 Ann Richards 152
 Mary Robinson 155
 Margaret Thatcher 158
 Simone Veil 161

A Political Triple Whammy, *Diane Abbott* 165

Martin, What Should I Do Now? *Bella Abzug* 175

Part Three
Women Count: Why the Numbers Matter

The 30 Percent Quota Law: A Turning Point
for Women's Political Participation in Argentina,
Gloria Bonder and Marcela Nari 183

Women in Parliamentary Life, *Marilyn Waring* 195

From Movement to Government: Women's
Political Integration in Norway, *Hege Skjeie* 213

EMILY's List: Overcoming Barriers to Political Participation,
David Lauter 217

Part Four
Women Hold Up Half the Sky

Guatemala: A Story of Tragedy and Promise,
Rigoberta Menchú 229

The Dance of Life: Women and Human Rights in Chile,
Marjorie Agosín 233

Women, Information, and the Future: The Women of Kenya
and the Green Belt Movement, *Wangari Maathai* 241

Part Five
Tomorrow's Promise

Sultana's Dream, *Rokeya Sakhawat Hossain* 251

She Who Would Be King, *Ama Ata Aidoo* 261

Notes 267

Bibliography 275

Notes on Contributors 279

Permission Acknowledgments 285

LIST OF TABLES

Women in Australia's
Federal and State Parliaments 1994 14

Political Rights for Women: Australia and New Zealand 16

Percentage of women elected to the Knesset in Israel 92

Voting Rights Achieved by Country 209

Women Heads of State or
Government in the Twentieth Century 212

FOREWORD

Gertrude Mongella

As a former minister in the government of my native Tanzania, and in my current capacity as secretary-general for the United Nations Fourth World Conference on Women, I have been acutely aware of the importance of women's involvement in decision making at all levels. It is reasonable and just that women and men should have equal access to political power, yet women continue to constitute a minority in the decision-making arena, both nationally and internationally.

Today, women are more politically active and visible than ever before. Many governments have established special offices for women's issues and taken steps to increase the numbers of women in parliaments. But in spite of the general increase in political participation by women over the past twenty years, the overall numbers of women at the highest levels of government remain unacceptably low. Women's representation at the cabinet level is less than half that in national legislative bodies, and nearly one hundred countries have no women in parliament at all. There are, of course, encouraging exceptions, many of them in the developing countries.

The Fourth World Conference on Women will pay particular attention to the gains women have made in the political arena, and to what steps are necessary in order for their role to be further strengthened. The delegates will take a critical look at power sharing, analyzing obstacles to women's advancement and recommending action to overcome them. It is my hope that nations will be persuaded to address gender imbalances with greater urgency, for it is through increased participation of women in politics at all levels—local, national, and international—that women and men will be best able to work effectively together to meet the challenges and demands of the coming century.

ACKNOWLEDGMENTS

All anthologies are collaborative efforts, and this is especially true for this volume. It would have been impossible to bring this book to closure without the hard work and commitment of many people. First, special thanks to all the contributors to this book, who took valuable time from very busy schedules to make this volume possible.

The founder and director of The Feminist Press, Florence Howe, was extremely supportive and understanding about the needs and requirements of such an undertaking. Susannah Driver, senior editor at The Press, was an extraordinary friend to this book, as well as a sensitive and thoughtful editor. She worked tirelessly in the fulfillment of the many tasks that needed to be performed when producing an international collection. To put it succinctly, this book could not have become a reality without the good judgment, good humor, wisdom, and energy of Susannah Driver, for which I am personally deeply appreciative. The staff at The Feminist Press, especially Sara Clough, Alyssa Colton, Tina Malaney, and Bettina Mohr, enabled the completion of this book under a very tight time schedule, and Dennis Ascienzo gave us this beautiful design in record time.

The contributions of Ulrike Bode deserve special mention. She put aside important work of her own to come to the aid of this project. She suggested the essay on India and accomplished the task of acquiring it and others with great ingenuity and resourcefulness.

Kathleen Paton, of whom it has been appropriately said that she "could research the shell off an egg," did just that. In a very short period of time she put together the materials for the "Women First" facts, as well as working on the research of a number of profiles, locating photographs, and other tasks too numerous to enumerate.

Levis Guy was involved in the preliminary research stages of the project and conducted the interview with Dame Eugenia Charles.

Frances Madeson and Christopher O'Connell provided research for the profiles section.

Many other individuals helped in a myriad of ways, from suggesting and helping to locate important contacts, to helping with translations, transcription, and similar work. Heartfelt thanks are expressed to: Christina Gilmartin, Helen P. Young, Isabel Crook, Lisa Stearns, Li Xiaojiang, Xao Ma, Annette Rubinstein, Marilyn Romain, Radhika Lal, Lida Junghans, Hongjin Kang, Sucheta Mazumdar, Frances Fox Piven, Colette Shulman, Martina Vandenberg, Robin Morgan, Joann Vanek, Charles Hale, Minor Sinclair.

At the United Nations, Tina Jorgensen was an early advocate of this project and she and Joanna Piucci guided it through the various offices there with practiced skill.

Steven Scheuer was, as always, patient and tolerant beyond any reasonable expectation, and generous in full measure. His unflagging loyalty and his determined faith and belief in a world of equality and kindness are the foundation for any endeavor I attempt. Lani Reynolds and Professor Rebecca Klatch saw me through difficult passages and I thank them for their valuable friendship and assistance.

Finally, this volume cannot be, nor was it intended as, a replacement for much of the other exemplary scholarly and analytical work on women in public life previously produced and published. Each of us owes a debt to the work of scholars, professionals, activists, and writers in our own regions and countries who have gone before to lay paths to understanding. I am personally indebted to the work of many, far too many, in fact, to list all of them. However, I have been deeply influenced and guided by the work of three feminist thinkers, who bear individual mention here. Dr. Joann Vanek, a sociologist, wrote the first article ever published about the meaning of housework. It was this article that began a new way of envisioning women's work—teaching us that not always did the hard work of women get counted as meaningful. Joann Vanek's mission to couple theory with meaningful statistical presentations about the conditions of women globally has informed much of my own thinking about the status of women. Since 1980 Dr. Vanek has been a part of the international secretariat of the United Nations. As a focal point for work on gender statistics, she has continued her commitment to, and work on, projects related to women worldwide. As the chief of the Gender Statistics Unit of the United Nations Statistical Division she coordinated the production of the first United Nations global statistical report on women, *The World's Women 1970-1990: Trends and Statistics*. A second volume of this important publication is now available. It is precisely because of work such as this that we have begun to see where the missing women really are, not just in public life but throughout the areas that matter—from career paths to health conditions of women and girls, survival rates, education, and of course, women's work in global economics. *The World's Women*, volumes I and II, contains many essential facts and data and should become as common a presence on both personal and public library shelves as dictionaries.

The work of the political scientist Barbara Nelson has been a touchstone for me throughout the last decade. Her insights into the "politics of everyday life" have guided many of my own conclusions about the paradoxes of women's place in a political world. With Najma Chowdhury and an able team of researchers, Nelson produced in 1994 one of the most important and complete research reference books on the topic at hand. *Women and Politics Worldwide* should be under the arm of every one of us working toward the world the novelist Ama Ata Aidoo envisions. It is a portable world congress of women.

Finally, I could not begin to edit a volume about global perspectives on women in politics without acknowledging a personal tribute to the early work of Robin Morgan. In 1970 Robin Morgan transformed the rhetoric of the women's movement with her ground-breaking and now classic anthology *Sisterhood Is Powerful*. In 1984, after thirteen years of research, editing, and networking, she published *Sisterhood Is Global: The International Women's Movement Anthology*. This volume assembled research about women in eighty countries—and combined both statistical and original essays from women in each country. In many cases, the voices and the data she included were appearing and being heard for the first time. The book continues to be a relevant resource and the work she initiated continues under the auspices of The Sisterhood Is Global Institute. Morgan's work made the world for women a more accessible place, making sisterhood both global and powerful.

Alida Brill
New York, New York

IWTC/ASW

Women Hold Up Half the Sky
International Women's Tribune Centre, Inc., New York, NY

INTRODUCTION
Alida Brill

"A woman's place is in the House
...and in the Senate."

—*American feminist proverb*

I was a college student before it occurred to me that women might have a real chance at becoming public, political figures. It happened the way these revelations often happen, with one action, in one moment, but that life snapshot remains etched in my mind. While I was rushing to class, another student called to me, from a table in the "quad," "Don't you want to sign up and help Shirley Chisholm's campaign?" I put on a political button that said "Hit the Chisholm Trail—Elect Shirley Chisholm President"[1] and I have never been the same. Shirley Chisholm, an African-American woman, ran for president of the United States when the power was still overwhelmingly entrenched in white, male pockets of privilege and entitlement. I hit the "trail" and have continued on, in one way or another, ever since. The campaign, although unsuccessful in nominating Ms. Chisholm for president, nonetheless was successful, as many first steps are, because it untied the tongues of many women, and forced us to confront our own strength and the world of possibility that could lie before us, if we moved from a more private sphere into the world of public and political life.

Despite the occurrence of a late-twentieth-century women's movement (a rebirth of feminism in some countries as well as new movements for social change in others), much is still wrong with the picture of women in government. We are missing from the official portraits of government in most places. Yet, women are ready, qualified, and eager to serve in decision-making posts in each region, country, city, and town on the face of the globe. Sadly, we still occupy only a shamefully small number of high-level jobs. Even in countries where women have been enfranchised through suffrage and where we have had the ability to run for office for the better part of the century, the statistics are still shockingly tiny. (There are a few points on the world map where this is not true, but only a few.)

In both the developed and developing worlds, women, who constitute more than half the world's population, still account for only single-digit numbers as heads of state, heads of government, and other top leadership roles. Among elected representatives there has been considerable progress but the numbers change by gradual increments. As Barbara Nelson and Najma Chowdhury concluded in their excellent book, *Women and Politics Worldwide*, "in no country do women have political status, access or influence equal to men's." As we enter these last years of the twentieth century, these are unacceptable facts. To many of us it is an often enraging predicament, especially coupled with the grim fact that the enfranchisement of women is still not completely universal. Although the struggle to achieve political parity is a difficult and exhausting battle, we remain unbent.

All of these caveats and roadblocks to our participation notwithstanding, we nonetheless come together in the United Nations Fourth World Conference on Women in Beijing, China, in 1995 to celebrate our achievement, endurance, perseverance, and courage. We also come to assess the work ahead of us. In many ways this book of international collaboration is a celebration of the victory of our journey. We recognize that struggle is connected to victory. While the journey is far from completed, we note that women have moved into places of power and politics that would have been hard to envision a few short years ago. Today, girls coming of age in virtually all regions can imagine that they might grow up to be a prime minister, a president, a member of parliament, and the like. In short, the dreams of a young woman today incorporate the belief that she can be an influential member of her nation's government. While vast inequities remain, this book tells new stories and looks forward to a future different from the past.

1986: CORAZÓN AQUINO IS FIRST WOMAN ELECTED PRESIDENT OF THE PHILIPPINES.

For many women the path to power has been difficult and even onerous. Women continue to shoulder responsibilities at home as well as fulfilling their public duties. The eternal balancing act women must perform between the domestic sphere and the public sphere is dramatically evident in the lives of the women portrayed here. A public woman is one of the most crucial weapons we have in the war against stereotype and gender bias because it is a fundamental challenge to the assumptions about gender organization and sex-role assignment. The famous British feminist thinker Virginia Woolf wrote in *A Room of One's Own* of a "magnifying mirror" women have traditionally offered men, by which men could then see their images at least twice their actual size. With the advent of more and more women living lives previously reserved for men, men, especially those in powerful positions, have had to see themselves in a realistic mirror reflection—simply their own size—not glorified and magnified. Perhaps this is one of the reasons that in many places men have fought so hard to keep women out of official realms.

During the many centuries that women were left out of politics one way that some women came close to power was as the spouse of a political man. In that role, custom and tradition defined behavior. Increasingly even the role of the first lady is in a process of transformation, as one can see in the case of Hillary Rodham Clinton, the first lady of the United States. She is a professionally trained lawyer, has ideas about major issues, and has been a leader in her own right. Mrs. Clinton has played a visible and vocal role as first lady, in a style and manner not seen since the days of Eleanor Roosevelt, who was first lady from 1933 until 1945. Mrs. Clinton's desire to be herself and to offer her considerable intelligence to the nation has been acclaimed and supported by some. Unfortunately, many Americans are very threatened at the appearance of this first lady, who is as able as her president-husband, and who might once have been considered "presidential timber" herself. Thus, she has been the target of severe and often unfair criticism and derision by both the public and the press. Betty Friedan, one of the founders of the current American feminist movement, was so angered by the "double standard" to which Mrs. Clinton was being subjected to that she wrote an editorial, which was widely printed in newspapers across the country. "Stop Pillorying Hillary," Friedan implored. The unhappiness with Hillary Clinton continues; she is a victim of deeply held resentments and has essentially been punished because she has refused to hide the power of her mind. She stands as a symbol of the difficulty of the personal and the political. Mrs. Clinton has attempted to destroy the cultural limitations that have diminished the personhood of numerous first ladies, but the traditional assignment of that role has proven too rigid to break through. Yet, she represents another kind of "new public woman" and as such reminds us how difficult it is to be given a voice—as a serious person—when wedged inside a circumscribed and narrowly defined gender role.

Throughout this volume you will hear the voices of women who have had to fight to gain acceptance, who must constantly remind men in power of the importance of their presence and of the equality of peoples. Is there a woman's voice in politics which is unique? Does it really make a difference that women have achieved political office? Would it be just as good if there were more men in politics worldwide who were sympathetic to the woman's agenda? In the first two instances the answer is yes! In the last, a resounding no! While it is critical to have enlightened men in power who are not contemptuous of women's issues, which are basic human issues, it is not the same. Without our own voices being heard inside the public arena and halls of government policy and debate, we are without the right of accountability—a basic entitlement of those who are governed. Neither do we have any assurance that concerns crucial to our well-being will be addressed. This does not mean that every woman leader has taken a point of view or has an ideology that has been good for women. In large part, however, the woman's voice has been one that has worked for issues and in areas that have often been forgotten or overlooked or misunderstood when there has not been a viable female presence in a vast array of governmental levels and positions. Questions of reproductive health and its choices, general areas of concern to women's employment and education equity, equality of opportunities, the occurrence of femicide, nutrition and health of children, and the well-being of the environment, to name only a small number, are issues that have been vigorously taken up by women internationally.

WOMEN FIRST

1992: CALIFORNIA ELECTS TWO WOMEN, DIANNE FEINSTEIN AND BARBARA BOXER, TO THE U.S. SENATE.

Simply stated, ensuring a "women-friendly" country is most efficaciously achieved when women have access to the corridors of power, policy, and change. This is not to suggest, however, that the role of the political activist, grassroots organizer, protester, or dissident should be overlooked or underestimated. Frequently it has been the work of women in movements for change, who are seen as "outsiders" to the official work of governments, who have led the way to social legislation that has remedied unfair or harmful practices. In the course of the lives of many political women, it has been their work in areas outside the official public world where they have first received their training as leaders. A woman can be an outsider one day and in power the next, as the lives of some of our contributors attest.

To some extent this book has been organized in the manner in which women's lives have been organized and lived. Taking up the real world of politics and examining it with analytically open eyes is the task of Part One, "Reality Politics." In this opening section the problems and sacrifices of the public woman are contrasted to its rewards and triumphs. Janine Haines begins this section with a powerful case study, the examination of women in Australian and New Zealand politics from 1893 to 1994. Her essay, "Not For Want of Trying," takes the reader through the paradoxes of this region. Despite the fact that women have been in political life in Australia since 1903 and in New Zealand since 1918, women still only comprise 20 percent of the elected national and local offices. (When seen in a comparative global context, however, the 20 percent figure is, in fact, better than most countries!) Haines describes the historical legacy as well as speaking from a personal perspective, having been elected to the Australian Parliament in 1978.

The euphoria resulting from the collapse of the Berlin Wall dividing Germany from itself was followed by the need for some extremely difficult and delicate work. Hanna Beate Schoepp-Schilling was the first director general for the Department of Women's Affairs in the Ministry of Youth, Family, Women, and Health. In "The Impact of German Unification on Women" Schoepp-Schilling provides a careful and insightful analysis of the role and experience of women in rebuilding a united Germany and in influencing its policy.

China, whose culture is one of the oldest in the world, is home to Deputy Wu Qing, who sits in the Municipal People's Congress of Beijing as an elected member. In the conversation recorded for this volume, Wu Qing shares her own views about women in Chinese politics, about their achievements, and about accomplishments and obstacles that have to be overcome.

In "Political Women and Women's Politics in Asia," author Radha Kumar states that "the South Asian predilection for women premiers has so often been commented upon that most Indian feminists merely snort at its mention." Yet, Kumar fully recognizes the stunning fact that the four chief countries inside the subcontinent, India, Pakistan, Bangladesh, and Sri Lanka, have all had women prime ministers. Kumar draws parallels between the contemporary and historical perspectives of the region.

Bulgaria has experienced great upheaval and transition in recent years. Blaga Dimitrova is a noted Bulgarian writer and poet, who became vice president in the "new" Bulgaria. Of her personal journey, Dimitrova says: "...in Bulgaria, politics and poetry are linked by tradition." Dimitrova's journey from poet of protest to leader is a personal story of courage and many private transitions.

W O M E N F I R S T

1993: AGATHE UWILINGIYIMANA IS THE FIRST WOMAN TO BECOME PRIME MINISTER OF RWANDA (SHE WAS ASSASSINATED IN 1994).

In the Middle East, confusion, hostility, and sorrow are often present. For this most volatile region, where misunderstanding and ancient and current conflict are the hallmark of its history, the Palestinian and the Israeli contributions stand side by side. They so appear in the hope that they will stand together as a metaphor for hope. Hanan Ashrawi was the only female spokesperson for the Palestinian delegation to the Middle East peace talks. In "The Feminist behind the Spokeswoman" she talks about her people, the promise of peace, and the importance of dialogue. In the next selection, a documentary filmmaker from a seventh-generation Jerusalem family, Lilly Rivlin, has a dialogue with a younger Israeli woman, Ilana Bet-El, who has been an active voice in Israeli public life. "Israeli Women in Two Voices" illuminates the importance of telling our stories to each generation in order to continue to grow, and to learn.

What are the paths to power? That is the question asked of each contributor in this second part of the book. How does a woman find herself in a public life? In some cases, the political life has followed a great tragedy, such as the death, sometimes by assassination, of a family member. In those cases, as in others, women have harnessed a terrible personal pain into the productive energy of a public life. The interplay between the domestic and the public sphere of a woman's life can deter or guide her path. "Paths to Power" profiles the many routes to politics, as well as drawing portraits of some of the world's leaders.

In "From Prison Cell to Parliament" South African Thenjiwe Mtintso recounts an exhilarating, frustrating, and wondrous journey of South African women from days of imprisonment to days of parliament. She describes the extremely difficult and delicate balance of gender organization and roles and public life: "...it is a far cry from the experience of exile and imprisonment, for those who dared to oppose the apartheid regime."

Stereotypes are easy to form, difficult to dismantle. Japan is an example of a country where the assumption has been that women have not been able to achieve much public prominence. Breaking stereotypes within her own country, as well as outside her native Japan, Mariko Mitsui, assemblywoman and self-proclaimed feminist, tells of her role in working against Japan's discriminatory practices. Maria de Lourdes Pintasilgo broke many stereotypes when she became Portugal's first woman prime minister in 1979; in "Daring to be Different" she examines the ways in which she was perceived and why it mattered that a woman served as the head of the government. Diane Abbott of the Labour Party has all the ingredients to be, as she describes it, the "triple whammy" in the British House of Parliament. As the only black female MP, Abbott illuminates her childhood and the paths she took to overcome what appeared to others to be insurmountable barriers, as well as to break through cultural stereotypes. The result is an inspiring story of strength, courage, and empowerment.

Much has been written and said about the difficulties of combining marriage and family with politics. Usually the focus is on the frequently daunting task of trying to educate the men in one's family (especially husbands) about the importance of the life outside the home. Not often do we stop to look at the exception to that; that is to say, rarely do we commend the private life of a political woman because that private life aided the public one.

Bella Abzug, one of the first "trail blazers" in American political life, was elected to the United States Congress in 1970. Abzug, long a familiar face in world forums, tirelessly working for women, for peace, for the environment, offers a deeply personal essay about the strong influence of her lifelong marriage on her successful work. This moving document chronicles the power of a positive partnership. Written shortly after the death of Abzug's husband it is a resounding tribute to the integrity of her life, and an affirmation to the query: Is there such a thing as a feminist husband? Meet Mr. Martin Abzug.

We count for something, we, the world's women. We matter; we exist and as our numbers multiply our rising voices will be heard in more places and on more issues. "Women Count" gets down to the business at hand, in other words, the tally. Where are we on this journey? Our increased presence did not happen magically, and certainly not by accident. (Global milestones have been noted throughout the book, labelled as "women first" in a parody of a phrase from another era.)[2] Four important selections in this section also begin to fill in our map of discovery and point us to the places on that map which are still uncharted. Gloria Bonder, secretary of state on women's issues and public policies in Argentina's Ministry of Education, and coauthor Marcella Nari report on that country's *lev de cupos,* or quota law, which requires, by legal mandate, the inclusion of women in government. They talk about the development of this law and the fight for gender parity in Argentina. Marilyn Waring, former member of the New Zealand Parliament and author of the ground-breaking book *If Women Counted* looks at the history of New Zealand's women leaders and the lessons they teach us all. Norway is one of the bright spots on the map where in 1986 the prime minister appointed eight women to a cabinet of eighteen and where each cabinet since then has included no less than 40 percent women. Hege Skjeie shows why these numbers make a difference in "From Movement to Government: Women's Political Integration in Norway."

W O M E N   F I R S T

1988: BENAZIR BHUTTO IS FIRST WOMAN ELECTED PRIME MINISTER OF PAKISTAN.

In a country as developed, wealthy, and capitalistic as the United States, money is the commodity that often does the counting. Money matters here in my homeland, it matters too much. Some political analysts have said, in criticism, that the United States has the best Congress that money can buy. Attempts at election campaign reform have not really been successful, because we are a country oriented toward the accumulation of personal wealth and where the power of the political purse is directed toward its preferred source of information—the television set. Feminist scholars of American politics have long realized that women do not win more elections partially because it is so difficult for the average woman (who does not have personal wealth to spend) to raise significant funds to campaign nationally or across her region or state. It is evident that when women candidates do raise money successfully, it is usually too late in their campaigns to make a difference. An American heiress has decided that it is time to correct that, so that even if the inherent corruptness of the system cannot be eradicated, at least women can have a chance to get out on the political playing field. Using the concept of the importance of getting money into a campaign in its beginning, not ending, stages, Ellen Malcolm invented a new organization and named it EMILY's List. "EMILY" stands for "early money is like yeast." She formed a national "political pac" that enables women across the country to support progressive Democratic women. David Lauter, a noted journalist, interviewed Ms. Malcolm and analyzes the role of Emily's List in "Overcoming Barriers to Political Participation."

It is said that if all the women in the world, at one moment, screamed out their pain and their frustration, the entire world would come apart from the sheer force of that sound. It is an old dilemma for those of us engaged in the business of social and political change. Is our glass half empty or is it half full? During the Chinese People's Revolution, another sort of slogan was said about the weight of women's power—"women hold up half the sky." And so this refrain labels the section about women's struggle for change in the world. More often than men, women begin their political careers as activists, or as agitators for social reform and justice. Although the main focus of this book is on women in official decision-making roles, it is only appropriate to highlight a tiny sampling of women involved in the struggle for social change worldwide. It is also well to remember that yesterday's exile, prisoner, or activist can be tomorrow's leader. Rigoberta Menchu received the Nobel Peace Prize in 1992 for her work with, and on behalf of, the native peoples of her country, Guatemala. The poet Marjorie Agosín has been living in exile, where she continues to fight against the military dictatorship in Chile. Agosín exemplifies the transforming power of women's collective pain. Through language, dance, and action, the women of Chile in their despair have fought for human rights in their "Dance of Life."

WOMEN FIRST

1993:
ANSON CHAN IS FIRST WOMAN, ALSO THE FIRST CHINESE PERSON, TO BE APPOINTED CHIEF SECRETARY, THE NUMBER TWO POSITION IN HONG KONG.

The name of Wangari Maathai, from Kenya, is virtually synonymous with the Green Belt Movement. In her essay, taken from a previously delivered speech, she talks about the work of the organization. Maathai draws the parallel between the politics of the world and global environmental work.

In our waking hours, and in our dreams, we envision new worlds. We see an end to inequality and inequity, we hear our voices rising and see our numbers increasing. These visions of a better world for our daughters and our granddaughters are given voice through the actions of the world's women leaders and activists and also by the words and pictures of our artists and writers. Women writers tell the stories of our lives, record our histories, chronicle our triumphs, defeats, and struggles. They help us imagine ourselves beyond a time of unfairness; they keep us from becoming fearful or paralyzed. Women writers give us new worlds, and provide us with spectacles with which to view these new worlds. We end this volume with the fictional stories by two remarkable women writers. In 1905 Rokeya Sakhawat Hossain wrote a visionary tale which was published in the English language in Madras. Creating in her story a place called "Ladyland," in which women rule, avert war, eradicate disease, and harness solar power for everyone's use, Hossain has helped generations of subsequent readers envision a world of liberty and equality.

Thinking about how to end this volume was not in the first instance an easy task. Who should sound that all-important last word? Once all the contributions were in, it was clear that only one voice could force us forward into a truly new world. The renowned writer Ama Ata Aidoo, from Ghana, takes us in a fantasy to the year 2026 in the Confederation of African States—and to its first president, a woman. In "She Who Would Be King," Aidoo has produced the most believable of tales and it is through her prism that we must continually remind ourselves to look. It is the hope imbedded in each selection of this volume, perhaps best illuminated by the radiance of Aidoo's writing, that each of us might become a vehicle for the changes that must be made. Perhaps it will be the case that books like this will eventually cease to be published because the incidence of women in politics will be so normal, so frequent, so very, very ordinary that a commentary upon our presence might well prove unnecessary. Until that time, our voices will not be silenced and our work will continue.

People's Deputy Wu Qing, People's
Republic of China (© Gang Chen)

Vice President Blaga Dimitrova,
Bulgaria

Senator Carol Moseley Braun,United States
(Courtesy of the office of Senator Carol Moseley Braun)

Prime Minister Eugenia Charles,
Dominica (© Ruby Mera)

President Vigdís Finnbogadóttir, Iceland
(Courtesy of the Consulate General of Iceland)

Member of Parliament Diane Abbott, Great Britain (Courtesy of the office of Diane Abbott MP)

Governor Ann Richards, United States (Courtesy of the office of Ann Richards)

The official photograph of the heads of state or government attending the World Summit for Children, United Nations Headquarters, September 29 and 30, 1990. President Violeta Chamorro of Nicaragua, Prime Minister Eugenia Charles of Dominica, and Prime Minister Margaret Thatcher of Great Britain are the three women in the group of seventy-one leaders. (UNICEF/Eastman Kodak Company)

Nobel Peace Prize recipient Rigoberta Menchú, Guatemala (UNICEF/5437/Ruby Mera)

President Mary Robinson, Ireland
(Courtesy of the Department of Foreign Affairs, Dublin)

Prime Minister Margaret Thatcher, United Kingdom
(World Summit for Children Photo by R. Mera)

Writer and Minister of Education
Ama Ata Aidoo, Ghana
(© 1993 Diana Van Maasdijk)

PART ONE

REALITY POLITICS
TOWARDS A WOMAN'S
GLOBAL REALPOLITIK

NOT FOR WANT OF TRYING
Women in Australian and New Zealand Politics 1893–1994

Janine Haines

The first day I took my seat in the Senate chamber of Australia's federal parliament, the place was awash with testosterone. It was February 1978; fifty-seven of the sixty-four senators were male; the clerk of the Senate was male. No women were even among the attendants moving quietly around the chamber providing senators with the papers and documents they needed to deal with the business of the day. The situation in the House of Representatives was worse. Not one woman sat among the 124 male MPs, although women had been elected to that chamber in the past and would be again. In those years (the late 1970s), every important political and parliamentary position in federal politics in Australia was held by men (with one exception—the minister for social security, Senator Margaret Guilfoyle). All other ministers, the speaker of the House, the president of the Senate, and the governor-general of Australia were men. The picture was little better across the Tasman Sea in New Zealand's unicameral parliament: the prime minister and the governor-general were both male, there were no women in the ministry, and only five of the ninety-two members of New Zealand's House of Representatives were women. This scenario was replicated in Australia's six state parliaments. As a federation of six autonomous states and two territories (which share legislative and constitutional powers with the Commonwealth government), Australia is one of the world's younger nations, having been given independence from Britain in 1901. All states except Queensland have bicameral parliaments with governments formed in the lower house, with the upper house acting as a "house of review." At the end of the 1970s none of the states had ever had a female premier; very few women had been elevated to state government ministries; no state government had ever appointed a woman as governor of the state; and neither of the territories had elected a woman to the position of head of government. As with the federal parliament, the number of female MPs in any state parliament in 1978 could generally be counted on the fingers of one hand, although the figures were to improve over time. In South Australia, for example, the number of women in the state's house of assembly rose from two in 1977 to eight in 1994, and the situation was much the same in the other state parliaments as well as in the federal parliament. (See Table 1.)

Table 1
WOMEN IN AUSTRALIA'S
FEDERAL AND STATE PARLIAMENTS 1994

Parliament	Upper House			Lower House		
	No. MPs	No. Women	%	No. MPs	No. Women	%
Australia	64	17	26.6	147	13	8.8
New Zealand	-	-	-	99	21	21.2
New South Wales	42	15	35.7	98	10	10.2
Victoria	44	6	13.6	88	9	10.2
South Australia	22	7	31.8	47	8	17.0
Western Australia	34	4	11.8	57	10	17.5
Queensland	-	-	-	89	13	14.6
Tasmania	17	0	0	35	8	22.9

The number of women in state parliaments in Australia is still, on average, less than 20 percent, although even this low figure is better than in federal parliament where, in 1994, women made up just 13 percent of senators and members. This tendency of women to opt for a career in state politics is not surprising. Because of the distances most members of Parliament have to travel to Canberra (the site of Australia's federal parliament) during sessions, and the time it requires away from home, national politics is less attractive and less feasible for women than it is for men. This is particularly the case for married women with families. Few men have ever been prepared to take on, as women traditionally have done, the added workload involved when a spouse is absent due to the pursuit of a career. As a consequence, those Australian women who have both political aspirations and family responsibilities have generally chosen the relatively less disruptive life of a state MP. The significantly higher number of women in most state parliaments in Australia compared to the number of women in Australia's federal parliament is also due, in part, to the fact that state parliaments are not regarded as being as important as their federal counterparts. Therefore, political party machines are more likely to countenance the selection of women to winnable state seats than to winnable federal seats. In neither Australia (at either state or federal level) nor New Zealand does the number of women in Parliament, or the time it took for them to be elected, reflect the fact that women constitute over 50 percent of the population.

The paucity of women in parliaments, both historically and currently, however, has meant that legislative programs and priorities have generally reflected the experiences and needs of men, rather than those of women. For example, until the late 1960s women were paid less than men for doing the same work. Furthermore, married women were not classified as permanent employees in the state public service and would not be employed by the Commonwealth Public Service. Until 1975 a man in Australia could sue for divorce on the grounds of a single act of adultery by his wife, while a woman had to prove persistent adultery and either excessive cruelty or desertion on the part of her husband to get a divorce. And, married women could not be employed in Australia's Commonwealth Public Service.

When women were finally elected to parliaments in both Australia and New Zealand they actively campaigned for changes to laws, both written and unwritten, that discriminated against women. In the 1940s, Enid Lyons, the first woman to sit in Australia's House of Representatives, persuaded her government to pay child endowments to women to offset the cost of rearing a family. Elizabeth McCombs's first actions as a newly elected MP in New Zealand were to address the Parliament on the need for better employment opportunities for girls and to advocate that the marriage age be raised. McCombs also supported the introduction of invalid pensions. She was aware of the salacious interest some members of the public and press took in some rape and divorce cases and fought for an amendment to the law so that some cases could be heard *in camera*. Since then other women in and out of parliaments in Australia and New Zealand have successfully campaigned for better pay and working conditions for women (including a provision that women could not be dismissed from their jobs when they became pregnant), fairer divorce laws, provision of government-subsidized child care facilities, and changes to the law so that rape occurring in marriage became a criminal offense.

Why, then, given the example set by these political pioneers, did so few women follow in their footsteps? The reasons are many and varied but one thing is certain: the paucity of female MPs in the parliaments of those two countries is not for want of women trying. In both New Zealand and Australia women have stood as candidates for their national parliaments as soon as they were legally entitled to do so in 1903 in the case of Australia and 1919 in New Zealand. Many stood as "independents" (as did many men), but an increasing number over the years stood as candidates for the major political parties. Yet, it took until 1933 before the first woman took her seat in New Zealand's Parliament, and a further ten years before the first women were elected to Australia's federal parliament (although a few women had been elected to some state parliaments). Female candidates in Australia from 1943 onward were one-tenth as likely to be successful as male candidates, regardless of which party they stood for. This success-rate disparity, also evident in New Zealand, is all the more ironic given the fact that women in Australia have had the dual rights to vote and to be elected to their national parliament longer than in any other nation. (See Table 2.)

Table 2
POLITICAL RIGHTS FOR WOMEN
AUSTRALIA AND NEW ZEALAND

Place	Right to vote	Right to stand	1st Elected to Upper House	Name	1st Elected to Lower House	Name
New Zealand	1893	1918	1946	**Mary Anderson**	1933	**Elizabeth McCombs** **Mary Dreaver**
South Aust	1895	1895	1959	Jessie Cooper	1959	Joyce Steele
West Aust	1899	1920	1954	Ruby Hutchison	1921	Edith Cowan
Australia	**1902**	**1902**	**1943**	**Dorothy Tagney**	**1943**	**Enid Lyons**
New South Wales	1902	1918	1931	Ellen Webster	1925	Millicent Preston Stanley
Tasmania	1903	1921	1948	Margaret McIntyre	1955	Amelia Best
Queensland	1905	1918	n/a	Old Parliament is unicameral	1929	Irene Longman
Victoria	1908	1923	1979	Gracia Baylor	1933	Millie Peacock

New Zealand's Upper House (legislative council) consisted of members appointed by the government of the day. Women were first entitled to be members in 1941. The first women were appointed in 1946 and the council was abolished in 1951.

Women are also three times more likely to be elected to upper houses in Australia than to lower houses. This is largely because, with the exception of Tasmania[1], lower houses consist of MPs representing single member electorates while upper house MPs are elected in proportion to the vote their parties get within a multimember electorate. Men with political aspirations are more likely to "share" political power with women in a multimember electoral system such as the Senate than to surrender power altogether by giving women access to a significant number of winnable single-member electorates.

Furthermore, unlike the United States Senate, which is seen as a house of considerable power and influence, the Australian Senate is regarded as a house of secondary importance. This is partially due to the fact that the prime minister has traditionally been a member of the House of Representatives and partially because the number of senators for each party has no impact on which party forms the government. That right, and the power that goes with it, is the prerogative of the party that wins the largest number of the House of Representative's seats. Nonetheless, the Australian Senate is not the "unrepresentative swill" the prime minister, Mr. Keating, called it in 1994—if for no other reason than that the number of women in the Australian Senate is greater than that in the House making it, if only marginally, a more accurate reflection of the population at large.

Women were spectacularly unsuccessful in running for Parliament for decades, but that fact had nothing to do with inadequacies or deficiencies in their intellect, ability, or commitment to a political cause. Instead, it lay and still lies with the attitude of the men who run the party machines. Many of these men would privately agree with a Western Australian male member of a 1992 Liberal Party preselection panel, who told a hopeful female candidate that he did not believe women should be members of Parliament.

This attitude still prevails among many members of the preselection panels in Australia. During the 1993 election campaign, the Australian prime minister made many statements regarding the need for women to have a greater say in setting policy priorities. In the 1990 and 1993 federal elections, however, the two main political parties, the Labor Party and the Liberal Party, ran female candidates for seats that the other side were assured of winning; the ploy effectively ensured that the women would not be elected and thus could have little say regarding legislative programs. The second largest group of female candidates were placed in marginal seats (that is, seats in which only a small shift in voter allegiance will change the seat from one party to another). MPs who represent such vulnerable seats spend most of their time between elections trying to shore up voter support in order not to lose the next time around. They are thus unlikely to be competing for time-consuming "promotion" positions such as the chair of a high profile committee or a ministerial portfolio. The smallest number of seats for which women in one of the major parties were candidates were those that their own side were assured of winning. (The phenomenon of preselection bias by seat type and its impact on women with political aspirations is less clearly defined in New Zealand where voting is not compulsory but it nonetheless has an impact on how many women are elected in that country, as well.)

When women are elected, they are often resented and accused of being tokens. I witnessed one such unprovoked attack by a male opposition senator on a female minister in 1989. The man in question was mid-way through a thoroughly uninspiring speech when he suddenly leaned across his desk, waved his hand in the direction of the seat of the minister for local government, Senator Margaret Reynolds (who was not in the Senate chamber at the time), and announced that she was "on the front bench not because of the number of neurones she can put together but because of the number of chromosomes she has." None of her male colleagues who were in the Senate chamber at the time so much as murmured a dissent.

Given these kinds of attitudes, it is perhaps not surprising that, despite the leadership shown in extending political rights to women, the number of women in Australia's federal parliament is still barely above the world average of 10.1 percent (a mere 3,626 of the world's 35,884 members of parliament, 10.1 percent, are women).[2] Nevertheless, it is ironic to see the disregard political parties in these two southern hemisphere countries, which nearly a century ago led the world in the enfranchisement of women, have for the talents, interests, and experiences of women!

Although some states in the United States as well as on the Isle of Man had given at least some women the right to vote prior to 1893,

WOMEN FIRST

1893: NEW ZEALAND IS THE FIRST COUNTRY IN THE WORLD IN WHICH WOMEN GAIN THE VOTE.

New Zealand set an international precedent that year when it became the first nation in the world to give women the right to vote *on the same grounds as men,* rather than restricting the franchise to women who owned property. In December 1894, the South Australian Parliament broke more new ground when it passed legislation giving women not only the right to vote, but also the right to be members of Parliament. The bill took effect in March 1895 and South Australian women voted for the first time in the 1896 election, although no women stood as candidates. Indeed, it was not until 1918 that the first women stood for election to the South Australian Parliament. It would take forty more years before a woman was actually elected—and then only after she had appeared before the full bench of the supreme court in that state to prove that she was a "person" under the state's Constitution Act. Fortunately for Jessie Cooper, the 1929 privy council decision conferring "personhood" on Canadian women so that they could be appointed to Canada's Senate had set a precedent, and the South Australian court duly declared Mrs. Cooper a real person, and not just a woman.

Western Australia also gave women the vote (but not the right to become members of Parliament) in 1899. The actions of those two states led Australia's first federal government, elected in 1901, to insert in the Electoral Act of 1902 a clause giving all white women over twenty-one the right to vote and to stand as candidates in federal elections. A much less enlightened position was taken with regard to the voting rights of Australia's indigenous population: aboriginal women, like aboriginal men, were not entitled to vote in or stand for the 1901 federal election unless they had the right to vote in state elections—which for women was the case only in South Australia and Western Australia. From 1902 until 1962 Australia's electoral laws barred aborigines (whether male or female) from voting in federal elections unless, as required under Sn 41 of the Australian Constitution, they had the right to vote in state elections, or, as of 1949, they had been members of one of the armed forces.

Those who hoped that the newly won rights to vote and stand for Parliament in the newly established nation would lead to an influx of women into Australia's Senate and House of Representatives were doomed to disappointment. As in New Zealand, it would take decades before women in Australia were elected to federal parliament, and the number of female MPs remains small in both countries with women making up a mere 10 percent of Australia's House of Representatives, 22 percent of the Australian Senate, and 21 percent of New Zealand's House of Representatives in 1994.

Given the attitude toward women expressed by some male MPs during the suffrage debates in the 1890s, and the fact that many men in the late twentieth century still retain those views, the paucity of female MPs even in the 1990s is not all that surprising. The fact is, of course, that men did not—and still do not—like to share power (political or other) with women. To justify their antipathy, men frequently cite a range of perceived deficiencies in women that allegedly make women unsuited to political life. One New Zealand MP argued in 1893 that enfranchising women would blunt their "womanly and motherly and sisterly instincts,"[3] and another suggested that "it is always a first step in the decadence of a nation when men hand over government to women."[4] Many Australian politicians, at both state and federal levels, showed similar degrees of prejudice on the question of female suffrage— occasionally exhibiting outright paranoia. It would "desex" men if women became their equals, said one South Australian MP in 1894. Anticipating the standard antifeminist sneers of the late twentieth century, another claimed that the only women who wanted to vote or become members of Parliament were "disappointed childless creatures who have missed their maternal vocation; ill-favored ones who will never get an opportunity of exercising it; [and] the bitter hearted whose day is past."[5]

In 1902, a member of Australia's federal parliament offered the opinion that women should not be elected to Parliament because they were apt to act "on instinct" rather than on reason. While he knew that the "instinct of some dogs is better than some men's reason" he wasn't prepared to give women the vote because it was not the case "that every woman's reason was better than every man's."[6] On the other hand, a South Australian MP was of the opinion in 1894 that women did not need the vote (or presumably the capacity to reason) because they could use their "wiles" to influence their menfolk.[7]

Things have not changed much in the years since those words were spoken by angry (and frightened) men in New Zealand and Australian parliaments. Fears about the impact on men and families of "wily women" being given equal opportunities in the paid workforce were behind some of the more bizarre contributions to the Australian Senate debate on the Sex Discrimination Bill in 1983. This piece of legislation was aimed at prohibiting employers from hiring, firing, and promoting employees on the basis of their sex rather than on merit. One male senator, in a speech which would have been described as "hysterical" if a woman had made it, predicted the breakdown of marriages and the disintegration of families, if women were paid and promoted as men were. He was particularly concerned about what he called "compulsory close cohabitation" in the workplace and, for the benefit of a breathless Senate, cited two examples.

The first involved truck drivers who, he said, often had to drive long distances in Australia and who, of necessity, slept in their vehicle. "It concerns me," he said, "that if one of those drivers is male and the other one is female and they are required by their employer to share that job, that may perhaps create complications for them." These "complications" included what he described as "a very close relationship" which would almost certainly break up the marriages of the two drivers. He worried, too, about whether male and female employees of Telecom "working underground or around a Telecom pole" might not also be led astray to the detriment of their marriages. He closed his remarks by referring to the marriages of fellow male politicians and their staff, which, he said, had broken up because of the presence of "glamorous women who may very well be endeavoring to use their guile to woo them in some way." He added, in case we had not already got the point, that he believed "it was a matter of grave concern to many women in this country that their husbands may in some way be subjected to improper influences."[8]

I sat in the Senate chamber, hour after hour, listening to this kind of hysteria masquerade as rational debate, and despaired as some of the more conservative female senators argued that there was no need for equal opportunity legislation because *they* had "made it" and other women could too, if they were interested and talented enough. Hearing some men indignantly suggest that "merit" should be the only criterion for employment in any field, including politics, I realized that society had not advanced very far since the suffrage debates so many decades earlier.

The fact is that ability has never been a major criterion in the selection of political parties' candidates or in an employer's choice of senior personnel. Neither can the paucity of women in New Zealand

and Australian parliaments be attributed to women's lack of interest in political careers, because women had sought preselection in those two countries from the time they were entitled to do so. Two nurses tried to stand as candidates for the South Australian state election of 1896, the first election held after the passage of the suffrage bill. They were rejected by the political parties, however, because they were believed to be too controversial. They had been at the center of a very public debate two years earlier when they campaigned against nepotistic promotion procedures within their profession. However, in 1903 four women were nominated—one for the House and three for the Senate—in Australia's first federal election following the passage of the national suffrage bill a year earlier. None was successful, although they all received a creditable number of votes. It was not until 1918 that the first women stood as candidates in a South Australian election—all unsuccessfully. One of them, Selina Siggins (who had been the first woman in Australia to stand for the House of Representatives fifteen years earlier), referred frequently in her campaign speeches to the fact that two female candidates had been successful in Canada's provincial elections the previous year. Unfortunately for her, the voters of South Australia were not of a mind to follow suit. She returned home to New South Wales to stand, equally unsuccessfully, in the 1922 federal election.

In the New Zealand election of 1919, three women stood as candidates but were unable to convince the party machines to select them for winnable seats and unable to persuade the voters to support them as "Independents," and were thus also defeated. The political parties of New Zealand and Australia were so antipathetic to the idea of women becoming members of Parliament that it took until 1933 before the first woman (Elizabeth McCombs) was elected to New Zealand's House of Representatives, and 1943 before the first two women (Enid Lyons and Dorothy Tangney) were elected to Australia's federal parliament. Following a precedent already set in Britain, Canada, and the United States, these successful women were either unencumbered by spouses or had no pressing family responsibilities (McCombs and Lyons were widows and Tangney was not married).

By the mid-1940s women had been elected to all Australian state parliaments except South Australia's and had begun agitating—often successfully—for reforms to the laws and attitudes that acted to restrict women's role in society. Women might be "persons," but their rights under the law in Australia, as in New Zealand, left a lot to be desired. There was still much for female MPs and women in the community to

WOMEN FIRST

1960:
SIRAMAVO BANDARANAIKE OF CEYLON (NOW SRI LANKA) BECOMES THE WORLD'S FIRST WOMAN PRIME MINISTER.

campaign for in the second half of the twentieth century. Equal pay and the right for married women to have the same access to jobs and promotion that men had were just two issues that had to be addressed. It was only when women entered Parliament that many of these, and other, anomalies were challenged.

As happened in other countries, the needs of women and children vis à vis those of men were raised more frequently as more women were elected to Parliament in Australia and New Zealand. In 1925 Millicent Preston Stanley, the first woman elected to the New South Wales Parliament, began a six-year campaign that led to women being entitled to legal custody of their children; Dame Enid Lyons declared in her maiden speech in Australia's House of Representatives in 1943 that every subject "from high finance to international relations, from social security to the winning of the war, touches closely on the home and the family"[9]; and Mabel Howard, as New Zealand's Minister for Health and Child Welfare in the late 1950s, successfully took on a raft of male bureaucrats and the New Zealand branch of the British Medical Association to set up treatment centers for children with disabilities and established programs to assist children affected by polio.

Nearly thirty years later, in 1981 I, along with other women in state and federal parliament, played an active part in a massive campaign to change the definition of "provocation" in murder cases. This campaign came after a South Australian judge gave a heavy gaol sentence to a woman convicted of murdering her husband, despite years of physical, sexual, and mental cruelty he inflicted on her and their daughters for years, including the night of the murder. It was not until 1991, however, that the High Court ruled—again in response to pressure from women in and out of Parliament—that rape in marriage was a crime. Despite these advances in legislative and common law decisions relating to the safety of women, only South Australia has passed stalking legislation, making it an offense for men to harass women by loitering outside their homes or places of employment.

Not all female MPs have been prepared to recognize that some women have faced, and still face, social, economic, and employment disadvantages because of their sex. Several women from both the Liberal and National parties in Australia voted, along with their male colleagues, against the Sex Discrimination Bill because they saw it as "social engineering." Unable to accept that similar, although non-legislated, "engineering" had benefited men for centuries, these men and women refused to acknowledge the fact that the ledger needed to be balanced (and indeed could only be balanced) by laws banning overt discrimination in the employment, payment, and promotion of women. Even fewer recognized (or acknowledged) that similar forms of discrimination against women in political parties have actively prevented the election of women to Parliament.

Not only are the skills and experience that women could bring into political debates still not taken into account when selecting candidates for winnable seats, but the men who control the preselection process aren't interested in equity, either, although there has been talk for many years about a quota of winnable seats being allocated to female candidates.

Such a proposal is a two-edged sword: while it certainly increases the number of women in positions of power, it can also rebound on the women concerned, leaving them open to the jibe that they couldn't win on their merits and thus were second rate. The fact that the Liberal and Labor parties in Australia and the National and Labor parties in New Zealand have historically and habitually taken other factors, such as factional allegiance, ethnic or social background, and occupation into account raises far fewer eyebrows than the suggestion that the parties might like to consider deliberately preselecting a few women.

The major problem for aspiring female politicians in Australia and New Zealand is that, with the sole exception of the Australian Democrats, who select their candidates by full membership ballot, political parties choose their candidates via selection panels made up mostly of men. That many of those men still have a narrow view of a woman's place in the world was made plain by the male member of a preselection panel in the early 1990s, who asked a potential candidate how she would care for her children if she were elected. Clearly attitudes hadn't changed much since I was appointed to the Senate in the late 1970s. So few women had been elected to Australia's federal parliament between 1902 and 1977 (twelve to the Senate and five to the House of Representatives) that I became part of a privileged minority in December 1977 when the South Australian Parliament chose me to fill a casual vacancy in the Australian Senate. Furthermore, I was only thirty-two years old (young even for a male politician in those days) and had two children under eight. The media didn't quite know what to make of me. How would the family cope when I was in Canberra? they asked. Did my husband know how to work the washing machine? Would I spend my weekends at home cooking casseroles and freezing them so the family would have food to eat while I was away? Even more important to one worried journalist, how did my husband feel about being married to a woman who earned more than he did? On the other hand, I was spared the vitriol directed at New South Wales liberal MP Rosemary Foot who was instructed by an irascible opponent in 1983 to "go back [home] and do your washing."[10] The media persisted, however, in referring to me as the new "girl" in the Senate and—as they did with other women in the public eye—discussed my clothes, my hairstyle, and my figure more frequently than my contribution to the legislative process.

At least I wasn't blonde. Those (female) MPs who were found that this fact was almost always mentioned in media stories about them.

When Kathy Martin (later Sullivan) was first elected to the Senate in 1974, *The Australian,* Australia's only national newspaper, ran a story headlined "Kissable Senator" and referred to her as "the new 34-year-old blue-eyed blonde Liberal senator-elect from Queensland." Twenty years later, in March 1994, when the Minister for Sport, the Hon. Ros Kelly, became embroiled in a controversy over the allocation of funds from her budget, media stories almost always mentioned the fact that she had fair hair.

WOMEN FIRST

**1966:
INDIRA GANDHI
BECOMES FIRST
WOMAN PRIME
MINISTER
OF INDIA.**

If women in the public eye are a size or two larger than anorexic, that too becomes a focal point in a way that never happens to men in public life. The most extreme example of the Australian media's fascination with women's bodies rather than with their minds was the emphasis placed on the physique of the Hon. Joan Kirner when she was premier of Victoria in the early 1990s. Kirner is a pleasant, articulate, and intelligent woman who dresses stylishly and has a sharp wit. She is not reed thin but she is far from being obese. Nonetheless, her elevation to the leadership of her party in mid-1990 was greeted by one newspaper with the heading "Miss Piggy for Premier." The many male MPs whose size is often a health risk and whose shirt buttons are strained to the limit are never criticized for their appearance. Ms. Kirner was the second woman in Australia to become premier of a state and, as was the case with Dr. Carmen Lawrence, who had become premier of Western Australia several months earlier, she took on the position when the Labor Party was in dire need of something, or someone, to lift its image. While the general public had no difficulty accepting, indeed welcoming, Dr. Lawrence's and Ms. Kirner's elections as premiers of their states, the male-dominated media didn't quite know what to make of it.

The Australian, which devoted its front page to Dr. Lawrence's elevation, responded to the achievement in quite an extraordinary way. Two full columns down the left side of the paper were devoted to a discussion about what a range of men, including then-Prime Minister Bob Hawke and her male cabinet colleagues, thought of her. The headline said "Hawke gives the nod to first woman premier"—as if the imprimatur of a man was necessary to validate Lawrence's position. In the center of the page was a large photo of Dr. Lawrence in a kitchen. The caption underneath the photo noted that it had been taken when, as Western Australia's minister for Aboriginal affairs, she had opened an Aboriginal housing estate. The stereotype had, nonetheless, been effectively established. It paled in significance, however, when compared with the opening paragraph of the story under the photo. "Dr. Carmen Lawrence," wrote the male journalist, "is no Margaret Thatcher. She hasn't the beauty of Pakistan's Benazir Bhutto. And while she might have the intellect, she hasn't the years of Israel's Golda Meir."[11] He might well have added, apropos that last example, that she wasn't dead, either. Needless to say, no male MP has ever received such treatment. Three years later Dr. Lawrence was elected to federal parliament where she was immediately given the senior and controversial, but typically "female," health portfolio.

While female MPs everywhere quickly discover that many, if not all, their male colleagues resent sharing space in the corridors of power, they find out just as quickly that constituents are generally gender blind. Voters will support their local MP, whoever that person may be, if they believe their member to be honest, committed, and to have their interests at heart, even if they don't always agree with that member's policy decisions. When New Zealand National Party MP Marilyn Waring defied Prime Minister Robert Muldoon's instruction in 1981 that she not publicly discuss the issue of abortion, two members of her electoral committee called for her to be reprimanded and dumped. When she arrived at the meeting convened to discuss the matter, she found herself confronted by a crowd of farmers in moleskins and sport coats. Many of them were sporting anti-abortion badges. The first man who spoke did so in a voice shaking with rage—a rage that, he said, was directed at those people who had supported her election to Parliament and then tried to deny her the right to vote according to her conscience. The motion to censure her was resoundingly defeated and she went on representing her conscience and her constituency—learning to fly so that she could keep a better eye on her rural electorate—until her retirement in 1984.

Few women or men go to such lengths in the interest of doing their jobs properly and those who do realize that such commitment can rarely co-exist with the additional responsibilities of becoming a minister. It is something cabinet members in the United States do not have to consider—chosen from nonmembers of Congress, their constituency consists primarily of the president who selected them for the position and, indirectly and to a much lesser extent, people who are affected by departmental decisions. What the two positions have in common, however, is that far fewer women than men reach those exalted heights.

As I have already noted, however, some women in Australia and New Zealand have found their way into the ministries of both federal and state governments as well as becoming party leaders. While I was the first woman in Australia to be elected parliamentary leader of a political party when I took over the position on the retirement of Senator Don Chipp in 1986, other women, such as Joan Kirner in Victoria, Carmen Lawrence in Western Australia, and liberal MP Joan Sheldon in Queensland, soon followed. Since my retirement from politics—and hence from the leadership of my party—two other women, Senator Janet Powell and Senator Cheryl Kernot, have been elected federal parliamentary leader of the Australian Democrats. Another woman, Senator Meg Lees, is currently the party's deputy parliamentary leader. While Powell was at the center of controversy in 1990 for supporting legislation that was contrary to party policy and subsequently resigned, Kernot has proved a charismatic and trusted leader. Lees's grasp of complex legislation and capacity for hard work is widely acknowledged. Women, such as Liberal Party Senator Margaret Guilfoyle and the Australian Labor Party's Senator Susan Ryan, had already shown during the 1970s and 1980s that women were more than capable of being effective, innovative, and respected ministers.

Their capability should come as no surprise to anyone. In order to justify their existence in the hallowed halls of power, however, unlike their male colleagues women in politics still have to prove over and over again that they are more than just competent, individually and collectively. Women will know they have arrived politically, and in every other way, only when they are regarded and accepted not just as women, not just as legal "persons," but as human beings with a diverse range of experiences, intellects, mind sets, and priorities. Certainly women are different from men in very discernible ways. But they are no different in their diversity, which is why their involvement in politics is something to be encouraged, valued, and celebrated. Unfortunately, despite the length and fervor of the struggle, and with fewer than 10 percent of MPs in English-speaking parliaments being female, we still have a long way to go before we are heard, and even further to go before we are listened to.

THE IMPACT OF GERMAN UNIFICATION ON WOMEN
Losses and Gains
Hanna Beate Schoepp-Schilling

During the night of November 8, 1989, the Berlin Wall separating the two Germanies (in the West, the Federal Republic of Germany, the FRG; and in the East, the German Democratic Republic, the GDR) finally came down. At that moment, the largest number of women ever were holding political positions in government at federal, state, and local levels in the West (FRG). In divided West Berlin, for example, eight women and five men held cabinet positions. At the federal level, the percentage of women in Parliament was 15.4 percent, and six women were heads or deputy heads of ministries, one of which included a Department for Women's Affairs, created in late 1986. Structures equivalent to this department were also functioning in all of the eleven states in West Germany (FRG), as well as in nearly five hundred municipalities.

At this historic moment, I was serving as the first appointed director general for the Department for Women's Affairs in the Federal Ministry of Youth, Family, Women, and Health. In 1988, I had also been appointed as the FRG's independent expert to the United Nations Committee on the Elimination of Discrimination Against Women (CEDAW). My qualifications for these positions did not include membership in a political party or experience in government, both customary routes to power. Rather, I travelled a different route.

Beginning in the early 1970s as a scholar in American Studies, first at the Free University of Berlin, I taught women's studies and built a library. Later, through small, international conferences on gender issues at an international institute in Berlin, I had familiarized politicians, administrators, scholars, and members of the media with such issues as sexism in education, antidiscrimination legislation for women, affirmative action, women's studies and centers for research on women, and the value of women's work as child rearers and homemakers. During this period and into the mid-1980s, as an activist in various women's organizations and women's groups, I had lectured and published on these issues and had lobbied for their implementation at national and international levels.

I began work as director general of the Department for Women's Affairs in April 1987 and left that post in 1992; I was appointed to the UN's CEDAW in 1988 and continue to hold that post. It is from the dual perspective of a former government official and an independent, reform-minded feminist expert at the United Nations that I will describe the effects on women of German unification.

As preamble I will point to two lessons I had to learn quickly. First, politics is a matter of compromise. The purity of one's ideals and goals cannot always be maintained. Rather than concentrating only on what is desirable, one has to fight for what is achievable under the circumstances. Second, one must learn to take the long view of political processes and effects. The mere raising of consciousness regarding certain issues may seem only a minor accomplishment when compared with enacting legislation. The establishment of political structures may be considered trivial when they lack support for staff and activities. But such seemingly minor accomplishments may lay the foundation of the achievement of one's original goals, perhaps years away.

WOMEN IN THE TWO GERMANIES

Under the socialist system of the GDR, East German women enjoyed a number of important human rights that had been granted to them in keeping with socialist ideology and because of the particular economic necessities of the GDR. Among these were economic independence through employment security; constitutionally guaranteed affirmative action in education and employment; a number of regulations, including an extensive and inexpensive child-care system, that enabled women to combine motherhood and employment; and unrestricted abortion rights. It is also true, however, that women, including mothers, were more or less forced into employment. Basic political and civil rights, although guaranteed in the constitution, were dependent on the interpretation of the socialist power elite. Other rights were negated completely. In addition, as in all socialist countries, the sexual distribution of labor, the allocation of male and female roles and tasks, was never questioned. This distribution was reflected in the sexual segregation of the labor market, in women's responsibility for the family, and in their minor presence in socialist politics.

Human rights are indivisible. Political and civil rights cannot be traded against social and economic or any other rights, but have to be seen as one set of instruments to guarantee the fundamental rights and welfare of women and men. This has been acknowledged again and again by member states of the United Nations and in the 1993 Vienna

Declaration on Human Rights. Furthermore, the denial of one set of human rights actually distorts the enjoyment of those granted. Because GDR women and men did not enjoy full civil and political rights, their social and economic rights reaffirmed existing power structures, including gender hierarchies. For example, women's economic rights meant job security in practice, but not necessarily equal pay or the freedom to choose the number of working hours. Violence against women, though it existed inside and outside of marriage, was negated both by research and policymaking, since it did not fit in with socialist emancipatory ideology. Because women held no full political rights, they could not address these discriminations against them publicly and thus, these issues remained politically taboo until the fall of 1989.

Women in the FRG live in a democratic, socially oriented, free-market system, which provides free choice and opportunities to shape one's life, and, for those in need, guarantees a sufficient, though meager, livelihood, as well as education and health care. Equality of women and men and nondiscrimination on the basis of gender are guaranteed in the constitution and all existing legislation provides for de jure equality in all areas of life. However, although due to the new women's movement sex roles have been questioned since the late 1960s, de facto inequality still exists—as in all highly industrialized democratic countries—because women still carry most of the family responsibilities despite their increasing commitment to employment and political activism. Following the principle of both equal opportunities and free choice, federal government policies in the tax and welfare system have gendered implications that, given most women's choice for motherhood, may have a negative impact on them.

WOMEN FIRST

1993: SYLVIA KINIGI IS THE FIRST WOMAN TO BECOME PRIME MINISTER OF BURUNDI (SHE HAS SINCE BEEN ASSASSINATED).

By the mid-1980s, day care facilities were far from being sufficient; on the other hand, the federal government had established a paid parental leave with job guarantee of up to almost two years, as well as recognition of that period in the social security pension. Various legal instruments and programs provided training for women to re-enter the labor market. While federal antidiscrimination legislation concerning employment existed, it was only in some states that affirmative action in the public sector was legally mandated. Legally, abortion was possible under certain conditions; practically its availability differed from state to state. Women's associations and groups enjoyed subsidies for their activities.

By the late 1970s, the women's movement had turned its attention to questions of political power. Women in West German political parties had begun to accept feminist ideas regarding antidiscrimination legislation and affirmative action measures in employment and political life. They had begun to pursue two strategies to increase women's political influence, the first of which led to political parties accepting a system of quotas or guidelines for the inclusion of women candidates running for office and women party officials. The second strategy followed the philosophy of CEDAW, which encourages governments to establish political structures to pursue and implement policies for women. Hence, due to pressure by women, equal opportunity offices were set up at federal, state, and local levels.

The GREENS, then a new, small party with a strong feminist component, established a 50 percent quota in 1986; the large center-left Social Democratic Party established a rising 25 percent to 40 percent quota in 1988, and other parties, including the large center-right Christian Democratic Union, established guidelines. Effects were felt rapidly internally and in parliamentary elections at the municipal, state, and federal levels, even by 1987.

By late 1986 the Christian Democratic Union, which was the major party in the coalition government at the federal level, had added the Department for Women's Affairs to an existing federal ministry for youth, family, and health, following the example of some states. Such institutions quickly proliferated at state and municipal levels, all due to pressure from the new women's movement, numerous traditional women's organizations, and women in political parties. On the other hand, the policy goals and resources of all these institutions were dependent on the respective political will of their various governments, which were formed either by center-right or center-left majorities. A legal basis existed only for the equal opportunity offices at the local level in one state.

Such was the situation when I began working as director general for the Department for Women's Affairs in April 1987. By June, the minister was able to present an extensive women's agenda to the public. It ranged from legislative measures to programs and research projects. Women of all ages and from all areas of life were to profit from it.

The department had been given special procedural rights: they were given not only the right to check on all new legislation from women's points of view, but also the right to initiate legislation, sometimes in collaboration with other ministries. Our program included plans to improve the existing antidiscrimination legislation in employment, to introduce strong affirmative action for women at least in public employment, to extend paid parental leave, to create re-entry programs for women homemakers, to improve social security pension schemes for employed women and for homemakers, to penalize rape within marriage, and to legislate financial support for battered women's shelters. As ambitious, research projects and public hearings were to be initiated on many different topics, including rural women and the voting patterns of younger women. Through an anticipated increase in our budget, we planned to expand financial support for seminars and training sessions for women's organizations and groups, as well as for the National Women's Council, an umbrella organization of approximately 12 million women.

Unfortunately, in late 1988, the minister moved to a more prestigious but less politically powerful position as president of the federal parliament. More unfortunately still, her replacement arrived with less political will and clout to implement the established agenda. Nevertheless, much was accomplished, as this essay will indicate, especially during the critical years just prior to and just following the unification of the two Germanies.

WOMEN CROSS BORDERS AS THE WALL COMES DOWN

In contrast to most other post-socialist societies in Eastern Europe, East Germany (GDR), in the last months of its existence—from December 1989 until October 1990—created political institutions for women's policies. These institutions were established through the efforts of the newly emerging GDR autonomous women's movement. First, in early fall of 1989, small women's groups formed the Independent Women's Union with a predominantly socialist feminist platform. Second, the leaders of the Democratic Women's Union, the official organization for women in the GDR, began a process of democrat- ization, adopting ideas and goals from political and women's organizations in West Germany (FRG). Both women's organizations were part of the various self-appointed political round table groups of reform-oriented citizens who advised and pressured the still-existing social governments at the central and municipal levels.

At the central level, a minister for women's affairs was appointed. In early 1990, when new constitutional legislation was prepared for the counties and municipalities, these women's groups exerted pressure for the inclusion of a legal mandate for political offices of women's affairs in the municipalities, which was accepted by the first democratically elected Parliament of the GDR in April 1990.

Earlier, the Department for Women's Affairs, under my direction, had responded to a parliamentary enquiry with a report on the development and status of such offices for women's affairs in the FRG. In view of the developments in the GDR, I had this report reprinted and disseminated in the GDR during the first six months of 1990, thereby assisting the newly appointed office holders to define and defend their areas of work and their competencies against sometimes hostile mayors and counselors, who were both impressed and intimidated by the official document.

At the same time, many cities in the GDR and FRG formed partnerships, accompanied by financial and administrative assistance, which opened a variety of opportunities that allowed West German women working in municipal equal opportunity offices to support their East German colleagues with valuable advice, documents, and material resources.

Thus, at the very moment of reform, between November 1989 and October 1990, women in GDR municipalities gained access to positions of political power and were politically influential, either by winning parliamentary seats, by becoming city council members, or by working in the newly established women's or equality offices. The latter in particular, driven by a newly acquired feminist consciousness, moved to save as many child-care facilities as possible; to create shelters for battered women; to look after foreign women; and to support other newly emerging women's groups in their various activities.

The establishment of quotas and guidelines for women's representation in the West German political parties played a decisive role during the first democratic election campaign for the last central GDR government in March 1990, and for the first democratic municipal elections in May 1990. All GDR parties, whether newly founded, refounded, or reformed, followed the West German examples of quotas or guidelines, while also answering to the demands of many East German women themselves. Hence, even without the socialist habit of reserving a quota of seats for women, female representation in the new, democratically elected central parliament dropped only from 32.2 percent to 20.5 percent; that is, not as dramatically as in the other socialist countries undergoing democratic reform. Similar positive results for women were achieved in the municipal parliaments.

In the newly elected central parliament of the GDR, even though female representation was comparatively high, center-right parties dominated; they also dominated the central coalition government, thus setting the political framework in which policies for women could be formulated for the remaining months of the GDR, but especially with regard to the unification treaty.

Nevertheless, at the central government level women's policy institutions were also established. However, the competition between the two major coalition partners—the Christian Democratic Union plus some smaller allies and the Social Democratic Party—originally had led to the creation of two independently functioning national structures for women's policies, one in the form of a Ministry for Family and Women's Affairs (headed by a woman from the Christian Democratic Union), the second in the form of an Equal Opportunities Office (headed by a female appointee of the Social Democratic Party) directly under the supervision of the GDR minister president (Christian Democratic Union). The second model was supposed to guarantee women-oriented policy influences from the minister president's office into all ministries. This arrangement, however, was doomed from its inception, since the minister president, and the equal opportunities officer belonged to different parties, and the office was soon placed within the Ministry on Family and Women's Affairs. To this ministry, as well as to all other GDR ministries, a corresponding West German counselor had been appointed. In this case, the appointment went to my deputy. Given the center-right principles of both the governments of the FRG and the GDR and their respective women's ministries as well as the soon-to-be accepted legal basis for unification, it became clear in the early summer of 1990 that GDR policies for women—ncluding affirmative action for women in the labor market, the extensive and inexpensive system of child care that covered children from birth until well into their teens, the unrestricted access to abortion in the first trimester—had little chance to be carried over into the policy framework of unified Germany. Nevertheless, the GDR Ministry on Family and Women's Affairs, as well as the Equal Opportunities Office under its sovereignty—in the five months of their existence—were able to raise consciousness with regard to women's issues and to provide seed money for the newly emerging shelters for battered women, to support a number of cultural and labor market projects for women, to assist the municipal offices for equal opportunities, and to publish valuable data collected on women in the GDR, to name only a few of their efforts.

Most important, while not being able to "save" these specific women's rights, both the FRG's and GDR's women's ministries, women in both parliaments and of all parties, and the National Women's Council of the FRG exerted enough pressure to include in the unification treaty one article that formulated a framework for future policy efforts for women in a unified Germany. This Article 31 of the unification treaty postulates four goals: First and second, the federal government was to develop equal opportunity legislation as well as legislation for improving the compatibility of employment and family work. Third, it was to cofinance—for a limited period of time in 1991—the existing child-care system for preschool children in the new states, until their governments had developed new child-care legislation. Fourth, it was to bring about a new abortion regulation by the end of 1992. This last goal was a compromise, since the conflict over different GDR and FRG abortion regulations had threatened the unification treaty as a whole. Women (and men) of the Social Democratic Party and the small Free Democratic Party, as well as the Christian Democratic Union, in both the GDR and FRG, had not been willing to give up on unrestricted GDR abortion rights for women. Thus, the two different sets of laws were to coexist in a unified Germany for fourteen months at the most, with the clear mandate to draft and pass new legislation during that period.

The very existence of a Ministry on Family and Women's Affairs in the last months of the GDR fuelled the demand by GDR women's groups for similar structures in the governments of the re-established states, which were elected immediately after unification in October 1990. When the federal government of the FRG, in preparation for these new state governments, planned their budgets in late 1990—which, in the beginning, were to be heavily subsidized by federal monies—the Department for Women's Affairs, under my direction, was able to insert budget lines for the institutionalization of such structures for women's policies as well as for future state-supported programs for women. Additional pressure in this direction came from the eleven women's ministries or similar institutions at the state levels of the former FRG, since the governments of the "old" states assisted the "new" states in establishing their political and administrative structures. Thus, all governments of the six new states (including unified Berlin) created a structure for women's policies either at the ministerial level or one or two steps below in the political administration. Once established, these new institutions were immediately offered advice and financial support by their sister institutions in the old states.

Beginning in late 1990, the federal Department for Women's Afffairs, too, cooperated with these new institutions by organizing a conference in each of the five new states to which all the municipal equal opportunities officers of that state were invited. Together with each woman office holder at state level, I moderated these conferences. Thus, I was able to present and discuss various policy goals for women and different strategies to achieve them; to elaborate on the origins, visions, and developments of the new women's movement; and to point to the importance of vocal women's groups for any progressive policymaking. These conferences served as essential training and networking grounds for the women office holders of the new women's policy institutions.

In the following months, the new state institutions for women's policies exerted an influence on behalf of affirmative action clauses in the formulation of their state constitutions, their child-care legislation, and their employment-creation strategies. In addition, they responded to the demands of women's groups and supported specific projects for women in the areas of employment creation, shelters for battered women, and cultural centers for women. In this work, they were supported by the women in the local women's policy institutions who often pursued similar projects, which sometimes needed additional funding from the state levels.

Thus, by the beginning of 1991, after the state elections in the new states in October 1990, and after the first federal elections since unification in December 1990, unified Germany had a larger number of women in its parliaments than ever before. Women's representation in the federal parliament had risen from 15.4 percent in 1987 to 20.5 percent. In the state parliaments representation ranged from 13.5 percent to 20.5 percent. Women's participation in the sixteen state governments ranged between 8.3 percent and 36.3 percent; in the governments of the new states, between 8.3 percent and 33 percent. In addition, institutions for women's policies had been established in all sixteen state governments and in approximately 900 municipalities. Of those, more than 300 had come forth at the local levels in the new states. At the federal level, the Federal Ministry for Youth, Family, Women's Affairs, and Health had been divided into three ministries. Critics of the center-right government called this an easy strategy to multiply the number of female ministers. In practice, however, it meant an increase in staff and budgetary resources, as well as more visibility for the Department for Women's Affairs.

WOMEN IN A UNIFIED GERMANY

The first federal elections in unified Germany of December 1990 had reaffirmed the center-right government. In 1991, the Department for Women's Affairs and the federal parliament moved quickly to address the policy challenges of the unification treaty, as well as such additional issues as violence against women and building women's groups and associations in the new states. In some of these policy areas, the federal government merely laid the foundations until the new state governments, including the institutions for women's policies, were capable of taking over what rightfully fell under their sovereignty.

Regarding equal opportunity legislation, the Department for Women's Affairs, which I still headed, began preparations for an extensive new law. In addition, we formulated proposals for legislation being prepared by other ministries and by the parliamentary committee for the reform of the constitutional Basic Law.

In the area of equal opportunities legislation, a few rights were gained. First, the new Constitution of unified Germany came about through amendments of the Basic Law of the former FRG. To the existing clauses on the equal rights of men and women and on the prohibition of gender discrimination, an affirmative action clause was added, though this clause, unfortunately, is somewhat vague in its formulation and, subsequently, its practical impact. A new Equal Opportunities Act provides for some affirmative action regarding jobs in the federal public sector (some state laws provide for stronger affirmative action measures in their public employment sector including quotas; however, they are currently under consideration by the Federal Constitutional Court); an explicit ban on sexual harassment at the workplace; a strengthening of women's representation in the labor councils in the private and public sector; and some minor improvements and clarifications in the general antidiscrimination legislation for the employment sector. Regarding women's representation in public bodies of the federal government, a new nomination scheme has been legislated to increase the number of female office holders. However, almost all of these measures lack sanctions for noncompliance and are too vague in their concrete goals; in addition, they hardly constitute improvements for women in the private employment sector.

Though the current center-right government generally is adamantly negative in its attitudes with regard to quotas in politics or employment, the devastating situation of women's unemployment in the new states finally compelled it, through the intensive efforts of the Department for Women's Affairs, to include a clause in the reformed Labor Promotion Act that stipulates quotas in schemes for unemployed women regarding their further training and retraining as well as their inclusion in public job creation schemes, in proportion to their unemployment rate. Since 1989, women's unemployment rate in the new states rose far more quickly and disastrously than did men's. While some three million jobs were lost in general in the territory of the former GDR, most of them were lost in female-dominated employment areas of light industry, agriculture, and administration due to the lack of modernization, the noncompetitiveness and overstaffing in these areas. In addition, overt, covert, as well as unintentional discrimination by individual employers, by governments, or trade unions, is also to blame.

1980: JEANNE SAUVE IS FIRST WOMAN APPOINTED SPEAKER OF THE HOUSE OF COMMONS OF CANADA.

Concerned about the employment issue, the deputy minister and I visited a number of labor market offices in the new states and, subsequently, held press conferences in order to raise consciousness about both the existing antidiscrimination legislation for women and the potential for special labor market programs for them, which were initiated both by the federal Department for Women's Affairs, by the policy institutions for women at state levels, and by the Federal Labor Market Board and its local offices, often with the assistance of the municipal equal opportunities offices. Despite these efforts, little gain has been made. The demise of whole sectors of employment in the new states, combined with the inherited effect of a sex-segregated labor market in the former GDR and the existing mechanisms of a sex-segregated labor market in the FRG, will make it difficult for women to regain their former hold in the employment sector, even though an overwhelming majority of them—as polls indicate—do want employment, and not merely for financial reasons.

Regarding the issue of making employment and family responsibilities more compatible, paid parental leave and parental sick leave from work with full pay were extended, with special consideration for single parents. Since female-headed households reach 30 percent in the new states as compared to approximately 12 percent in the old states, this regulation is particularly beneficial to former GDR women and recoups one of their former GDR benefits.

The process of legislating a new abortion regulation has been painful and is still open. To women in the FRG, abortion had become available only in 1976, and was restricted to four conditions (severe handicap of the fetus, the pregnancy as a life threat to the mother, pregnancy as a result of rape, pregnancy causing a situation of dire stress to the mother), one of which had to be certified by a medical doctor, after the pregnant woman had undergone a consultation with a psychologist or medical doctor. More than 90 percent of all abortions had been certified for the fourth condition. Medical costs of abortions were covered by the national health care system. In some Catholic-dominated regions of the old FRG it had been difficult if not impossible to obtain abortions. Women in the GDR, on the other hand, had been given free access to abortion in 1973, the cost also being carried by the state health insurance system.

The parliamentary procedure of devising new abortion legislation was painful and bitter. Seven different bills were put on the floor in the summer of 1992, ranging from further restricting the existing FRG legislation, to accepting the GDR legislation, to taking abortion out of the penal code altogether. Finally, a compromise, pushed by women parliamentarians across party lines, was passed in June 1992, only to be declared unconstitutional in parts in May 1993.

Today, the current regulation is more liberal than in the former FRG, but more restrictive than in the former GDR. Abortion is defined as being illegal and punishable in general. It is, however, permitted and not to be punished if the pregnant woman has undergone an obligatory counseling process, which can include the prospective father or one or both of their parents. Following the counseling and after a waiting period of another three days, the pregnant woman can have an abortion performed if she finds a doctor willing to do it. The medical cost for the abortion may no longer be carried by the state health insurance system (unless the abortion is for medical reasons), and thus will be paid for either by the woman herself or by welfare. If she cannot work because of the abortion, she will get sick leave compensation. In any case, a new legislation will have to be formulated on the basis of the verdict of the Constitutional Court.

Another important mandate is a legal claim to a child-care placement for every child at age three, to be put in practice by all state governments by 1996. This policy constitutes more of a formidable challenge for the old state governments of the FRG than the new ones, for the extensive child-care system of the GDR (creches, all-day daycare, after-school care, vacation arrangements) never broke down completely. Due to the efforts by the federal government, the state governments, and institutions for women's policies on various levels, most of the places for children three years old and older were saved and guaranteed by new state legislation. It is true that they have become more expensive, with the states, the municipalities, and the parents sharing the cost. However, the current threat to the child-care facilities comes more from the dramatic decline in the birth rate in the new states rather than from either financial restrictions or a general policy. Nevertheless, financial restrictions may well keep the new states from expanding child-care institutions when such institutions are needed in the future.

With unification, the Department for Women's Affairs was able to increase its budget extensively in order to finance two large programs for women's organizations and groups in the new states. I was especially keen on initiating and financing such programs for emerging women's groups and associations because I had learned a historical lesson before I came into my government position. As a former board member of one of the FRG's oldest post-World War II women's organizations in Berlin, influential in shaping postwar policies for women in the late 1940s and 1950s, I had come to appreciate the importance of creating a strong lobby for women. From 1990 to 1994, the federal Department for Women's Affairs supported many fledgling women's groups and their activities in the new states, funding seminars on consciousness-raising regarding women's issues, on training women to run organizations, and on political and cultural activities. In addition, the department funded the National Women's Council so as to establish five women's offices in the new states, where women's groups could receive training in how to create and run women's organizations in a democratic way and how to lobby for women's issues. This measure proved to be very innovative, given the fact that democratic voluntarism in this part of Germany had disappeared after 1933. Today, a number of newly founded women's organizations and groups, in addition to new chapters founded by women's organizations of the former FRG, are thriving in the new states.

A second initiative of the Department for Women's Affairs supported the new shelters for battered women in the new states until the political institutions for women's affairs at the state level could establish budget lines of their own. Shelters for battered women had not existed in the GDR, and the very issue of violence against women had been kept silent. With the lifting of the taboo and with increasing economic tensions, violence against women in the former GDR became very visible. Autonomous women's groups founded the first shelters in many cities during the last months of the GDR. Today, they are supported by state and municipal funds as they have been for a long time in the old states.

CONCLUSION: LOSSES AND GAINS

For a number of reasons, it was unrealistic for both East and West German women's groups to have hoped that the specific economic and social rights of women in the GDR would survive. First, it is generally unlikely that, when a coherent political and socioeconomic system—in this case socialism—breaks down, that some of its features will survive. It is even less likely that features that benefit a social group not at the center of power will survive. Second, though a number of women in the FRG had fought for more than 15 years— through social pressure and parliamentary initiatives—for the institutionalization of these very same rights, they had not been successful in gaining legislative acceptance for them in the FRG. In addition, the very fact that the GDR acceded to the FRG on the basis of the FRG's constitutional basic law, and subsequently on the basis of a unification treaty, meant for most FGR politicians formulating the unification treaty that this treaty should not be utilized to change existing FRG law. Third, the newly emerging independent GDR women's groups held political views that were incompatible with the characteristics of West German party democracy. Their grass-roots approach that included no representation through parties and no hierarchies could not exert much political impact once the West German system with its reliance on strong parties was generally favored by the electorate in the GDR during the last months of its existence.

WOMEN FIRST

1979: MARIA DE LOURDES PINTASILGO BECOMES FIRST WOMAN PRIME MINISTER OF PORTUGAL.

No doubt women politicians and women office holders in women's policy institutions were not able to prevent developments that cause a number of former GDR women to experience aspects of their lives as more negative than before. On the other hand, the efforts of the increasing number of women in responsible political positions and in political structures and policy institutions for women prevented worse developments, particularly in comparison to many Eastern European countries. While they were not strong enough to fight all consequences of the male-oriented structures of both the former GDR and FRG, political women were able to increase their spheres of beneficial influence for women in both structural and practical ways, and use their admittedly still limited power in many ingenious strategic ways.

Implementing Articles 2, 4, and 7 of the Convention on the Elimination of All Forms of Discrimination against Women through an increase in female politicians and through the creation of institutions for women's policies certainly can make a difference for women, as the example of Germany at a very critical moment in its political development has shown.[1] Because of the quota and guideline regulations, each German election brings more women into political power. Women's policy institutions at all governmental levels continue to influence legislation and programs for women. To avoid that these gains turn into token gestures and token institutions, women themselves need to rally to bring such parties and candidates into office who will generate new political will and new strategies for women's policies, and who will increase competencies, staff, and budgets of the women's policy institutions in order to realize these potentials. In this way, the full enjoyment of German women's human rights and their de facto equality as compared to German men will be furthered with democratic means within a democratic system, thereby giving the latter its true legitimacy.

A Conversation with Wu Qing

Isabel Crook, Liu Dongxiao, and Lisa Stearns, participants

"The rose is my favorite flower
because it has thorns."
—*Bing Xin*[1]

Wu Qing is a deputy to the Haidian District People's Congress and to the Municipal People's Congress, Beijing, People's Republic of China. For more information about Wu Qing and about the participants, please see the Notes on Contributors in this volume.

This conversation is presented by Ulrike Bode. She coordinated, compiled, and edited it from two interviews and written follow-up questions. She thanks Christina Gilmartin for her pivotal assistance in structuring the conversation, and both her and Helen P. Young for invaluable background information and insights. Isabel Crook wrote the footnotes and suggested the epigraph by Bing Xin.

BEIJING, DECEMBER 1994 AND JANUARY 1995

Isabel Crook: Wu Qing, you've been politically active for years, because you care about your fellow countrymen and -women, and about the future of China. Apart from your duties as an elected representative, you've been active in other fields, particularly in promoting the position of women.... We'd like to ask you about your personal experience as a Chinese woman in the world of local politics and the lessons you've drawn. Then we'd like to hear your views on the situation of Chinese women in general as they participate in politics. How did you become a political activist?

Wu Qing: I was greatly influenced by my parents, especially my mother. Let me give you an example: We were in Chongqing, Sichuan Province, during the anti-Japanese war in the early 1940s. I was a first-grader and we were encouraged to raise funds for wounded soldiers. I think I raised the most in our class. My mom taught me to share with people and to reach out to others to help.... She also taught me that I am a human being first and a woman second, and that as a woman

I should have my own career. My dad was a sociologist and one of the founders of sociology in China. He tried to apply the theories he learned in the West to China and encouraged students to do research in rural areas.

I was also influenced by Christianity, because I went to the International School of Sacred Heart in Tokyo from 1949 to '51. My dad was head of the Guomindang Chinese diplomatic mission to Japan until 1949 when he resigned because of corruption in the Guomindang government. After returning to China, I...was greatly influenced by Mao's "Serve the people heart and soul." As a child, I read Soviet novels like *Zoya and Shura* and *The Gadfly*. Later I read books on history and sociology.

All this made me feel part of society and taught me to participate in politics, to try and change society. Zhou Enlai [prime minister from 1949 to 1976] was a model. He really showed concern for people's livelihood. Our family was very democratic. Whenever there were problems, we children could always chip in and say what we thought. My parents only gave us guidelines and then left it up to us to decide. So I dared speak out and disagree.... In 1958, for example, I said government leaders should move out of Zhongnanhai (a beautiful scenic place in the center of Beijing) and that the Great Hall of the People in Beijing should be open to the public.... I was the Communist Youth League secretary of my class at the time but I was dropped from the post.

IC: Why did you study English?

WQ: Actually, because of Zhou Enlai. When Zhou...heard from my mother in the early 1950s that we had started learning English in Japan he said, "Why don't you encourage your daughters to continue...? China needs people to make bridges between China and the world." That's why my sister gave up her dream of becoming a historian and I gave up my dream of becoming a surgeon.

IC: How did you get involved in American studies?

WQ: Also because of my parents. Both of them were educated in the United States during the 1920s and many of their friends were American. My mother got her M.A. at Wellesley; my father got his M.A. at Dartmouth and his Ph.D. at Columbia University. In the 1950s and '60s I felt that our newspapers' reports were different from what my parents had told me about America. Since it is one of the most powerful countries in the world, I thought we should know something about it.

I am an associate professor at the English Department of the Beijing Foreign Studies University [BFSU]. I teach American studies and English to undergraduate and graduate students. It's my duty to give Chinese students a balanced picture about the USA and Americans.

IC: Why did you involve yourself in local politics?

WQ: In the Cultural Revolution, nearly all Chinese suffered. I didn't want that to happen again. At that time we followed blindly the instructions coming from the top. We were brought up in an age of consensus. We used to feel enmity toward those who had different views or used different methods, but it's natural for people to have different views. These should be respected. We can learn from each other. I agree with Mao's saying that ideas should come from the masses and return to the masses. Another thing: It's essential to educate people to know who they are and what they can do....

IC: How did you come to be elected a deputy to a People's Congress?[2]

WQ: I studied in the United States for a year in 1982/83. When I came back in the fall of 1983, I found that the new policies made changes possible in China and that people wanted change. But you could only start locally. In the summer of 1984, to my surprise, I was nominated[3] for deputy to Beijing's Haidian District People's Congress [DPC].[4] My name was put forward because BFSU[5] was given a quota.

IC: In those days the quota system included percentages for women, ethnic minorities, workers, peasants, soldiers, teachers, intellectuals, non-Party persons, patriots who had returned from abroad, et cetera—

WQ:—to have representatives from all walks of life. I think this was a good system....BFSU was required to elect a woman: a non-Party member, an excellent teacher, and middle-aged....So I was nominated together with a teacher from the Japanese department. I was elected and I accepted.

I wanted to bring changes to the system of People's Congresses. I thought there should be more mass participation and that policy makers should know people's needs. Besides, there is a lot of room for creativity. As a people's deputy, I would be able to try out new ways of functioning politically and different methods of approaching constituents, government officials, and agencies. I'd also be able to suggest and do different things for my constituency. It was a challenge and an opportunity to make changes happen because I am protected by the constitution, both as a citizen and a deputy. The day I was elected, I decided that I would not just fill in the quota the next time but be reelected on the basis of what I'd done for my constituents and what I stand for.

IC: When your three-year term was up you were reelected.

WQ: That was in 1987. There was one seat but no specific sex was required. Previously, only two candidates were nominated by the Communist Party [CCP] and the democratic parties. Now anyone with ten sponsors could stand. Electors had more choice and started taking more initiative;...they were enjoying more democracy and freedom. In the first round, all names put forward by the nominators were announced. Then there were discussions, negotiations, and compromises among political parties, mass organizations, and individuals. It went from bottom to top and from top to bottom, several times, until the list was narrowed down to two candidates.

In 1987 many voters preferred men. Many thought that women don't know how to function in society or how to play a political role. So, the percentage of women deputies fell significantly after quotas were abolished. That's why the All-China Women's Federation [ACWF] and women fought so hard to legislate a gradually increasing percentage representation for women.

IC: How do you see this drop in women's participation in government?

WQ: Both negatively and positively. Negatively, it means fewer women representatives. Positively, it means that women deputies have to be more aware and brave enough to take up challenges. At all levels there are token women deputies. Some function. Some don't because they lack confidence. It's a quantity/quality business. If the quality of women deputies is raised, quantity will also be raised. That's why training deputies is important.

IC: Though the trend was against women in 1987, you were reelected. Why?

WQ: Because of the work I had done in my constituency and the stand I took on different issues. The first time I got elected, I studied the Chinese constitution very carefully because I think as a people's deputy I should be a model in carrying it out. Article 76.N states that deputies to the National People's Congress [NPC][6] must be exemplary in abiding by and enforcing the constitution and the law, as well as in production, work, and public activities. Deputies to the NPC should maintain close contact with their constituents, listen to and convey their opinions and demands, and work hard to serve them. Article 77 sets forth that NPC deputies...can be recalled by their electoral units....Immediately, I put out a notice telling my constituents how and when to contact me. Since June 4, 1984, I've been receiving them every Tuesday afternoon from 4:00 to 5:30. Sometimes they come in groups, sometimes singly, sometimes none.

Lisa Stearns: Is this a common practice?

WQ: I don't think so. Deputies are so different and have different schedules....Besides, my constituents know my routines. Sometimes they wait for me on the sports ground, because I jog every morning at 6:30, or they stop me on my way to the classroom. Sometimes they write or call me. They bring up problems of all kinds,...even personal matters.

I try to solve whatever problems they bring up. And I always give them feedback—whether I succeeded, how I did it, and if not, why not and why I failed. I also call public meetings...to report on how many proposals I put forward, how many problems I solved, and what issues remain unsolved and why. And I make self-criticisms, like, I don't know how to handle relationships, or I am too aggressive sometimes.

I believe transparency of political participation is essential. So I discuss my stand on different issues. For example, as a district deputy I elect the candidates to Beijing's Municipal People's Congress [MPC] on behalf of my constituents.[7] I tell them my criteria and ask for their views: If the choice is between a man candidate and a woman, all other things being equal, I would choose the woman. If it is between a Han [the dominant ethnic group in China] and a person from an ethnic minority, I would choose the ethnic....

I also expect my constituents to care about others. One of our district deputies mentioned that schools in some poor villages in the mountains west of Beijing were short of books. I called on my constituents and their families to donate books for the children there, and they gave over 4,000 books....

IC: What are some of the things you have accomplished?

WQ: For example, there was no bus along the road our university was on and everyone complained. The previous deputy had taken the issue up, but nothing was done. I pushed hard and we got the 323 bus route started.

Another issue I tackled had to do with the Changwa brigade team. Whenever they needed cash, they would dig nightsoil pits around our living quarters, because when people complained, the previous deputy would go to the university and say, "I need some cash. If I want them to remove the pits, I have to pay them." When I became a people's deputy, I applied the constitution—Article 53 says that people should respect public ethics. So I talked to the agriculture section of the district people's government. I brought the officials over to see the consequences of having nightsoil pits so close to living quarters. I also encouraged friends to write letters of complaint. Then I talked several times with the brigade leader. In the end I said to him, "Well, you just have to remove it."...After negotiating for about two hours, we decided that it should be cleared in five days. *(chuckles)* I made him write, in black and white, an agreement. He did, but it took him about an hour. He was smoking all the time....But I persisted. After five days, I went to check and it was beautifully done. I immediately wrote a letter of thanks on behalf of my constituents to the brigade saying how appreciative we were.

IC: On a big sheet of red paper!

WQ: Right. I also helped disabled retired workers get medical treatment in the clinic on campus....They thought this was one of the good things I did for my constituents. Then I managed to buy 22 *mu* [three and one-half acres] of land for BFSU to have some of the apartment buildings for the staff put up.

IC: That was very difficult.

WQ: Very, very, very...

IC: You see, in the past BFSU had some land. But in the Cultural Revolution we were asked to donate it. Our Party secretary felt that this was a patriotic duty, so he gave it away. Everybody afterwards criticized him. But Wu Qing got the land replaced.

WQ: Actually, we gave up 78 *mu* [13 acres] of land....

IC: What happened when you were up for reelection?

WQ: The third time I ran for office was right after '89. I had a very difficult time then. The university CCP secretary tried in every way to prevent me from being elected because I had supported the students in the summer of 1989. Party members were warned...not to put me forward as one of the candidates. For some time, over 100 people...were nominated *(laughs)*, anybody people could think of. It was a farce. Of course, my constituents knew that the process ends with the secret ballot and stuck it out. So, in spite of all this I got reelected—with 80 percent of the votes....

When I was in the States in 1993 I got reelected, so I'm now serving my fourth term. There's a saying in Chinese that when a person leaves the tea gets cold. One of my constituents wrote to me, "Wu Qing, it's so funny. In your case, when you're not here the tea is still warm." *(laughter)*

IC: You were also elected to the Beijing MPC?

WQ: Yes. More than a dozen of my fellow deputies in Haidian District put forward my name because they knew...what I thought and what I stood for. You see, at every DPC session I prepared and spoke on each issue that came up. I also spoke from the floor. Whenever the mayor came, I raised issues with him. Even the people working in the DPC office recommended me. And I voted for myself. Besides, from American studies I've learned to use Western political strategies, for example, lobbying. And I believe in pluralism.

IC: How do you function as a municipal deputy?

WQ: Before an MPC session is due, I put up a notice at the DPC session telling people how to contact me if there are issues they want me to raise. When I have...gotten the results, I arrange for the people concerned to talk with those who have the authority to deal with their complaints. If they are satisfied, I write a short comment on the work done and sign my name. If not, I ask those in charge to go on trying to solve the matter.

LS: Are your methods and goals different from those of your peer deputies?...Are they influenced by the fact that you're a woman?

WQ: Hard to say. My goals are now to educate my constituents, not just women, about their duties and responsibilities. Of course, women need more encouragement to be assertive and confident because they have been socialized to think that they are inferior to men....Whenever I talk to female students, I tend to tell them that they can change the situation, but first they have to change themselves.

LS: Do other women deputies follow this approach or—

IC: Even men deputies, do any of them follow your example?

WQ: I don't know....No matter what I do, I try to mobilize my constituents....People should have the guts to make complaints and form groups to push for changes. They should also learn to make a problem an issue and persist....For example, three years ago, nondegree graduate students came to me about their housing....They had been told that they couldn't enjoy the privileges or rights of degree students. But there was a document saying that they should be treated equally. So I...got the document. As a people's deputy I should carry out what policies there are or change them. After studying it, I got these students together and said, "If you want housing, you have to band together as a group. But...you might offend some of the officials up there and you might have to take the consequences. Are you willing to...work together?" They talked and decided to do it. After two years and a half, every person in that group got housing. Now I'm working with the last twelve people who were on the list of 240 households eligible for housing....I've met with them four times already to work out tactics. Some of them don't want to wait anymore...and are backing out. I don't want them to back out. I want them to stick together....

IC: How does this affect your relations with the officials?

WQ: Some supported me as I was helping BFSU carry out its policies....Some thought I was a nuisance, too noisy. And some are jealous because I enjoy prestige.

IC: Can you give us an idea of how the DPC functions?

WQ: We have a session every year that lasts usually a week at the district level, about ten days at the municipal level. The DPC elects the district heads and vice heads, examines and approves the plan and budget for the district's economic and social development, and reports on its implementation....

At my first DPC session in 1984, we deputies just sat and listened to reports, one after the other.[8] We didn't get a chance to make suggestions or criticisms, so several of us spoke up and asked for a meeting at which we could put forward our ideas. This was granted. Another demand was that we should meet with the mayor of Beijing since many of our suggestions and criticisms were tied to the city government's policies and decisions. He came, and that has become a routine. But he doesn't go to any of the other city districts. Haidian concentrates most of the colleges in Beijing, and most of the deputies are well educated and have a sense of political participation. And Haidian voters know how to take advantage of the new electoral system to elect people who can really represent them. So, whenever there is an election, the attention of the municipal government is on Haidian District.

When I was nominated as one of the candidates to the MPC in 1988, I knew immediately that there would be inequality among the candidates, because the biographical data on those nominated through official channels had been prepared a long time in advance, while the data for those nominated by peer deputies would come out then and there....I went to talk to the director of the DPC. I said that *all* the candidates' biographical data should be distributed at the *same* time—to no avail....So I complained to the person in charge of office work. That person was a retired army man. He had never talked to a woman like me. I went up to him and said, "There is this inequality...." He got so angry! "Don't you know that some of the typists passed out because they were working so hard?! Don't you know that it was impossible for us to get the materials out at the same time?!" I said, "I can understand that. The people who passed out have all my respect, my sympathy. But this is a political issue. The material should come out at the same time."

I felt there was strong discrimination in his eyes when he talked to me, because I'm a woman! In fact, I had hesitated. Number one, being Chinese, we should always try to be modest, polite. Number two, I'm a woman, should I bring this up? Number three, because I'm involved, I don't know how people look at me. I turned it over, again and again, in my head for two or three hours. In the end I decided to go and talk because I thought this was a political issue. It was important, not just for myself.

LS: So this debate was inside yourself—

WQ:—inside myself—

LS:—before you decided you could make this next move?

WQ: Yes! Yes! Yes! When I was talking to him, my heart beat so fast! *(laughs)* And it was so hard to articulate clearly what I wanted to say, but I felt there was great discrimination inside him, because I am a woman, because I was so forward. So assertive, so independent—

IC:—instead of being modest and—

WQ:—docile and obedient. You see, I wasn't brought up under the Confucian influence, nor was my mother. I was never docile. Still, in the 1950s and '60s, I was so convinced that whatever the CCP did was right that I never questioned it. In Mao's era we followed Mao's policies. No one was encouraged to question or do otherwise, and those who did were labeled and became targets in political campaigns. (For example, my father and brother were labeled rightists in...1957 for having different views and speaking out, telling the facts.) Confucian ideas still affect women. For one thing, people don't expect women to challenge, to disagree, to question. The second time I felt that I was really considered a woman was when I was the first deputy to cast abstention votes and "no" votes at the MPC in 1988.

IC: That caused a shock—

WQ: Right.

IC:—through the whole Congress.

LS: This was at a very important time.

WQ: Yes, at the beginning of 1988. I cast two abstention votes and two "no" votes. We were asked to elect people to committees. Government officials were recommended to two of them, so I cast two "no" votes because I thought that as administrators they should be supervised by the MPC to guard against corruption....

When we vote for the presidium, it's a kind of package vote. Either you agree with the ninety-one members or you disagree. I said that that's wrong, that I would like to go by each individual. Because there were people who were too old and people who couldn't represent me! So I cast an abstention vote. I abstained again when the agenda was put to the vote. I thought there should be a plenary session for deputies to speak from the floor. Government officials must hear people's complaints directly....

After the votes, nobody moved from their seats. When I was leaving the assembly hall, nobody moved. I thought, perhaps one of those older persons passed out. Everybody was looking at the stage. (I had been sitting in the front, in the fifth row.) When I looked back, the stage was empty and then it dawned on me that people were trying to—

IC: They were looking at you!

WQ:—yes, to find out who that person was who cast abstention votes and "no" votes. The only person! I raised my head high and walked out. When I got home, I got phone calls. The first came from my brother. He said, "I heard that one of the deputies in Haidian District cast abstention votes and 'no' votes. Do you know who that person is?" I said, "It's me." *(laughter)* I think I even shocked my brother. *(laughter)* All this caused a stir. A reporter had come to interview me on the recommendation of the DPC office as I was considered one of the most active deputies. But after my abstention votes, he didn't dare write about me. From that day on I heard people say, "Now *that's* the woman who cast abstention votes, 'no' votes." But I got a lot of support from other reporters, peer deputies, and staff members of the DPC and MPC.

LS: What was the tone in their voice when they said, "that woman"?

WQ: Not friendly, not friendly. Very...

Liu Dongxiao: Did they value it less because you are a woman?

WQ: Yes! Yes! Woman—women—a woman...In that tone. The way they looked at me made me feel inferior, as if I were not normal.

LS: Your approach is to contact agencies and to try to enlist them in your goals by forging relationships, which are important in China to get work done effectively. What are the advantages of being a woman in that process and what are the obstacles?

WQ: I feel that being a woman I have the advantage, because usually officials don't expect you to be assertive and independent.

LS: The element of surprise!

WQ: Right. *(laughter)* So sometimes they commit themselves before they know it, because it takes them a little while to think, "Ooh...." I usually tell them the complaints and needs of my constituents, but I also give them constructive suggestions or help them..., for example, if they want their staff members to study English.

Women also tend to show more care for people—perhaps in minor things, but they touch people's heart.

LS: You're talking about the flowers you delivered to people you care about? *(laughter)*

WQ: Yes. I usually visit retired constituents who are not feeling very well. I give them calendars, especially if they have made good complaints or suggestions. Without them, I would not get elected. Without them, I would not know their needs better. And without them, I would not know the world—society—better.

LS: There are many avenues of political activity, also within government agencies. Would you consider working within the government structure as distinct from the Party structure?

WQ: I'm not a Party member. I just want to be what I am now. *(laughs)* I think in the CCP you have to obey completely whatever decisions are made....That's the hard part. Once you get an official post, sometimes you have to say certain things simply because you are there. That's why I don't want to.

LS: Is it easier for you as a woman to work as a people's deputy? Would there be other obstacles for you within a ministry, for example?

WQ: I think it's easier for me to be a people's deputy because I don't have those official hats....When Wu Yi [minister of foreign trade and economic cooperation since 1991] became vice mayor of Beijing in 1988, there were all kinds of rumors. People said she got there because of her relationship with certain people, not because of her merits. She is a very capable person. They were saying that she was going to become Mrs. So-and-So—

IC: A top leader...

WQ: —and that that's why she was there.

LS: No one can challenge that with you because you're directly elected?

WQ: Right. But then, of course, I have other problems.

LS: Such as?

WQ: After '89, apart from this attempt to prevent me from getting elected, I was not allowed to go abroad for about three years....I think my promotion to full professor is also affected. But I don't care anymore....Whatever I gain, it will be the support of my constituents. I like that. *(laughs)*...I will persist in being active in politics.

IC: How do you make time to do all this? You've got your family and you're a very caring person. You have your teaching and you care about your students. And you have this political work.

WQ: I'm very healthy. I've been jogging every day for 43 years. Then I plan my time, my schedule, my route....I use my phone a lot. Now I get a lot of things done faster because I have very good relationships with some officials. I know their home and beeper numbers. I know their wives and talk to them; they help. I know their drivers and secretaries.

LS: Do you know some of the women deputies and their husbands?

WQ: Not too many...there are not many women in the political sector to begin with. Of the women I know, a lot are single.

LS: Could you comment on that?

WQ: A lot of them are divorced, because usually men don't want a career-oriented woman. They want a good mother to their child and a supportive wife. But they don't want to be supportive husbands sometimes....It's difficult for women to get into political office in China —of the illiterates 70 percent are women. Every year about four million students drop out, and again 70 percent of these are women. So girls have to be very well educated and self-confident....A lot of women feel that they are not built for political activity because they have to be assertive enough to know the game. As a people's deputy, you have to know how to function, what the problems are, and what to make an issue. How to bring them up and who to talk to. How to solve them, who to see, when to see, how to do. There are so many things involved, so a lot of women shy away from politics. In general, women think it's men's domain. I can give you some figures. A survey was done in 1992 about whether people want to be people's deputies. When women were asked, "Have you ever thought of becoming a people's deputy?", only 14.53 percent said, "Many times." 12.9 percent said, "Only once," but 72.51 percent answered, "Never thought about it."...

LS: Do you and other women deputies...talk about these issues? Do you cooperate among yourselves? Is there a gender consciousness among you and your women colleagues?

WQ: It's rather hard. I tried to bring up the gender issue about two years ago. I wanted to address it at the MPC session in 1990. But I got a very strong negative response in my group (deputies from Haidian District to the MPC form four subgroups, and I am in one of them) when I talked about the inequalities between men and women in politics, the economy, employment, the family, education. A lot of men said, "There *should* be inequalities because men and women are different. Women are inferior." Some women who are not very well educated also came up to me saying, "We are not like you, Wu Qing. You're well educated, your parents are prominent." They think I'm too strong and very special because I am the daughter of Bing Xin....But college-educated and professionally successful women in my group supported me. So, to get other deputies' support, I dropped the issue....You know, the quota system cuts both ways: Though it guarantees the representation of women in all sectors of society, some seats are token.

LS: What is the quota system now?

WQ: The ACWF proposed a percentage, 25 percent. It met with strong opposition because many people, mostly men, do not think women are capable of functioning as deputies. And some women agree.

LS: This was during the drafting of the 1992—

WQ:—Chinese Law on the Protection of Rights and Interests of Women. In the NPC, 21.3 percent of the deputies are women.

LS: As I remember the law, there should be a step-by-step—

WQ:—increase of women's representation, right.

LS: It's interesting that this particular clause—whether to have a quota—was debated several times, inserted, and then withdrawn, and reinserted and withdrawn, so there was quite a process and strong, hot debate about it.

WQ: Right. The excuses some of the men used! In the south, in some provinces, women make up about 30 percent....Some say, "If you have this 25 percent limit, then they have to cut down the number in the south." In general, the sentiment is that there shouldn't be too many women deputies.

LS: This argument was listened to?

WQ: Yes.

IC: What is the percentage of women deputies at the district and municipal levels?

WQ: Twenty-two and 25 percent, respectively. But it does not conform to the percentage of women in our population—48.5 percent. So there should be more women representatives. In 1995 there will be a woman cadre in each Chinese village....

LS: Also at the county level?

WQ: There are more female representatives at the county level because women at this level are better educated and men tend to be more open as the level goes up.

IC: There have been women cadres in the countryside as long as I can remember. They...usually were asked to be in charge of women's affairs.

WQ: Yeah. But they take care of a lot more things now....The reforms have brought growth in production and development, as well as in the rate of crime and chaos. New laws have to be made and enforced. Many female deputies focus on controlling prices and inflation, and on ways to check crime....But there has also been a setback in women's awareness. I was brought up in the '50s, when policies stressed that men and women are equal. You know Mao's saying, "Women hold up half the sky." Women were encouraged to become physicists, geologists....

LS: Were they also encouraged to be political participants?

WQ: Very often daughters or wives of Red Army veterans and prominent political leaders were encouraged to enter politics or to be on committees....It's important for women to be better educated, to have more self-respect, self-confidence, so that they can compete on an equal basis. It's hard, but they have to fight for the opportunity.

LD: Most times their confidence is affected by the stereotypes of women. For example, when women speak on women's issues, they are challenged, like, "Do you have a family? Are you anti-family, anti-social?", because they are considered strong and therefore less feminine. So now, sometimes a kind of answer—a powerful answer, some women think— is to present their husbands, to show them how harmonious they are with their families.

LS: Has your family been important to you?

WQ: I get a lot of support from my family. My mother…wrote a scroll for me saying that for the interest of the people I should not be afraid of any opposition forces that might prevent me from working for the people.

IC: Your mother is a rebel too. *(laughs)*

WQ: My husband helps….We do the housework together; whoever has time has to do more. In a family, you need both men and women— it takes two to tango….

LS: If you had decided not to marry, or if you were divorced, would you have been as effective as a political person or has family legitimized you in the political arena?

WQ: I don't know….I might have had more trouble! People might have spread rumors about me.

LS: You mentioned that some women in political positions are divorced.

WQ: They do have problems. People think that they have lost femininity, the glamour that's needed to attract people and get their support. They think they're superwomen. Or that they don't know what love means because they have failed in the most important relationship, that between man and woman. They tend to distance you. They don't think you're normal. A woman can be more effective if she is attractive. In politics there is a lot of this human relationship business going on, because if you want to get things done you have to talk to people to get support….In general, a woman will be politically more vulnerable if she is single or divorced as this can be used against her. But, definitely, a woman can be effective politically as long as she is a person of integrity and supported by her constituents.

LD: Have you been challenged to show that you have a harmonious family?

WQ: So far, not yet. Not yet. *(laughter)* But that's a good question….There was a vice county magistrate who had problems with her male chauvinist husband. He would call her every day at 11:30 A.M. to ask her to go home to cook for him. When she was on business trips, he would visit her unexpectedly….Men usually do not have these kinds of problems. If they want to run for political office, they find a supportive wife. But for women it is not easy. In general, men marry down, women marry up. Not to mention that women have to be much better than men to attain the same office.

LD: The stereotypical demands that women be more committed to their families really divert women's attention from their work.

WQ: Women in politics don't have much time to be with their families, especially their children, and they often feel guilty about it....They have a double role: They have to work outside *and* inside the home.

IC: In the late 1980s, you turned your attention to women's issues. Why?

WQ: Because women's issues were becoming more and more obvious as a result of the economic reforms. In 1989...I was invited to become a women in development consultant for CIDA, the Canadian International Development Agency. This offered me opportunities to travel to poverty-stricken regions...and get to know the lives and issues of my sisters in those areas. These trips raised my consciousness, as well as a sense of identity with these women. My job was to get more of them involved in the whole process of CIDA projects, especially in decision making....

It's so important to get women organized to have a group identity...and work together to overcome difficulties. Changes do happen when women learn that in unity there is strength. This solidarity creates a lot of power....

I helped to initiate the Women's Hotline....It offers counseling to women needing help, though now 15 to 20 percent of the calls are from men....Our counselors are trained to give expert advice on divorce, marriage, law, family planning, child care, sex, et cetera. My job has been to advise them, publicize the project nationally and internationally, and raise funding....And a group of us started a Singles' Weekend Club...that helps members, especially single mothers, share their experience and form support groups....

LS: It sounds as though this link between the work of non-governmental organizations [NGOs] and influence on policy in the long term has been a way for women to play a political role....

WQ: Yes. Some of us are trying to talk to women in other regions. At the Conference on Women in Development in Rural China in October 1994...I discussed networking and funding for women. I also stressed what development means for individual women, groups, and areas. It is essential to build women's awareness that they can...overcome their weaknesses and build on their strong points so that, in the long term, they will be able to change their social status. This...is the basis for any change.

Rural Women Knowing All is the first magazine to focus on rural women in China. I'm an adviser and fundraiser for it. If we want to change China—especially the lot of Chinese women—we have to help rural women who make up the majority. The magazine raises women's self-awareness, and helps them to participate in production, improve their livelihood, and guard against corruption....It also publicizes the

Women's Law so that women know their rights and can protect themselves....The magazine is launching a literacy program for women aged 15 to 35 as part of the nationwide drive to make women literate....This will bring about a fundamental change in China....

I also support the Hope Project which raises money to get dropouts back into school....And I am the president of the Chinese Women's Health Network....We are going to translate *Our Bodies, Ourselves* (the Boston Women's Health Collective book)...and write two culturally specific books on the same topic, one for women, one for men....

In the United States, I met Anne Murray, the president of the Global Fund for Women, and now I am their adviser for China. That's why more and more women are coming to me with their projects. It's a very good opportunity for me to put women inside and outside of China in touch so that they can get to know and help each other, financially and spiritually. It takes women from all over the world to work together. We have more or less the same kinds of issues and problems. Of course, the ways of solving them are different, but there are many similarities....We must work together in spite of political differences, all kinds of differences.

LS: You know of EMILY's List in the United States, the organization that raises funds for women to support their campaigns for election....What would be an appropriate strategy in China to increase women's political participation?

WQ: I'm thinking of a project to train women deputies to know their rights and responsibilities, and to teach them how to function. So far, I've talked to local DPC officials....Deputies must also learn to report frequently to their constituents....I don't think they're electing me now because I'm a woman but because of my work—at least I can show them what women can do and that they can do better. It's a two-way traffic. Reporting to constituents also makes them feel important. And they are....People's deputies are of the people, by the people, for the people.

IC: Is it easier to work with women in NGOs than in government positions?

WQ: It is, because there is more flexibility and we can focus on what we think are priorities. Besides, there are no rules or orders to follow which we think are not good enough....

LS: I've often talked with my Chinese colleagues about the question of sisterhood or women's solidarity....Does this concept transcend local differences or does it need to be considered within a particular social context?

WQ: This feeling of sisterhood is everywhere and it's very strong....When I was in the States and talked about women in China, they said, "Hey, that's familiar!" That's why it's important for the Chinese now to think globally and act locally, regionally. Gradually, we can shift from "think" globally to "act" globally. Take unemployment or social security in Third World countries, prostitution, trafficking of women—these are global issues we must address together.

LD: In my experience, in the past it was more difficult for women to work with women because many of us are envious of each other, though there are many factors that affect relationships among women. It's easier now because we are interested in women's issues, but sometimes we can't seem to remember the principle of helping each other—the principle of sisterhood.

WQ: But it's unfair to say that it's just hard to work with women. What about working with men, or men working with each other? They have the same problems, because we are human beings and you can't do away with greed, jealousy, and all that....

IC: Do you feel you are unique?

WQ: I really don't know. All deputies are unique. Most people could do the things I do: meet regularly with constituents, pass on complaints, push persistently to get things done. Because of my mother's fame, people think I can get away with saying and doing certain things. Still, I believe it is because I am serious and persistent. For example, the underpass linking our two campuses. That took six years with the help of my constituents....

IC: You've been a district deputy for ten years and a municipal deputy for seven years. How do you feel about your involvement?

WQ: I like being a people's deputy because no one tells me what to do. I have to work out my own strategies. Some deputies...just enjoy the honor. I want to change that into a pattern where deputies serve the people. Deputies are changing because constituents are changing and placing higher demands on them. And deputies are finding that they can bring about concrete changes....In Deng Xiaoping's era, people can take more initiative, be more creative, and accept more challenges. Governments at different levels are becoming more responsive....

LS: How would you summarize the three main obstacles to women seeking political power?

WQ: Number one is Confucianism. Its ideology has had a great impact on people in general, both men and women. It demands three obediences from women: to the father, to the husband after marriage, and to the son after the death of the husband....Men's place is still outside the home, women's place is still inside the home. That really sticks in people's minds. Even college graduates, after they get married they think home is most important to women....Women just have to sacrifice. They have no time for particular work outside of "the home." I put that in quotes because women think that's their job—work outside to earn money, work inside to take care of husband, son, and perhaps in-laws.

Number two is that women are not well educated. They are not well informed or socialized to have a wider vision, to think that it is important for them to try to...make society better, or to work for the interest of the greater part of the people.

Number three is that women are socialized to think that they are inferior. That they can't and shouldn't think *big*....Of course, in actual practice the obstacles come from men.

Power really lies in decisions over economic resources. Women are usually in "soft" service jobs, in personnel and propaganda, in organizational or educational jobs, because they are not perceived as being qualified to make major decisions, especially decisions that will affect millions of people. Planning is another area where there is real power, but women are only in charge of the State Family Planning Commission. With the economic reforms, more and more women are competing for jobs that used to be held by men—management or political positions that had never been filled by women. But now Wu Yi's there and she's doing a great job.

It is essential to raise the awareness of women, as well as of men, to socialize boys to be supportive of and to respect women, to work with women. We'd better start at the beginning, instead of having to re-educate men. Our Women's Studies Forum had a project to look into the roles of people in primary school textbooks. We found that the images portrayed are still very traditional. That must change.

We also started to look into TV advertisements. Women on television play their traditional role. It's always a supportive role—being a secretary, being an object for men to look at. That's *not* the woman we want. We want women to be beautiful, to be capable, to be able to compete with men.

POLITICAL WOMEN AND WOMEN'S POLITICS IN INDIA

Radha Kumar

POLITICAL WOMEN

The South Asian predilection for women premiers has so often been commented on that most Indian feminists merely snort at its mention. They are especially irritated when this predilection is cited to conclude that South Asians are more receptive to powerful women. Yet there is something startling about the fact that the four chief countries of the subcontinent, India, Pakistan, Bangladesh, and Sri Lanka, have all had women prime ministers—and three have them today. (India, by far the largest of the four, lost Indira Gandhi in 1984. However, since the assassination of Rajiv Gandhi in 1991, several factions of the Congress Party have periodically clamored for the election of his widow, Sonia Gandhi, and are currently clamoring again.) That this political leadership of women should occur in countries that are held in low regard for their performance on women's rights and whose traditions comprise relatively strict and numerous gender codes is especially startling. How can a country have purdah, dowry, bigamy, polygamy, widow immolation, and a woman prime minister?

In answer, most Indian feminists argue that there is no logical connection between the existence of a woman prime minister and the status of the majority of women in the country, and offer two possible explanations for the phenomenon. The first, more commonly advanced, is that acceptance of a woman prime minister draws on a subcontinental mythology that is peopled by strong and often fearsome women who are generic figures of powerful female nature, such as the smallpox goddess or the goddess Kali, who came to earth to destroy demons and drink their blood. This mythology cannot apply to the mass of women, but only to the exceptional. But to argue this, given that Pakistan and Bangladesh are Islamic states and the mythic women are worshipped by different Hindu sects, one would have to say that the cultural practices of Hindu mythology dominate the subcontinent, and it would be difficult to make such an argument cohere. The other explanation, subscribed to by a larger number of feminists than is the above, is that this is a variant of the dynastic traditions of the subcontinent, in which the strongest relative (child or wife) seizes power. For example, Indira Gandhi was the daughter of India's first prime minister, Jawaharlal Nehru, as is Benazir Bhutto the daughter of Pakistan's first premier, Zulfikar Ali Bhutto; Begum Khaleda Zia is the widow of Bangladesh's assassinated president Ziaur Rahman and her chief opponent, Hasina Wajed, is the daughter of another leader who was assassinated, Sheikh Mujibur Rahman; and Chandrika Kumaratunga is the widow of a political leader who was killed and the daughter of Sirimavo Bandaranaike, a former prime minister of Sri Lanka and herself the widow of one of Sri Lanka's foremost political figures (who also was assassinated). What makes these modern variants of the subcontinent's dynastic traditions is that gender can be less important than political talent: for example, Benazir Bhutto is preferred to her brother. But the other point which can be made is that it is precisely the legacy of martyrdom—assassinated fathers and husbands—that gives these women political potency.[1] The problem with both arguments is that they obscure the individual women. When Indira Gandhi first became prime minister she was cursorily viewed as malleable and her advisors were called "the kitchen cabinet." Within a few years she emerged as an ambitious and daring political schemer, and when she imposed a state of emergency on India in 1975, her political drive was unquestionable. In the next nine years, she centralized authority, flouted the legislature, undermined Congress Party organization, fell from and rose again to power, harbored terrorism, and was assassinated in 1984. On two occasions at least she intervened in support of feminists: in 1980 and 1981 she sponsored a new law against custodial rape, and in 1983 she got the Delhi municipality to withdraw a grant of government land to an organization propagating widow immolation.[2] After her death the Congress commemorated her as mother of the Indian nation, and the site set aside for her ashes was named *Shakti Sthal* (the goddess Shakti symbolizes female power; *sthal* means place).

To the feminist groups that emerged in the late 1970s, after the emergency was lifted, Indira Gandhi was an authoritarian politician to be shunned. Her deeds were such that she could not be construed as an important figure for women—or else, she could be construed only negatively, as a warning sign that women might be especially vulnerable to the corruption of power. Indeed, it might be that the wariness that the contemporary Indian women's movement has displayed toward direct engagement in electoral politics stems in part from the shadow cast by Indira Gandhi. The importance of the dynastic argument is that it makes clear that South Asian receptiveness to women in politics has been largely limited to the political apex. What this apex consists of can sometimes surprise. Indira Gandhi was not the only powerful woman politician in India. The south Indian state of Tamil Nadu has been ruled by the redoubtable Jayalalitha since the death of M. G. Ramachandran, its film star turned politician and chief minister. Jayalalitha was M. G. Ramachandran's protégée—some say his mistress—and though several members of his family vied for the political mantle, it fell on Jayalalitha. And she cannot, even by stretch of definition, be said to come from the elite. Judging by the rhetoric of her followers (some of whom have killed themselves as an act of worship), Jayalalitha has a mythic quality.

Jayalalitha's rise is not the only example of how theories of elite political dominance in India need to be qualified. The tension between modernity and traditionalism that characterizes post-independence India has created two primary types of woman politician: the urban elite woman from a political family, and the traditionally recognized figure of dangerous female power to be appeased. The chief feature of the 1991 elections was the emergence of a new breed of militantly Hindu woman politician typified by Uma Bharati and Sadhvi Rithambara, both of whom shot to prominence through the 1990 campaign to erect a temple to the god Ram on the site of a mosque. Alleging that Ram was born on this site, a pan-Hindu organization, the Vishwa Hindu Parishad, launched a campaign to "liberate" the site and replace the mosque with a temple in 1986. The campaign gradually garnered support and in 1990 the demand was taken up by the Bharatiya Janata Party as a major plank of their electoral campaign. In the same year the right-wing Hindu nationalist Bharatiya Janata Party founded a women's wing; its kin organizations and co-campaigners, the Rashtriya Swayamsevak Sangh and the Vishwa Hindu Parishad already had them (the Rashtriya Sevika Samiti and the Durga Vahini, respectively). Though the Bharatiya Janata Party stalwart, Vijayaraje Scindia, was the nominal female figurehead of the campaign, it was the young Uma Bharati and Sadhvi Rithambara who captured popular attention through a combination of passionate and incantatory appeals to communal violence. Rithambara's audiocassette, which was played all over the country and could be heard at street tea stalls, alternately throbbed and shrieked to all Hindus to hate Muslims, destroy the mosque, and build a temple to Ram; Bharati drew large crowds all over the central Indian state of Madhya Pradesh, which was her campaigning turf.[3] Her mixture of boldness, *Hindutva*,[4] and kittenishness proved to be especially attractive to Hindu men, for she remained approachable while retaining the attributes of the powerful mythic woman.

However, both the modern elite and traditional types of political women share certain ambiguities, and both have certain common experiences. First of all, politics is not regarded as an entirely respectable profession for anyone, let alone women. Elite men can confer respectability on politics, but for this they have to be known for their personal integrity, and the respectability they bring to politics only rarely extends much beyond their selves.[5] For elite women it is even more difficult, for they are judged not only by personal integrity but also by the nature of their family protection. Being a member of the elite, therefore, does not automatically confer respectability on a woman in politics, though it does cushion her against some of the nastier forms of chauvinism that non-elite women politicians are subjected to.[6] Nor does respectability afford women full protection: though few doubted Indira Gandhi's respectability, this did not protect her from innuendo or shield her from speculation about her relationships with any man on whose advice she seemed to rely unduly.

Secondly, the rise of such women politicians as Sadhvi Rithambara and Uma Bharati indicates a shift away from dominantly elite political representation. Both are lower middle class and low caste, and do not owe their rise to sheer political patronage, as Jayalalitha did. But the most notable example of lower-class and lower-caste women rising to power is the West Bengal Congress Party politician Mamta Bannerjee, who is lower middle class but not low caste, and who has risen from the ranks to become a junior minister.

Indira Gandhi, Mamta Bannerjee, Jayalalitha, Sadhvi Rithambara, and Uma Bharati can all be categorized as politicians. The former two conform to the realpolitik type of politician; the latter three have stretched Indian political definition to include figures of mythic female power, and within this category Rithambara and Bharati symbolize religion-based politics. But there are also small signs that the influence of the Indian women's movement has led to the accommodation of independent women in Parliament. The nomination of Ela Bhatt to the Rajya Sabha (India's equivalent of the British House of Lords) is one such sign. Founder of the Self-Employed Women's Association, an organization of poor working women (street vendors, load carriers) begun in 1972, Ela Bhatt was nominated as a nonpolitical woman with almost twenty years of experience in organizing women to gain rights both at work and at home.[7] Though her example is yet to be followed with another, her nomination shows that there is a space for the independent, issue-based political representation of women.

WOMEN AND TWENTIETH-CENTURY POLITICS

Women's political participation has long been debated in India, both at large and within women's groups. The most prominent of the early women's groups, the All-India Women's Conference, was for several years divided on this issue. It first came up in 1928 and 1929, a year after the conference was founded, and at that time it was decided that the conference would not engage in any political activities. Debate on the issue kept pace with the rising nationalist movement and in the early 1930s, when the Indian freedom movement was in full sway, the conference decided to participate in nationalist campaigns. Several of its members were already active in the Indian National Congress.[8] In the same years, no less a figure than Rabindranath Tagore criticized politically active women as "unnatural, unbalanced."[9]

Though the prominence of women in the nationalist movement opened a large space for women in politics and several feminists were inducted into the government of independent India, attitudes toward women politicians remained ambivalent. If anything, as the flush of independence died down, they grew more ambivalent. Since India gained independence in 1947 Indian women members of Parliament comprise no more than 5 to 7 percent, and the percentage in state legislatures has been even lower. However, though the percentage of women in Parliament barely changed between 1953 and 1989 (4.8 percent: 5.1 percent), there was a significant increase between 1989 and 1991 (5.1 percent: 7.1 percent).[10] And though the number of women being elected might not have risen by much, the numbers of women standing for election has steadily increased since the late 1970s, when the contemporary Indian women's movement developed. This rise has occurred largely in small towns and rural areas, and comprises both women standing as independents as well as on party tickets. It indicates a broadening of women's aspirations for political representation as well as an overall shift away from urban elite political dominance.

As feminist groups did not concern themselves with elections or political representation at the time, the link between the increase in women running for office and the growing women's movement must have been the less direct one of a changing political climate. Indeed, the genesis of the movement was through groups influenced by Socialists and others on the left in villages and small towns, especially in the states of Andhra Pradesh, Bihar, Maharashtra, and to some extent West Bengal and Kerala; Gandhians in Gujarat and the hill tracts of north India; and developmental and Christian reform groups working with rural and tribal populations, especially in the south. And though they shunned electoral politics, the women's groups of the late 1970s and early 1980s addressed themselves to campaigning for political change, both at the legislative and institutional levels, from the very beginning. In the space of ten years, they have gained new laws on dowry, rape, sexual harassment (known benignly as "eve-teasing"), *sati,* and, most recently, against the misuse of amniocentesis for the abortion of female fetuses. And, despite their insistence on autonomy and criticism of government and the elites, the feminists did not hesitate to work with political parties or to use whatever connections they had in government and the elites.[11] As a result, all sorts of new structures have been set up in the administration to deal with women's problems. Following the 1979 to 1982 campaign against dowry-related crimes, dowry cells were set up in the police administration to deal with complaints of harassment for more dowry and alleged cases of dowry-related murder. As the women's movement grew, women's development cells were set up in different government departments, and local government-supported women's organizations, Mahila Mandals, were revitalized. Women's groups were invited to aid in developing local training programs, including for the administration and police.

Though feminist groups did not seek to expand the number of women in Parliament, they were connected to women MPs from the inception of the women's movement. Two Bombay-based women MPs, Ahilya Ranganekar of the Communist Party of India-Marxist

WOMEN FIRST

1906-1907: FINLAND BECOMES THE FIRST EUROPEAN NATION TO GIVE WOMEN THE VOTE, AND 19 WOMEN ARE ELECTED TO THE NEW 200-PERSON FINNISH PARLIAMENT.

(CPI-M) and Mrinal Gore of the Socialist Party, had in fact mobilized women in an anti-price-rise agitation in the early 1970s; later, they and the handful of left-wing women MPs formed a kind of parliamentary lobby for the women's movement, campaigning for new legislation against dowry and custodial rape in 1980 and 1981. Parliamentary interest in feminist campaigns was not, however, limited to women MPs. The 1980 to 1981 campaign against custodial rape was taken up by a number of center to left MPs. In June 1980 Parliament discussed the increase in incidents of police rape since the 1960s: several MPs suggested the death penalty should be used in cases of custodial rape; an incident of police rape that occurred in the same month in Haryana state led them to ask for the resignation of the home minister. And a comic touch was introduced by the leader of a centrist fragment, the Janata (S) Party, Raj Narain, who announced he was resigning his post as leader in order to launch "a struggle to protect the dignity and honour of women" by going on an indefinite fast unless the government took appropriate action against another incident of police rape in Haryana in July 1980. At a little over five feet in height, Raj Narain's weight was then 82 kgs. The press vied to report his weight loss from day to day, and police rape was forgotten as the nation watched the kilos slough off.[12]

Subsequently, several male MPs supported feminist campaigns. In 1985, the MP Arif Mohammad Khan opposed a bill piloted by a Muslim League MP, G. M. Banatwala, which sought to remove Muslim women's right to maintenance from their husbands; he resigned in 1986 when his government made a volte-face, enacting a similar bill.[13] And a large number of both socialist[14] and left-affiliated MPs voted against this bill, and later for a bill seeking to restrict attempts to revive the cult of widow immolation, which was enacted in 1988.

As the women's movement gained in strength, party-affiliated women's fronts were revitalized and in some cases new fronts were formed, such as the CPI-M-affiliated All-India Democratic Women's Association. Though relations between party-affiliated and autonomous women's groups were rarely tension free, the socialist- and communist-affiliated and autonomous women's groups worked together on campaigns and continue to do so now. The Congress Party-associated All-India Women's Conference sometimes joins the others in campaigns, but the Congress Mahila Dal (the women's wing of the Congress Party) rarely does so. And the women's wing of the Hindu communal Rashtra Swayamsevak Sangh (national self-help organization) is not admitted to joint women's fora nor would any of the other women's groups, party-affiliated or autonomous, work with the several Hindu communal women's organizations that now exist, such as the Vishwa Hindu Parishad and Bharatiya Janata Party women's wings. (The former was founded in the 1980s, and the latter in early 1991.) Nevertheless, their formation is also a testimony—however perverse[15]—to the growing political awareness of women as a constituency, which is surely an offshoot of the women's movement.

By the late 1980s, political parties began to take the constituency of women seriously enough to address women's issues in their electoral manifestos. The Congress Party, in fact, focused on women's political representation, promising to implement a 30 percent reservation for women in local and regional government, as recommended by the National Perspective Plan for Women that they had sponsored in 1988. Women's groups took note, and among the autonomous groups a new interest in electoral politics developed. This interest took different forms: some groups warned of political opportunism while others argued for an imaginative use of the new political space that was opening up. In Bangalore, the feminist group Vimochana issued a leaflet addressed to women voters in the 1989 elections, in which the group accused the major national political parties of "hypocrisy" in mentioning women's issues in their manifestos and urged women voters to exercise their votes to defeat leaders who had been implicated in rape charges, supported the campaign to revive widow immolation, or been involved in criminal and communal activities (conflict based on religious identity). A number of candidates accused of the above were listed by name.[16] By the early 1990s there were two developments that showed that the days of this kind of cautious interventionism were numbered. The major development, which was to take precedence over the issue of political parties and parliamentary elections, was *panchayati raj* (the rule of the *panchayat*). The panchayat was a precolonial form of local or community governance, comprising village councils that administered local concerns. Commonly, there would be both the general village panchayat, which would meet on matters of interest to the entire village, and smaller caste panchayats, which would intervene in disputes on marriage or divorce and could excommunicate caste members for offending caste norms. The Gandhian vision of an independent India was based on a vaguely decentralized agglomerate of general village panchayats or local government units, but the panchayat was included in administrative structures only in 1960 and remained largely a paper organization until 1989, when the Congress Party under Rajiv Gandhi sought to give the panchayats a greater degree of local control. They also promised 30 percent reservation for women in panchayats and *zilla parishads* (organs of regional government). At the same time, the Panchayati Raj Bill that the Congress enacted brought the panchayats under the direct control of the central government, and was seen—with reason—by many state governments ruled by opposition or regional political parties as an attempt to undermine India's budding federalism.[17]

Though it was the Congress Party that had promised 30 percent reservation for women in local and regional government, it was another organization, the Shetkari Sangathana in Maharashtra, that first made a policy resolution to field women candidates in panchayat elections. A Maharashtra-based independent peasants' organization, the Shetkari Sangathana got involved in promoting women's electoral candidacies in 1986 when they urged opposition political parties to field a majority of women candidates in the next elections, at both local and national levels. In the 1989 village panchayat elections, several local Sangathana branches decided to field all-women panels, which won in seven villages. In the same elections, all-women panchayats were elected in three other villages, but there is no information on whether they belonged to any organizations, or if so, to which. Clearly women's political participation was gaining popular currency. In the 1990 state elections the Shetkari Sangathana fielded some ten women candidates, one of whom was elected. But in 1991, when the subregional elections were finally held, Sangathana women candidates won roughly one hundred seats in regional bodies across Maharashtra.[18]

The radical spread of popular awareness of women's political potential that the women panchayats symbolized was also brought home at the fourth all-India women's liberation conference, which was held in Kerala at the end of 1990. Some three thousand women, 60 percent of whom were village women mainly from poor and low-caste families, attended the conference. This was a striking contrast to the first all-India women's liberation conference, which was held in Bombay in 1980 and attended chiefly by representatives of fledgling urban women's groups, most of whom were middle class and left wing. It showed not only how far the women's movement had come but also the directions in which it was spreading. One of the themes of the conference was "women in the political process": as I was asked to lead that workshop I can state fairly authoritatively that it was not expected to be particularly popular. But around three to four hundred women attended, and one after another speakers from the floor made evident why panchayat-level representation was so important. A particularly telling point was when, in a discussion on land holdings and land rights, one woman argued that property rights for her began with the rooms in her hut and the pots and pans: how were they to be shared if her husband died, and where would she live?

The panchayat elections started a debate on reservation within the Indian women's movement. Until the mid-1980s autonomous women's groups were, as has been pointed out earlier, wary of electoral politics, both in fear of co-option and on the general principle that political representation would deradicalize women and lead women representatives to put party or individual political interests above those of the movement. Gail Omvedt has shown how, even in the late 1980s the Shetkari Sangathana gained little support and considerable criticism from both left-wing and autonomous women's groups for their initiatives.[19] The fact that it was the ruling Congress Party that sponsored reservations for women in elective political bodies did little to still feminist fears.

The second development, which showed feminist attitudes toward participation in electoral politics were changing, albeit more slowly and reluctantly than in rural movements, was of the group Women and Politics. Prior to the 1991 general elections, autonomous women's groups in Delhi formed a platform called Women and Politics in an attempt to put four major issues on political party agendas: the declining sex ratio and the plight of the girl child, communalism and fundamentalism, women's candidacies and party reform, and the implementation of promises to establish a National Commission on Women, in consultation with women's groups. All the national parties were invited to a public debate on these issues. The three major political parties (Congress, Janata Dal, and Bharatiya Janata), sent prominent leaders (Margaret Alva, Surendra Mohan, and K. R. Malkani, respectively). That the latter two sent their chief policymakers, both men, indicates the political potential the two parties scented in the initiative. The left parties stayed away.

It took several months of heated debate for Women and Politics to be formed, and in the end the issue was clinched only by the argument that the Congress had already put reserved seats for women on the political agenda, which meant that women's issues would receive heightened political attention. Women's groups could use the political space thus created to underline their ongoing campaigns against communalism, for a National Commission, et cetera.

However instrumental the initial impetus for the campaign, it was translated from the start as the autonomous women's groups' entry into electoral politics. The 1991 elections were, in fact, marked by the profiling of women candidates, and the Women and Politics group was both directly approached for support by a number of women candidates standing on different party tickets and indirectly encouraged by party-affiliated women's groups to put pressure on their party executives to increase the number of women fielded, as well as to strengthen the campaign teams of the women they did field. One of the complaints of many women candidates was that, on an average, their parties took women candidates less seriously than male ones, allocated them fewer resources, and did less canvassing for them. Each party of course had its women stalwarts—generally no more than two or three—who had to be reelected to keep the party's face intact, but these were the special cases. Though the political parties had recognized the importance of the as yet only partly tapped women's vote, this was not correlated to provisions for women candidates, and though several political parties were increasing the number of women candidates they fielded, they did so reluctantly. The "women's vote" was still regarded as chiefly concerned with such issues as prices and the availability of goods, welfare provisions for the family, and religion (festivals, temples, religious observance). The influence of the women's movement was seen in promises to appoint a National Commission on Women and to expand women's rights within the family (to property, maintenance on divorce, et cetera). Compared to earlier electoral campaigns, however, political parties did take women candidates far more seriously. Partly this was due to media pressure: newspapers, radio and television not only reported on individual women candidates but covered the campaign trails of several of the more prominent among them, such as Maneka Gandhi (Indira Gandhi's daughter-in-law and junior environment minister under the Janata Dal government); Suhasini Ali of the Communist Party of India-Marxist, and Vijayaraje Scindia, Uma Bharati, and Sadhvi Rithambara of the Bharatiya Janata Party.

Partly it was due to newly active party women's fronts, who could now provide women party workers to canvass for women candidates. An interesting development here was that local party-affiliated women's groups that were strong provided electoral workers for campaigns in other areas: the Delhi-based Janwadi Mahila Samiti (progressive women's organization), for example, which is linked to the Communist Party of India-Marxist and is more active than some of the national women's fronts, provided cadre for Suhasini Ali's campaign in Uttar Pradesh.

The election of Uma Bharati posed a special challenge to feminists. On the one hand, it appeared to underline the argument that it is better for feminists to maintain distance from electoral politics and women's candidacies. On the other hand, it supported the argument that a broad women's platform can contribute to political ideologies that are offensive, and feminists must make a choice of political affiliation. Moreover, the hate-filled campaign Bharati and Sadhvi Rithambara ran has led some to ask—as they did with Indira Gandhi—whether there is a special relish that women can bring to horrible acts.

These arguments strengthened the case against electoral reservation for women. Reservation itself continued to be a moot point and, with the usual tendency of political events to conflate political issues, the debate on electoral reservation for women fed into an even more heated debate on caste reservation in government and public sector jobs, which comprise a substantial number in India. In 1990, the Janata Dal government announced that it was going to implement the recommendations made by a government commission in the 1970s that up to 40 percent of government and public sector jobs should be reserved for the "backward castes."[20] *Backward castes* were defined by economic as well as social criteria. Within the women's movement opinion was divided on how to respond to the Janata Dal announcement. One view was that women's groups should demand proportionate representation of men and women of the backward castes but, some cautioned, the announcement of caste reservation was already creating a number of caste wars before it was even implemented, and such a demand might cause confusion within the ranks. A demand for 25 percent reservation of jobs for women in industry had been mooted in the late 1970s by feminist groups in Maharashtra, but had been dropped because of both general arguments against reservation and specific arguments over what proportion was appropriate. The argument now was, why make a demand within the Mandal context rather than an overall one; conversely, to make even an overall demand at the time when the Mandal issue was dominant would seem both opportunist and divisive.

The other view, drawing on opposition to the Janata Dal announcement, was that not only had reservation been found to be a failure in practice,[21] but affirmative action could fail as well, because it created a kind of second-class status. This argument over affirmative action caused special tension in the discussion over what forms of action to ask for against the declining sex ratio. It was proposed in *Women and Politics* that one of the four demands that should be made of political parties before the elections was for affirmative action for the girl child—and that this should comprise a monthly stipend for each girl child born to families with an income below the sum of Rs500 per month (then categorized as the minimum wage). The rationale for this proposal was as follows: The 1991 Census showed an increasing decline in the ratio of women to men, due in part to acts of violence such as female feticide, female infanticide, and dowry murder; and in much greater part to discrimination against women, such as lower nutrition for girls than boys, poorer health care, earlier years of work, et cetera. While the acts of violence occurred more often among middle-class families than poor ones, they would also be slower to change as they reflected caste and community norms. The latter, however, might change if economic incentive to change were offered; this incentive could be made contingent on school attendance and would help to increase female literacy. And finally, these stipends would gradually influence the status of women and might have a part in diminishing acts of violence against women.

Arguments against the proposal were that this form of positive discrimination ran counter to feminist principles of equality; the demand itself was a kind of bribe to families to treat their girls better, which would be merely pocketed without any ensuing improvement; that if the state were to regulate disbursal it would encourage corruption; and that attempts to change discrimination against women at the level of the poor would have no effect either on acts of violence or discrimination against middle-class women.

Eventually, the proposal won in a vote with the narrow margin of two above, and only after it had been pointed out that the demand for the National Commission on Women had already been agreed to, and its function was to deal with acts of violence against women. A National Commission on Women had in fact been set up just prior to the elections, but this was done in haste by a caretaker government and was viewed as being instituted in dubious circumstances. Feminists protested against the lack of consultation before setting up the commission and proposed a series of meetings with women's groups across the country to decide the scope, authority, and structure of the commission. Though the meetings did not happen, after the elections that brought in India's present minority Congress Party government the National Commission was reformed, with Mamta Banerjee as minister in charge. It has powers to summon information from state governments and seek investigation into violations of women's rights. It can recommend legislation and request that legal action be taken in individual cases. However, it is poorly funded and remains an advisory body whose recommendations might or might not be implemented. Nevertheless, it can become a focal meeting point for women's groups, government servants, and parliamentarians, and its expansion is currently high on the feminist political agenda.

CONCLUSION

Three major conclusions can be drawn from this discussion. First, the political space for women in India is growing, both vertically and horizontally. At the vertical level, political space is no longer concentrated at the apex alone nor is it solely controlled by urban elites. While in the early years of independence, the Congress Party and the left parties were the only ones to be concerned about the political representation of women, the need to have women representatives and to address women's issues is now felt by all political parties.

Significantly, it is the horizontal level at which a striking expansion of women's political space is taking place. This growth can be seen both within the women's movement and within electoral politics. The

1990 all-India women's liberation conference showed how the movement is growing in rural areas and is beginning to represent the aspirations of women of different castes, classes, ethnicities, and religions. This is partly due to the revitalization of political parties' women's fronts, partly to the efforts of developmental and reform groups, and partly to government support. Within electoral politics, the 30 percent reservation of seats for women at village and subregional levels complements the spread of the women's movement. Though it is yet to be fully implemented, it has already led to an increase in both women's political participation and their representation. At the same time, the emergence of militant Hindu nationalist women politicians makes it difficult for the women's movement to adopt an unqualified support for women in politics. Rather than face the unpleasant prospect of having to publicly join battle with Hindu nationalist women's groups in the near future, many of the Indian women's groups prefer to strengthen their influence both at the grassroots and within institutions, and maintain some distance from electoral politics. There is a logic to this strategy: given that both Uma Bharati and Sadhvi Rithambara have shot to prominence in a state in which the women's movement is exceedingly weak, it may be that developing a women's movement in the region would prove the most effective counter to their rhetoric and to the Bharatiya Janata Party's claims to represent women. But there is also a danger in this strategy: that the space opened by the Panchayati Raj Bill will be occupied by others when it could be taken by candidates supported by women's groups. Indeed, there is no reason why doing the one should obviate doing the other, and the likelihood is that women's groups in those rural areas where the women's movement is strong will avail of the opportunities being offered by the bill. If the Shetkari Sangathana initiative is in any way an example, then the coming trend ought to be one in which rural women's groups will participate in Indian politics to a much greater extent than ever before.

In the urban centers the influence of women's groups on state and national level policies (in those cities where they are relatively strong) has been significant enough for feminist energies to continue to concentrate on these levels. It is likely, therefore, that we shall see women's groups continuing to work with state- and national-level MPs rather than engaging in municipal politics, and that the chief focus of their work at this level will continue to be the development of institutions such as the National Commission of Women.

What of women in politics? The space opened by the Panchayati Raj Bill applies to urban areas as well as rural ones, and so a rise in the number of women running in municipal elections is likely. However, given the extent to which factional municipal politics is entrenched in most of India's major cities, urban women's groups are far more hesitant than rural women's groups to avail of the opportunities offered by the bill, and only the most determined will undertake what will be a long and brutal haul. Meanwhile, the next elections may or may not bring India into conformity with the current South Asian quadrumvirate of women leaders—India is full of surprises—but we can confidently hope for a few more fascinating insights into political women and women in politics.

BLAGA DIMITROVA
A Voice for Change
Valentina Stoev

Blaga Dimitrova was vice president of Bulgaria from December 1991 to her resignation in July 1993. A renowned poet and novelist, her work has been published in Bulgarian, English (Because the Sea Is Black, The Last Rock Eagle, *and* Journey to Oneself), *French, and German. In her introduction to* Because the Sea Is Black, *Julia Kristeva wrote that "Blaga Dimitrova can turn thought into poetry, meditation into rhythm and flavor, colors into ideas, judgment into fragrance, vision into ethical statement. Seldom has a woman's writing been at once more cerebral and more sensual. This mixture comes about no doubt like visions brought on by a wound, personal or national. Dimitrova's poetry nonetheless stretches a modest and serene smile over the abyss. The memory of this smile has stayed with me, and it is once again there in her style, sustained through adversity; a sun rising over the Black Sea, the sun of a woman's talent, one that English-speaking readers will welcome."*

Dimitrova is currently a freelance writer and also works for the New Union of Bulgarian Writers and The Bulgarian Women's Union. The following comments by Blaga Dimitrova were compiled from conversations with Valentina Stoev that took place in Sofia in March and October 1992 and September 1993.

The image of a woman astride a lion, which depicts Bendida, the goddess of fertility, is a powerful symbol from ancient Thrace that appears on many vessels inlaid with gold and silver discovered a few years ago in Bulgaria. Also uncovered was the burial mound of a princess from the fifth century, filled with large amounts of fine gold and silver jewelry. These remnants of Thracian culture indicate that their women were strong and held in high esteem.

Over the centuries, our people's survival at this dangerous crossroads, the Balkans, has been largely due to women. Many men died in wars or rebellions, or went to earn their living abroad and never came back. Women remained. They raised children and cattle, tilled the land, spun wool, sewed fine clothes, made fleecy rugs, and grew flowers and food crops. Bulgarian women have also played a large part in the country's social and cultural life. During the National Revival Period [in the eighteenth century], when Bulgaria was under Turkish domination [1396-1878], women showed much daring and enterprise in the field of education. This took considerable effort in a backward and oppressed society. Women who chose to be writers, actresses, or teachers faced opposition from their families and public opinion. Yet, many women took the risk. They were ready to pay the price of disrupting their private lives in exchange for self-fulfillment. After Bulgaria's liberation from Turkish domination, women entered different walks of life.

WOMEN FIRST

1992: HANNA SUCHOCKA IS FIRST WOMAN TO BECOME PRIME MINISTER OF POLAND.

They gathered in "ladies' societies," not just for tea parties and small talk, but in order to launch various social initiatives. Women participated actively in the work of library clubs and published their own magazine and newspapers. The *Ladies' Newspaper*[1] dealt with different aspects of women's lives. It was aimed at broadening Bulgarian women's world outlook. It published articles about women's situations in other countries and prominent women writers in Europe and Russia. A great Bulgarian poet, Elissaveta Bagryana [1893-1991], got her start in its pages. The salient feature of Bagryana's work is women's drive for freedom in emotional life, for genuine equality with men. Her openness caused many trials in her personal life. She divorced her first husband and embarked on a difficult and lonely road. She traveled widely and had romantic liaisons with interesting writers and poets. Bagryana was much admired and respected as a poet, but was also the target of gossip and prejudice, which she proudly withstood. She devoted her life and work to opening new vistas for Bulgarian women.

Poetry was also my way of joining the traditional Bulgarian life of a lonely woman on the road.[2] There are many trials on this road. I have in mind my generation and its ideological barriers. In fact, these barriers were faced by both men and women writers. However, the communist regime brought a specific pressure to bear on women. They were tempted to become the regime's favorites. Women poets were especially favored by the authorities. They were able to travel abroad, to "decorate" honorary presidiums and official ceremonies. The young ones were most easily tempted. This reminds me of a well-known Bulgarian poet, Mara Belcheva [1868-1937]. She was very beautiful, and our former Tsar, Ferdinand Coburg-Gotha [1861-1948], invited her to be his mother's first lady-in-waiting. His courtship was quite insistent. He kept a marble sculpture of her hand on his desk. Yet, Mara Belcheva defiantly left the palace to live with the great Bulgarian poet Pencho Slaveikov [1866-1912]. Although he was poor and disabled, the proud Bulgarian woman preferred him to honors and life in luxury at the palace, and therefore became a legend. Following Pencho Slaveikov's death she published a book of poems entitled *Steps on the Threshold* [1918]. The poems are dominated by the image of snow as a symbol of purity and spiritual beauty.

Snow, as a symbol, is present in the works of many Bulgarian poets. It exists in my verses, too, but as smeared by human steps. Snow is pure only as long as it floats in the air. Once on the ground, it becomes dirty.

A few years ago I had a difficult operation for cancer. While in the hospital, I met a wonderful woman—one of those old, hope-inspiring Bulgarian women. One day she asked me if there were another child in my family. I told her I was an only child, but she persisted. Suddenly I dimly remembered something about a boy back in my childhood. "Wait," I told her, "my parents had another child before me, but he died. I do not know how and why. Nobody would tell me." She jumped up and said, "You are saved! Now you'll live his life!" She managed to convince me that I would survive the operation. She inspired people with a will for life, yet she herself died soon after of cancer. Perhaps, now I am living the life of my deceased brother.

I had a wonderful childhood in Veliko Turnovo. My mother, Maria, was a schoolteacher, and my father, Nikolai, was a lawyer. My mother was stern with me; she was a follower of the Swiss pedagogue Johann Pestalloci [1746-1827]. My father was a kind and gentle man who told me countless stories. Mother always interrupted him lest my imagination grew wild....

My parents were uncertain about my poetic attempts. They were glad that I was writing, and yet they were concerned. Poets were regarded with condescension. Bulgarians have a saying, "A fiddler cannot feed a family." My parents often told me, "You may write poems, but lessons come first!" They were sure that this would pass when I grew up. Obviously I have not yet grown up....My first book, which was somewhat of a success, was love lyrics: *Till Tomorrow* [1959]. Naturally enough, my parents were glad that I had my own book published. But some people were puzzled by my emotions. I gave a copy of the book to the poet Lyudmil Stoyanov [1888-1973]. One day we met at the Union of Bulgarian Writers and he said to me, "Girl, I have read your poems. How will you get married after this book?"

As for my road into politics, I do not think that it is a change of fields. In Bulgaria politics and poetry are linked by tradition. Ours has always been a poetry of protest, of revolution. Some poets fought in rebellions, others in an underground organization against a foreign invasion, and that's the difference. Resistance is typical of the best Bulgarian poetry—starting with Hristo Botev [1848-1876] and ending with the latest generation of poets who fought the totalitarian regime. Some of them were not published at all, but people used to copy their poems by hand. Others kept silent, and their names were soon forgotten by the people. Being a woman and a writer, I have always opposed power and authorities. Yet I was surprised by the duty imposed on me. I wanted to avoid this duty, as it turned against me. My friends and like-minded people insisted that it was my duty to run for the post of Bulgaria's vice president. I did not want to listen, and I refused to run until the very last moment. I believed that I should remain true to my writing, outside any political parties, to be an independent writer. Now, all of a sudden, I had to accept such a big responsibility as power! I was sure that I would never agree and reach for power. But something happened which, however trifling it might seem, was crucial for me.

One night my daughter came home late. She had been at a party with her friends. It turned out that her friends had said to her, "Your mother began the battle, led us, and now she leaves us on our own!" I understood that we had to go with these "steps on the threshold" that we had begun to take. We had to step over the high threshold. I do not wish to complain, or be regarded as a victim. I regret nothing. Now I see that we, the women, should go deeper—not higher, but deeper—into power.

My vice-presidential team consisted mainly of women. I recruited women intellectuals who are brilliant in their own fields. They gave up their professions to join me. Rada Sharlandjieva, for instance, translates American, British, and Serbo-Croatian literature. She has translated the works of F. Scott Fitzgerald, Jack Kerouac, William Faulkner, and Ivo Andric. For many years she was editor-in-chief of Narodna Koultoura Publishers and editor-in-chief of *Knigosvyat,* a magazine of world literature. Maria Georgieva, a poet, is the translator of Proust's works from French. Associate professor Klementina Ivanova is a specialist in Old Bulgarian literature. Renowned foreign universities have invited her to work for them, but she remains in Bulgaria. Elena Popova, our secretary, is an extraordinary woman. She translates from German and has worked at the Union of Writers. Her son, Niko Boris, is a well-known intellectual who translated the work of James Joyce into Bulgarian. We all work from early morning until late at night. My heart bleeds for these women's youth. Yet we are all sure that Bulgaria needs another voice. We could introduce a female element into the changes underway. I do not think the world needs a sentimental or pathetic attitude. There is something else I value highly in my work as a writer and public figure. Men's strength lies in their ability to divide themselves: They can be strong in several fields at a time. Women's strength lies in our inability to do so. I believe that this spirit of inner integrity should penetrate our whole society, our activities and our ideas. The new development of our society should not be based on division of parties, of people, or of purpose. All these should be unified.

Politics divides people; it can divide even old friends. It is culture, and moreover culture borne by women, that can bring people together. Not politics apart from man's inner life, but culture and politics in an integral whole.

Women in Bulgaria hold many responsible posts. I for one believe that both in the gloomy totalitarian past, and now, in the period of transition, a female teacher is as powerful and responsible as is the vice president. The same holds true, for example, for a woman doctor who has to treat mentally disturbed children. The malformations of the totalitarian regime have affected most of all human souls. They have had the most frightening effect on our fragile children's souls. There are so many cases of mentally disturbed children, of young people suffering in Bulgaria. It is unnatural for a child to suffer from insomnia, diabetes, neurosis and depression. Heinrich Heine said that the crack of the world goes through a woman's heart. Today too, the big crack of the world goes through the woman's heart. Sometimes it should be a heart of stone. It is said to be weak and tender, but it has to be strong in order to withstand the axe which is splitting it in two.

I have gone through many adventures in my life, but the last one has been the most dangerous. I believe that people like me feel quite awkward in the corridors of power. I used to write verse and prose, and now I have switched to—memoranda. Yet I have the rare opportunity to see another walk

W O M E N F I R S T

1982: MILKA PLANINC IS THE FIRST WOMAN TO BE ELECTED PRESIDENT OF YUGOSLAVIA.

of life from a different angle. I keep telling myself that one day I will describe it all. This is to console myself. Intellectuals are known to be always in opposition, by their nature. Therein their strength lies, that is why they avoid power. Politics is a dirty job for intellectuals. However, things in Eastern Europe are somewhat different. Having said "a," we have to say "b." Our colleagues criticize us a lot. Since intellectuals can grasp the essence of things, they say, why do they not take their share of responsibility, at least for a while, to help transform the reality? It seems that one should go through many impossible experiences in this life. Sometimes I think that we are in a dead-end tunnel. Light is nowhere to be seen. In such dark moments I tell myself, "Let us at least light up a hope and illuminate the darkness." My favorite poet, Pencho Slaveikov, said, "it is not before death that a lucky man is known." Death will show if one has been lucky. This life has to be lived through. Can you tell beforehand what Providence has in store for you? The balance is made at the end. For the time being my life is that of a common Bulgarian woman, who became vice president.

POSTSCRIPT, FEBRUARY 1995

Since resigning from the vice-presidency, I have continued my work in the New Union of Bulgarian Writers, an alternative to the former Writer's Union made up of independent Bulgarian writers. I am also active in The Bulgarian Women's Union, which was established in 1994 as the successor to the former, pre-war Union of Bulgarian Women. The leader of the pre-war Women's Union was the prominent lawyer Dimitrana Ivanova, who united independent women. Today's Women's Union again unites women intellectuals from all over Bulgaria and pursues a variety of activities, such as work with children, including orphans, and cultural and educational work to develop Bulgarian women's talents and skills. Union leaders are elected annually. The current chief is again a lawyer, Pavlina Todorova. The Women's Union supports the activities of the opposition coalition, the Union of Democratic Forces.

I am just finishing my newest novel, which is about a young woman living through the changes in Eastern Europe. Again, it is the story of a woman at the threshold of change.

THE FEMINIST BEHIND THE SPOKESWOMAN

A Candid Talk
with Hanan Ashrawi

Rabab Hadi

Hanan Ashwari, official spokesperson for the Palestinian delegation to the Middle East peace talks, spoke in January 1992 with Rabab Hadi, a cofounder of the Union of Palestinian Women's Associations in North America.

Rabab Hadi: Dr. Ashrawi, how does it feel to be the only female spokesperson in the negotiating delegations [of the Middle East peace talks]?

Hanan Ashrawi: On a personal level, quite awesome. It is a tremendous responsibility, a great challenge. It is also a great victory for women in general, and in particular for Arab and Palestinian women. Because this didn't come out of a vacuum but as a result of a long history of women's struggle in the Occupied Territories [the West Bank and Gaza Strip], Palestine. I came buttresssed by a clear feminist vision and agenda and a new definition of value, which gives me strength while my work supports the work of women at home—mutual reinforcement. My role legitimizes women's struggles; I can speak out on behalf of all the women whose voices have not been heard. This is a collective work, not tokenism.

RH: How can you say it is not tokenism when you are the only prominent woman in the delegation?

HA: We have other women in our delegation, among the advisers and on the political committee. Prominence is a result of exposure; it doesn't mean that we don't have women of substance who do critical work.

RH: But if we look at the Algerians, for instance, we see that women contributed a lot to the revolution—like Palestinian women. But come independence, women were sent back to the kitchen. Will this be different in Palestinian society, and if so, why?

HA: We certainly hope it will be different. We have learned from the experience of other women in national liberation movements. Even the women's struggle in the U.S., for instance, was carefully studied by Palestinian women. The Palestinian women's movement has not emerged suddenly; it began in the 1970s as a grass-roots movement that emerged from, and attempted to diagnose, specific Palestinian needs and realities—which were placed in a theoretical framework pertinent to feminists all over the world.

But at the same time, we also have genuine accomplishments. This became increasingly true during the Intifada [the Palestinian "Uprising" in the Territories]; women took initiatives, started projects, and sustained their work. The movement is no longer a luxury either for the middle class or the intellectual; it is a genuine expression of women's realities in areas hitherto ignored, like refugee camps and remote villages generally left to the domination of men. It is not an abstraction, it is grassroots—immediate, substantive, and effective.

In Algeria, women were reactive, they implemented the male-dominated political theory of national struggle; they carried out tasks, they were exploited politically the way they had been exploited for centuries. I don't think we have achieved equality or liberation in our society at all but we are on the right track. We are trying to create a place for ourselves, to take part in the decision-making proces.

RH: Do you feel that there is any change in the way the political leadership of the Palestinian community, the various parties and factions view women's questions?

HA: There is still the attitude that women are only a constituency to be recruited for the national movement. But at the same time we have the examples of women who have refused this, and who have actually forged a place for themselves alongside men. Most of the men I work with now I have known for years; you gain their gradual admiration and respect through your work, through being there, through forcing yourself on the scene and refusing to be intimidated or excluded. And there are other women who are doing this. It didn't happen overnight. We do meet with men's resistance; they still feel that the women's committees should be extensions of political organization—only to carry out tasks.

RH: Assigned to them by men.

HA: Yes. Our job now as political women is to constantly challenge this attitude. But what is more important is to work with women to evolve a joint awareness.

RH: Could you give some examples of concrete work toward women's emancipation?

HA: I think the most obvious example, especially during the Intifada, was the work of women in popular committees and in creating alternative economic projects. Some of the projects were very consciously part of the feminist agenda—proving that women can make decisions, start projects, and reap the fruits of their work. Some projects started by default, because the men were in jail. But even those lead to changes in awareness if they are properly channeled.

RH: The first two years of the Intifada, women made gains, but then there was a big backlash—Islamic fundamentalism, which is a wave spreading throughout the region. How does fundamentalism affect the women's movement and what was the reaction?

HA: First, there was the social backlash, because in every movement when you have rapid progress, it carries within it the seeds of reversal. The first two years [of the Intifada] women were working with the men, doing night duty, doing things that were unknown to women beforehand. They were making political decisions where a woman could be at a higher level than her brother, who normally, socially, had the power over life—here she had the power over his political life, so the definition of value became political rather than social. Whenever there is a definition of value like that, it is to the advantage of women, because social definitions of value always divert to women's sexual and personal behavior.

When the national issues took ascendancy, what were the sources of honor and shame? Is it more shameful to be a collaborator or to be an outgoing emancipated woman? Which is more safe? So political work stressed different definitions of shame and honor. Women who were in prison before were not "marriageable commodities," because they're "damaged goods." With the Intifada there was a sudden change: Released women prisoners became desirable because this was a source of honor—that you went to jail, that you had struggled—and the mythological questions of virginity or damaged goods were no longer questions. This was especially true because of support at the feminist level, from the women's committees, and eventually from the general community. But with these changes there was fear; families started trying to protect their daughters by bringing them back into the family unit through marriage, and sometimes early marriage. This was one part of the backlash.

Now, the Islamic fundamentalist movement is, by nature, a political movement; its strengths and weaknesses are in inverse proportion to the accomplishments of the secular national political movement. I do not for one moment believe that fundamentalism is endemic to Palestinian society. In Gaza we imported it from Egypt, and in the West Bank we imported it from Jordan; Palestinian society has always been traditionally more secular, liberal, tolerant. Hamas and other fundamentalist movements emerged as a result of a power vacuum. Feelings of despair and futility lead people toward more absolutist arguments and spiritual escapes. I think the emergence of the fundamentalist movement is most immediately and directly felt by women—because women are the most direct targets.

The most visible aspect of this victimization is the *hijab*. To me, that sums up the way you view a woman; as a sex object, as shameful, so you cover her up; as a commodity, the possession of the man; as a secondary member of society—she is supposed to stay at home to support the master; and last, because men now stress armed struggle, it emphasizes the role of women as passive and incapable of such activism.

RH: You mean it reinforces the he-man image.

HA: Exactly. And the dress code reinforces the invisibility of women; you lose your individual features when you wear the *hijab*—it places you among abstractions. Women are conscious of this. The Higher Women's Council made a statement against the *hijab*, because it had been enforced by men, not by women. Men had started throwing eggs and tomatoes at women who were not wearing it. The statement said that it is our right to choose what we wear, that men cannot force us to wear what they think we should.

This was a direct challenge to the Unified National Leadership of the Intifada; we were asking, "Where will you stand on this issue? Are you going to be silent and therefore be complacent? Are you going to support Hamas? Or will you have the guts to stand up to them and say this is unacceptable?" They came out with two statements.

RH: A year later.

HA: Late, yes, but at least they did it. They had to because if the leadership lets women down, then this reinforces that they are not a genuine leadership capable of directing a comprehensive struggle. It was the women's work that forced them to do that. It was a challenge. Silence to us is complicity.

RH: I would say that if there were more women in the Unified National Leadership, it would not have been a year later. The same thing with the Palestine National Council, where less than 10 percent of the membership is women. We don't even have one woman in the National Executive Committee of the PLO [Palestine Liberation Organization]. What's your view on that?

HA: I think that this does not in any way reflect women's accomplishments. There is always a time lag between women's aspirations and work and the male recognition of that struggle. For a certain period, we'll face conscious opposition—because of the threat of the challenge. And this opposition has to be not only weathered, but confronted. You have to make men aware that they are being unfair, antifeminist. I have challenged the resistance repeatedly; many Palestinian women have—with language, by refusing to be intimidated, by storming areas that men have closed off entirely against women. And through women doing it, with the support of the women's movement, you create models.

RH: We hear constant arguments by Palestinian men that the main duty of Palestinian women is to bear children for the revolution.

HA: Well, the most obvious answer is: quality, not quantity. The whole demographic argument is ridiculous. You do not base the potential success of your struggle on numbers. You base it on the justice of your cause, and on your ability. This is a convenient excuse to keep women as hatcheries. We *have* Palestinian people; there are five million. Almost two million are under occupation and the others are in exile. The male definition of self-value is based on their own progeny—ego about "the male line." But of course, keeping a woman pregnant and at home keeps her in a position of subservience, in a role which is biologically determined, according to the men.

RH: Is there a parallel in the Palestinian movement to the abortion rights struggle in the U.S.?

HA: We have so many different problems in Palestinian society that the right to choose is not really a basic issue. Right now we have the opposite problem—the right to sustain a pregnancy. Through tear gas, beatings, and imprisonment, there are spontaneously induced abortions as a result of the Occupation. But either way, whether it's the right to choose to sustain or terminate a pregnancy, it's an issue of a woman's control of her body. That is why we talk about self-determination as being an issue of most immediate concern *to women*—because we have been struggling for the right to self-determination *as women*. In many ways, women understand this better than men, because all sources of oppression, discrimination, and inequality are the same.

RH: Do you think that as long as Palestinian territories are occupied, women will face the argument that the national struggle comes first?

HA: Yes, always. I think traditionally we have suffered from the division of issues as "primary" and "secondary," as "immediate" and "long term." Whenever you have such a division, you end up placing women's issues as secondary and long term. There is no recognition of the holistic approach—that you cannot rank oppression. If you are fighting against racism and discrimination, you have to fight against sexism at the same time, at all levels. And not just for women—you have an unhealthy society struggling for national liberation if you fragment different types of oppression, the external and the internal.

You cannot struggle against national oppression when you oppress your own people. That's very clear.

I think this whole attitude of presenting issues as competing or mutually exclusive concerns is self-destructive. They are actually complementary. They feed each other. This is the challenge, for instance, we presented to Israeli women. How can you struggle for women's rights and allow for discrimination against Palestinians? The same thing can work the other way around with Palestinians: How can you struggle for national liberation and self-determination and not struggle for women's liberation and self-determination?

But the Occupation adds so many different levels of suffering, that it makes any type of struggle more difficult. On the one hand,

Occupation can sometimes be used as an excuse to ignore other types of oppression. On the other hand, it affects natural progress in every aspect of society; it has distorted our economic and cultural growth, our development of authentic institutions, our educational issues—everything is affected by an Occupation which is all-pervasive.

RH: What are some of your experiences with Israeli women?

HA: The women's movement in Israel actually started as a strange women's movement. They did not see the contradiction between struggling for women's rights as they saw them in Israel, and not struggling for the rights of the Palestinian people to be free of discrimination, and to self-determination. But these are part and parcel of the same perspective—they cannot be separated. I think the most determining factor in the emergence of Israeli women's consciousness—of making the link between gender issues and national/political issues—came with the Intifada. The prominent role that Palestinian women played was, in a way, a challenge to Israeli women. They started trying to reach us on a feminist basis. We told them we would work together on common agendas—gender self-determination and national self-determination.

We have had long-term cooperation with certain women's groups in Israel, especially members of the Women and Peace Coalition—Shani, Women in Black, and Women's Organization for Women Political Prisoners (WOWPP). And then you had the establishment after Brussels [the site of a women's Middle East peace conference in 1989] of the Women's Political Network. This group involves not grassroots activists, but women in positions of power, like Israeli Parliament member Shulamit Aloni, Professor Naomi Chazan, even Yael Dayan [daughter of former Israeli Defense Minister Moshe Dayan]—women who are more in the mainstream, not consciously feminist like women in the coalition. Because we said we couldn't deal with thirty-six different organizations, we have managed to put together a coordinating committee with both the coalition and the network.

RH: But don't you think that puts a heavy burden on Palestinian women, who have to play a double role in Palestinian society and also play a double role with the Israelis, who are the occupiers?

HA: Listen, we don't have double burdens; we have multiple burdens. We live under conditions of tremendous hardship, whether under Occupation or in exile. Both are cruel states. We have to deal with gender and social issues; we have to work on questions of economic survival, national survival, and just pure physical survival in the face of tremendous threats.

We also have to maintain consciousness at a political level, and to develop a political program. We have to resist Occupation. We have to create democratic Palestinian institutions that express Palestinian political will from the grassroots up. We also have to reach out to the Israelis, to deal with their questions of fear and insecurity, and try and affect their public opinion. We have to present our case to the world and wage an international political and public opinion struggle to counter all the historical attempts at distortion, manipulation, racism, and stereotyping that we have been subjected to.

All this in addition to being held, ironically, responsible for the safety of the people who are occupying us—a defenseless, captive, civilian population. People under occupation, generally, are judged by higher moral standards. You are supposed to be better than your occupiers. You cannot harm a soldier who is killing your children, because otherwise you would be a terrorist. All these labels are used against you.

So don't tell me we have a double burden. We have multiple burdens that keep us working day and night. That is a real challenge. I think historically the Palestinians have shown that we are strong, persistent, and that we have maintained our humanity—we have refused to distort our own perceptions of ourselves.

RH: So what would you say to U.S. women?

HA: I think U.S. women have a very serious responsibility pertaining to Palestian women. U.S. women are a tremendous force in their society; and the U.S. has the power of life itself over other countries, especially "Third World" countries. In regard to the peace process—we can call it a genuine peace process although it has within it all the seeds of inequity and asymmetry—I think U.S. women can be real decision makers. They can use their power as women to focus on the issues of

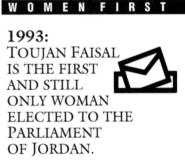

WOMEN FIRST

1993: TOUJAN FAISAL IS THE FIRST AND STILL ONLY WOMAN ELECTED TO THE PARLIAMENT OF JORDAN.

Palestinian women, as their way of supporting justice for Palestinians in general. They have to address the issue of U.S. responsibility for Palestinian oppression: It is U.S. aid that supports Israeli intransigence, violence, and militaristic expansionism. Racism has dehumanized Palestinians, and has allowed Israel to escape the consequences of its own mistakes. U.S. women have the duty to speak out for the truth. Women everywhere can reach out to Palestinian women.

Now, for the sake of Arab women's unity, women should be the conscience of Arabic language, which is by nature sexist. I think it is women who can be the guardians and revisers of Arabic discourse.

I haven't yet seen an Arab feminist movement evolve that reaches out to women in different Arab societies. So far, we have adopted the fragmentation of the nation/state, rather than becoming part of an Arab women's movement and the global women's movement.

Each of our experiences of pain is unique, but there is commonality. We have to emphasize the common denominators. We cannot afford to become captives of our own pain. Victimization has to be shared—and transcended—together.

ISRAELI WOMEN IN TWO VOICES
Myth and Reality
Lilly Rivlin and Ilana Bet-El

This is a dialogue between two women, one in her fifties, the other in her thirties; one lives in the United States, the other in Israel; both are intensely involved in women's issues in Israel. Lilly Rivlin is a seventh-generation Jerusalemite with a graduate degree in political science. A writer/ filmmaker, she lives in New York City. Ilana Bet-El, born and bred in the south of Israel, lives in Tel Aviv and holds a Ph.D. in history. She lectures in gender history at Tel Aviv University, and has been an Israeli delegate to the U.N. on women's issues and human rights.

Israel is like all other states, but more so. Founded on May 15, 1948, Israel began as an immigrant society of Western orientation that absorbed Jews from all corners of the globe. From the outset, women played an active part in the Zionist enterprise: Beginning with the very first groups of pioneers who arrived in the late nineteenth century, women have been involved in every stage of state building and social development.

The situation of women in Israel is defined by extremes of equality and inequality. Thus social legislation regarding women is advanced in Western terms (see Appendix) and covers issues such as the right to equal education and pay. And alongside national political parties, women's organizations have always existed in Israel, fighting for legislation, money, and recognition of women.

Despite this battle, full equality of women and men in Israel remains an issue of dispute and negotiation, waged by succeeding waves of women activists throughout the century. Even in the earliest "prestate" era women had to contend with the usual male domination of the political arena. Added to this were the immense influence of and problems from religious parties opposed to the social and political equality of women. At the same time, the ongoing situation of war surrounding the country defined the army as a central institution of national life, putting issues of defense and security prominently upon the political agenda. As a result the correlation between military and political prowess has always been deemed important in Israel.

Women are also obligated to serve in the army (though less and less) but cannot serve in combat units—which is another example of their dual position of equality and inequality in Israeli society and politics at large. While they do give military service, women are noticeably absent from the peace negotiating teams; despite having three months' state-funded paid maternity leave, the number of women in senior management positions is negligible; although women made up 10 percent of the first Knesset (parliament), they have never since risen above that figure.

Overall, the situation of women in Israel is ever balanced between unique achievement, high aspirations, and a male-dominated political reality, which is reinforced by religious and military interests. However, as the state matures it is slowly broaching such deep issues as the differences between the secular majority and the religious interests, the status of minorities and the inequality of women. It is hoped that with the promise of peace, the influence of military matters will gradually wane and the situation of women in politics and society will be allowed to develop on a footing equal with men.

The following debate explores all these issues and concludes with an appendix that documents the legal status of women in Israel.

Lilly Rivlin: I have before me your article, published in the *Chicago Tribune* in October 1993, in which you point out that on the occasion of the signing of the peace accord between Israel and the Palestine Liberation Organization in Washington, D.C., the platform was full of men making peace, with few women in sight. You noted that the Palestinians sent Hanan Ashrawi, the Syrians brought in an official spokeswoman, and Israel had none.

"Nothing," you wrote, "could diminish the joy of that day in September, even the absence of women from the formal peace process. At the same time, nothing could symbolize the situation of women in Israel so thoroughly as that ceremony."

Precisely! Spoken like a true feminist. Yet I recall your telling me how uncomfortable you are with the feminist label.

Ilana Bet-El: Not only uncomfortable, but also dissatisfied. But it's about labels, not meaning. The feminist label today seems to denote a radical stance, which doesn't address my own life and goals as an independent heterosexual woman. I am outraged by women's exclusion from the peace process—as from other parts of supreme political power—simply because they are women. Lots of women have campaigned for peace and inclusion in the process, some professed feminists and others not. So caring and being politically involved is not about being a formal feminist.

LR: I am a feminist and have been since I was thirteen years old. I insist on calling myself a feminist to ensure that the feminist movement be inclusive and embrace both the "radical" and nonradical woman, the heterosexual and lesbian woman. Feminism is a political stance. Without the activities of my generation—the second wave feminists—women's concerns would never have reached mainstream consciousness. Activists have always been a minority, in any revolution, but only through political agitation and through the ballot did feminists succeed in putting women's rights on the national agenda. You inherited this situation. And so you can say women are not involved in the peace process yet you're not a feminist. I can't!

But let us examine why Israeli women were not involved in the formal peace delegation. In other words, why were they left out? At the most basic level the answer is obvious. Women in Israel, like most women in the rest of the world, do not have political power. Women are not used to thinking about power, nor pursuing it, nor wielding it. Besides the legal and social barriers women lack a tradition, a culture of power, if you will. This is also true in Israel, Golda Meir notwithstanding. This is puzzling since Israeli women have served in the army along with their male compatriots since the inception of the state. In addition to which, women in Israel have been and still are at the forefront of the peace movements such as Peace Now and Women in Black.

At a recent meeting of the Jerusalem Link, a joint organization of Israeli and Palestinian women, leaders such as Hanan Ashrawi and Shulamit Aloni, Israeli Arts and Communication Minister, comfortably sat together on the same panel. They disagreed on many things, but also bantered back and forth in a spirit of ease and understanding.

IBE: It is really wonderful, but still only relevant to the higher echelon of women. For the vast majority of Israeli women the situation is more ambiguous: a reality of inequality, and an image of equality—in which Golda Meir and women's military service figure prominently. For many years it was known as the equality myth—which referred to a situation in which the men and women of Israel ostensibly lived in a utopia of evenly shared rights and duties. But Meir is dead and Israel is not Utopia—just an average Western democracy with a good record in social legislation. In other words, it is another male-orientated, patriarchal society.

The equality myth was based upon nostalgic images of pioneer women wielding shovels and girl soldiers marching along with Uzi submachine guns slung over their shoulders. But reality was different: The pioneer women did labor endlessly, but from the start they had to fight for the right to do so outside the kitchens of the new kibbutzim. In other words, the new society envisioned in the Zionist dream *was* based upon a traditional gender division of labor and power.

LR: Yet the myth was pervasive—probably because everyone wanted to believe it, men and woman, Israeli and foreign. In 1974 I sent a query to *Ms.* magazine entitled "The Myth and Reality of Israeli Women." It was deemed to be anti-Israel by one of the editors who thought revealing the reality of Israeli women's lives—the lack of equality—was a criticism of Israel.

We have come a long way since those days. The equality myth has been exposed both in Israel, which is most essential, and abroad. It is interesting, however, to consider how and why the myth came about, since it undoubtedly influenced the situation of women in Israel, not least in politics. All myths contain truths. The reality is that women in prestate Israel who fought for equal rights, though they were a minority, were pioneers. They *did* redefine women's role; their accomplishments, even by present standards, were on the cutting edge. They established the right of women to work; they proved that women could do jobs hitherto defined as men's work; they created a model for collective child care, all-female institutions such as women's agricultural communes (albeit short-lived), a Women's Workers Council, and even a Women's Party which pre-dated by several decades the Women's Party established by the second wave of Israeli feminists (in 1974).

IBE: All true. But at the same time, Israel was, and has remained, very much a family-oriented society: It really is the nucleus of life. Hence women are strongly defined as matriarchs and daughters. There is no doubt that the central role of the family, and women within it, is a major influence upon the situation of women in politics. The pull and conformity to family life means that younger women do not enter political life, since it means being away from the home. So women have traditionally kept to local politics, women's organizations, or peace groups. In other words, forms of activism which demand fewer hours. Women are traditionally supposed to care about "softer" options in politics, such as education and social issues, rather than the "harder" issues of state, such as foreign policy or war. This has much to do with the imaging of women, both in their own eyes and in the eyes of men: They do not want to appear tough, and thereby unappealing.

LR: I don't think it is that simple or that it's only the male-dominated society that has kept women out of the political process. First, societal images are created by human institutions, they are learned; secondly, women have limited access to economic resources; further, they lack a power base; and probably most important, the party system in Israel favors the incumbents and the professional party politicians. And, of course, let's not forget the influence of the orthodox religious community.

IBE: But above all, there is the army, which is central to our national life. The Israeli army is a people's army: a rallying point in which everyone has a part. After the state was founded in 1948, it was decided that all eighteen-year-olds, male and female, should enlist for a period of service. But once in the army, women were allotted the supportive roles and men the leading roles. To this day, the overwhelming mass of enlisted women become clerks and men become warriors; women make coffee and men go into action. Far from equality, the inferior role of women was and is immortalized in the great melting pot of Israeli youth, the army.

This situation is perpetuated, since men do reserve duty every year until the age of fifty-four, which means they constantly renew their "superior" macho image. At the same time, service in elite units has become a form of networking, which leads to jobs and positions of power in civilian life.

LR: It's the equality myth again: Because women accepted it no less than men, they have been campaigning for equal opportunities in the army only in the last decade. However, at the same time the numbers of women enlisting is dropping from year to year, currently standing at around 30 percent of the annual birthrate. Since conscription is your academic field of research, how do you explain the phenomenon?

IBE: National service in an army is not only an issue of military strength, but also one of cultural rooting, a form of showing obligation to society and establishing citizenship. Due to the situation in Israel, men show this obligation through combat, whereas women show it through their presence in the army. In other words, joining the army is for women a rite of passage, which does not always have military meaning. It is the act of enlistment which is important, not the content of service—which is another way of disregarding the ability of women. For example, in January 1995 women's service was shortened to nineteen months instead of twenty-one. Only a few years ago it was two years. The feeling is that women are dispensable to the army.

LR: It's like a no-win situation: If women don't serve, they lose status in many sectors of society; and if they do serve, then their noncombat positions in the army make them secondary—even if they hold down responsible positions. They never really make it to decision-making status, or have access to jobs which will enable them to make a horizontal switch into civilian life. I'm excited about the recent appeal to the Supreme Court by Alice Miller, a young woman who wants to become a pilot during her military service. She wasn't even allowed to take the entry exams, simply because she is a woman—yet she holds a private pilot's licence.

IBE: Hold it! Before she got to the Supreme Court she approached President Ezer Weizmann—an ace pilot and national hero—who told her: "Sweetie, have you ever seen a man knitting socks? Women don't become surgeons or orchestra conductors, and they don't become pilots" (*Davar*, 22 September 1993). He is wrong: Women in Israel today hold down many high-ranking positions in government and the private sector, and of course the free professions.

LR: Well, not so fast: How many women sit in the Knesset today? How can we explain the fact that although much has changed in the situation of Israeli women, the number of women elected to the Knesset has not risen since the first election? Eleven women were elected then, and eleven women were elected in the last election (1992), the thirteenth in number. Given the total of 120 seats, it means that women have always wavered just below the 10 percent mark, with an all-time low in 1988 when only seven women were elected [see Table 1, numbers from 1948 to 1994].

Table 1

Knesset	No. of Women	% of Women
1st	11	9.1
2nd	10	8.3
3rd	12	10.0
4th	9	7.5
5th	10	8.3
6th	9	7.5
7th	8	6.6
8th	10	8.3
9th	8	6.6
10th	9	7.5
11th	10	8.3
12th	8	6.6
13th	11	9.1

IBE: We have now come to a point of paradox: In absolute terms, a steady near-10-percent over forty-five years would seem to women in many parts of the world a wonderful dream. A quick glance at a map of women in parliament, issued by the Inter-Parliamentary Union in October 1993, shows that the vast majority of states, Western and Eastern, do not reach anywhere near that figure. As usual, the Scandinavian countries are way up high, with over 30 percent representation of women, closely followed by the Netherlands and Iceland. The stated figure for the U.S. is 10.8 percent, and that after the women's "landslide" in the 1992 elections.

So let me play devil's advocate: Are the figures for Israel disappointing in absolute terms, or in terms of an expected new society? I believe women in each country should fight their own fight for equality—but also keep sight of what is happening in other parts of the world. Perhaps this is another generational issue, but I honestly do not think there is a utopia, or that there will be, in which women will have an absolute majority in a parliament, with men out there with a 10 percent minority. My fight is for there to be more, many, many more women in the Knesset, but at the same time to keep sight of a realistic goal.

LR: Perhaps it is generational, perhaps because I have had the experience of being an activist in the peace movement as well as the women's movement, and have seen major changes, I don't share your "realism." As Theodore Herzl, the father of Zionism, said, "If you will it, it is no dream." I believe we must create visions to guide our programmatic steps. Feminists have never sought to displace men in the legislatures, only to have equal access, which means, in political terms, to achieve parity with men.

You are right to pick up on my expectations of a new society. I suspect it is a function of my living in the U.S. and illustrates how the often symbiotic relationship between American Jews and Israeli Jews places a burden on Israelis. We want you to be better. Although I fight it, yet I too am guilty of it. Just as I fight for parity in the U.S. Congress, I hope that you will do the same in Israel and elect more women to the Knesset.

IBE: I prefer the Scandinavian example myself. But overall, I want Israeli women to attain 50 percent representation in the Knesset, and more, as Israeli women.

LR: But do you really think women's lack of equal representation at the highest levels of power in Israel is a function of the primacy of the military in national life, as you suggest? Or might it be the consequence of a "compromise" made at the beginning of this century between the religious and secular factions of the national movement?

In the pioneer era, pre–1948, women's suffrage was deferred for decades in order to keep the religious groups in the coalition. Only after an extensive and difficult struggle did the Representative Assembly grant suffrage to women in 1926. But that did not give women the right to vote on the local level. That only happened in 1941, seven years before the State of Israel was established. Historically, and even today, in the name of the national interest or unification, the "unholy" alliance between the secular and religious parties takes precedence over attending to any issue subsumed under the sobriquet of the "woman question."

I do not think it's malevolence on the part of men but a matter of habit, lack of awareness, tradition—and of course the basic fact that nowhere in the world have those in power ever voluntarily shared it.

IBE: I won't give you an argument about that! But I think the problem in Israel stems from something else: It is a Jewish state. And Jewish means different things to different people. To secular Israelis it is about being part of a shared culture and heritage, rooted in thousands of years of Jewish existence, now re-created as a modern national ethos. To religious Israelis it is about being part of an equally ancient religion that must be preserved and often interpreted in keeping with tradition. The two approaches are not necessarily antithetical; indeed, freedom of worship is a tenet of any democracy, and firmly upheld in Israel. But political interests have turned them into opposing forces which dominate national politics, since there are also religious political parties which have religion as their main agenda. The situation is especially acute because of the proportional electoral system that makes coalition government a necessity—and allots a pivotal role to the relatively small religious parties.

LR: Is it "just" a political issue? Religion is *established* in the State of Israel, due to the 1949 coalition agreement signed by David Ben Gurion, as first prime minister, with the National Religious Party. As part of their agreement a religious status quo was created in which all issues of "personal status" were passed into the hands of the religious authorities: marriage, divorce—child custody, alimony, desertion—and death. It is not just Jewish Israeli women who come up against Rabbinical courts. The status quo also affects Muslim, Druze, and Christian women who face their own religious institutions on these matters too.

IBE: True, but that's not the whole picture. Nothing in Israel, or Israeli politics, is so clearcut. For together with these negative events came the positive ones. After the prestate struggle, women's suffrage was legally anchored when the state was founded in May 1948, and equality of gender was specifically mentioned in the Declaration of Independence. And in the first few years of the state extremely advanced social legislation—even by the standards of 1995—was passed by the Knesset, ensuring three months' paid maternity leave and equality in pay, just as two examples.

LR: What a balancing act! With one hand they give, with the other they take. Look at the public debate on the Fundamental Human Rights Law (1994), which was intended to incorporate those rights considered fundamental to a free, democratic, pluralistic society. The draft law does include all these issues—alongside a coda stating that nothing in this Fundamental Law shall affect the current status of religious laws. As Alice Shalvi, chairwoman of the Israel Women's Network, a nonparty advocacy group devoted to advancing the status of women in Israel, concluded: "Women and humans are perceived as antithetical (or, at least, as non-overlapping categories),…in terms of political expediency, the religious parties' continued participation in, and support of, the coalition government is more critical than the fate of women."

IBE: Which only goes to show that politics are politics. As in many countries, Israeli women are excluded from the political discourse. It has been the women's organizations which have always done the hard work: WIZO, Naamat, Emunah. They are there on the ground, in small distant towns and central big cities, operating baby- and child-care centers which allow women to go back to work; offering counseling and legal advice; fighting for women's legislation. But for years they existed alongside mainstream politics.

LR: Marcia Freedman was a pioneer in bringing women's issues to the central political stage. As the first self-declared feminist elected to the Knesset, she stood up in a plenary session in 1975 to talk about battered women, and she was heckled and booed. No one wanted to deal with the problem. Your generation may not like the word "feminist," but I harp on it because she was, and is, a feminist—and she turned a beam of light on the plight of battered women. Wife beating was no longer a lone woman's secret. Statistics began to be collected. Newspaper articles appeared. Today women's organizations estimate that some two hundred thousand Israeli women are victims of wife beating. Approximately forty thousand annually reach hospital emergency wards. New shelters have opened up in the country, and the Knesset recently voted to fund the establishment of two more, bringing the number to seven (one of them for Arab women). But constructing more shelters is no substitute for preventive action through formal and informal education.

WOMEN FIRST

1969: GOLDA MEIR BECOMES FIRST WOMAN PRIME MINISTER OF ISRAEL.

IBE: I absolutely agree that education has to be the source of any constructive and substantive change and development, anywhere in the world. In Israel, attention is now focused more than ever on the problems of violence in the family, and especially against women. It hasn't stopped, but it does make front-page news. The work of the women Knesset members has been very important in this context, as in many others. They are there as women, and for women, alongside dealing in the vast gamut of "general" political issues.

LR: I hate to be obsessive, but this important development came about due to feminist activism. The Women's Network played a vital role in raising media consciousness to women's issues, most importantly in creating a cross-party framework for all Israeli parliamentary women, to support each other as women.

IBE: This brings us back to our initial debate over labels and content. I acknowledge the truth of everything you say, but I feel that the current mutual empowerment amongst Israeli women politicians is not just because of the feminist label. It has a lot to do with the evolving role of Israeli women in general. As a new immigrant nation we had no longstanding gender roles. Whilst men simply assumed the universal roles of warriors and politicians, and re-created them as modern national characters, women had to spend much time searching for and establishing a meaningful role outside the home.

All this means that for women, the harsh realities of being an immigrant were compounded by the need to create a definition of Israeli womanhood. And I think this is still a salient issue, which will always be relevant. There should never be a single national gender role, in any country; it's something that fluctuates with time. After nearly fifty years of national life there is now a stronger cumulative image of women in Israel that is based upon collective experience: Several generations of women have gone through an egalitarian state education system, served in the army, married Israeli men, worked, borne and raised children, and shared their lives' joys and sorrows on a daily basis. The reality of everyday life is stronger than the movement. It is a reality now being faced by the hundreds of thousands of Ethiopian and ex-Soviet women who arrived in Israel in the last five years. They are not yet part of the cumulative experience and have to adapt to the now-existent role of Israeli womanhood. We face a challenge.

LR: Another part of the everyday reality is the plight of the *agunot,* those deserted wives and wives refused divorce by their husbands, who according to some estimates number ten thousand; the reality of that omnipresent debate over women's reproductive rights in which Israel's fairly liberal abortion legislation is perennially threatened by the political coalition mentioned earlier.

It seems to me that the chicken-and-egg conundrum surely applies. Legislation is the key. In order to get women-friendly legislation more women are needed in the Knesset. In order to get more women in the parliament, women must be encouraged to enter the electoral system. In addition to electoral reform, which has begun in Israel, women have to learn how to participate. For this women need money and training.

Most Israeli women's organizations now run leadership workshops for women who want to run in local and national elections, in which participants learn the basics of running a campaign, the ABCs of political life, and organizational and speechmaking skills. It helps, but women have a long way to go, as anthropologist Naomi Nevo reported in a case study of campaign material disseminated by women candidates of all parties. She found that the candidates abjured any feminist positions, "even in its minimalist terms—equality of opportunity." In short, says Nevo, "they see the wider ideology of nation building, whether in socialist or nationalist terms, as a more attractive asset than feminist principles."

IBE: Perhaps the rejection of feminist stances is related to the negative associations the label now has—which also include a constant dwelling upon women as victims. I also have a problem with the "politics of weakness." Like Gertrude Mongella, Secretary-General for the United Nations Fourth World Conference on Women (a woman hardly suspect of unfeminist principles), pointed out in the UN in 1993: In order to achieve, women must be strong and promote strength, else why would anyone vote them into office? People find it difficult to identify with basically weak people.

LR: Hurrah for politics of strength, but let us not forget our sisters, many of whom, through no fault of their own, remain victims.

IBE: Focusing on strength does not mean forgetting or negating the weak: It is a method of helping them.

LR: Perhaps. But what will definitely help is peace, which is now on the horizon, even with its stops and starts. It is coming closer, as is the end of our dialogue. But before I give you the last word, I have one last point, based on experiences in January 1995 at an international conference titled "Women, War, and Peace," sponsored by Women in Black and Women's Peace Movements. I realized that though Israeli women have been excluded from the formal peace process—and their resentment was made clear—they had also created a parallel peace process with Palestinian women, one that is more humane and allows for feelings and issues which are not part of the formal negotiations. This cannot excuse the exclusion of women from the formal process: They belong in the center of discourse alongside men. But at least, as the peace develops diplomatically, this space created by women may allow for the cross-cultural exchange so vital for a life of co-existence.

IBE: The prospect of peace and co-existence is also crucial to redefining women throughout the region. No more war means no more deaths: No more widows or orphans or grief. For Israeli women it also means the possibility of a smaller army, which will not be so decisive in the national life. It means serving coffee as an option, and not as a gender definition. It means living with a national agenda that is not absolutely determined by security issues. And so it means the option of participating in political power without being told that an understanding of military matters is the only thing that counts. It means succeeding even when men are present all the time, and not away in the army. It means loving men who are not heroes. It means looking into your children's eyes, and seeing a future.

APPENDIX: SELECTED ISRAELI LAWS

Social Legislation

Law of Equal Rights of Women (1951)—established equality of gender before the law, apart from issues of marriage and divorce (see below).

Law of Compensation for the Termination of Work (1953)—ensures that individuals who resign after giving birth or adopting a child are entitled to compensation as if they were fired.

Law of Women's Work (1954)—anchors women's rights in the workplace, including paid maternity leave during pregnancy, and for three months after giving birth or adopting a child, extends unpaid maternity leave for up to one year, and forbids the hiring of permanent replacement staff during these periods.

Law of Equal Pay for Workers of Either Gender (1964)—refers to basic pay and not additional salary components, e.g. access to overtime and car allowances.

Health of the Nation Acts: **Artificial Insemination** (1980)—specifies the conditions for the process; Amniocentesis Test (1980)—to be free for all pregnant women over the age of thirty-seven.

Law of Equal Retirement Age for Women and Men (1987)—enables women to retire up to the age of sixty-five, like men, rather than at the previous age limit of sixty.

Law of Equal Opportunities in Work (1988)—forbids discrimination in job openings and promotions on the basis of gender, sexual preferences, or through sexual harassment.

Military Service Security Services Acts (Women's Role in Compulsory Service) (1952)—establishes the conscription of citizens of both genders at the age of eighteen; specifies that women cannot serve in combat units; enumerates the occupational options for women in the army, e.g. clerical, administrative, maintenance, and kitchen duties, alongside of instruction and teaching positions, and those requiring academic training. Women serve for two years and are liable for reserve duty to the age of thirty-four or marriage, but few women are actually called up after their military service (men serve three years and are called up annually until the age of fifty-four). While women still cannot serve in combat units, their job options in the military have widened in the last decade, though many still occupy clerical positions.

Marriage and Divorce

Law of the Jurisdiction of Rabbinical Courts (Marriage and Divorce)
(1953)—establishes the absolute jurisdiction of the religious authorities
over these issues. There is no civil marriage in Israel. Seventeen is the
legal age for women to marry, or sixteen under special dispensation or
if the woman is with child. According to Hebrew law, divorce must
come from a joint decision of the couple, but in certain cases, the
rabbinical courts may enforce a divorce. Reasons for filing for divorce
by men are far more numerous than those available to women under
the law. If a woman refuses to grant a divorce that has been agreed to
by the courts, her husband may live with another woman as his wife
and bear children; if a woman is refused a divorce by her husband she is
not free to establish a new partnership, and becomes known as an *aguna*
(a bound woman); if she were to bear children they would be bastards
under Hebrew law. Upon divorce, alimony may be decided either in a
civil court or in a religious court. As of 1994 rabbinical courts are
compelled, by the Supreme Court, to make all financial rulings in divorce
settlements according to the civil code rather than the religious code.
Since 1993 a small number of women have trained to be women's
advocates in rabbinical court proceedings.

Abortion

The state provides abortions, within certain limitations. In order to
obtain a legal termination a woman must attend a hospital committee
composed of two doctors and a social worker, at least one of which
must be a woman, and fulfill one of the following criteria: (1) She is
under seventeen or over forty; (2) her pregnancy results from forbidden
relations, incest or outside marriage; (3) the child could potentially be
born damaged either mentally or physically; or (4) her life or mental or
physical well-being is in danger.

PART TWO

PATHS TO POWER
THE POLITICAL
IS ALSO PERSONAL

FROM PRISON CELL TO PARLIAMENT

Thenjiwe Mtintso

Women now constitute 25 percent of all of South African parliamentarians. For many of us this represents a critical mass, a base from which we can contribute to the transformation of our society and of Parliament itself—an institution that, under the apartheid regime, was a bastion of the white male supremacy. The decisive "moment" in our transition from apartheid to democracy was the first democratic elections in April 1994. Voters elected a Constitutional Assembly, with proportional representation according to the election results, that will both complete a new constitution and serve as the nation's first elected Parliament. Our transition was the product of a combination of mass and armed struggle, which culminated in negotiations that lasted for three years.

For South African women, particularly black women, Parliament is both an exhilarating and frustrating, a liberating and yet constraining process. Never before in the history of this country have black women been present in the highest decision-making level of society. For white women, there has always been the constitutional possibility of such representation, and indeed, a few women have made it there. However, even for them, as in any patriarchal society, Parliament has always been a terrain taken for granted as that of men. Those who made it were what could be called "honorary men" and clearly had to work hard to prove their worth. To what extent they made an impact in the Cabinet, Parliament, and indeed the society as a whole in terms of gender relations is difficult to tell. What is so far evident is that Parliament—from its facilities (toilets, gym, child-care centers, and so on) to language, rules, sitting times, and attitudes—was, and largely remains, a male domain. Sitting in Parliament, however, is a far cry from the experience of exile and imprisonment, solitary confinement and banishment, which were the price paid by many of us who dared oppose the apartheid regime.

MY ROUTE INTO PARLIAMENT

My own route into Parliament was no harder than that of many of my colleagues. I am the third of three children. My father died when I was three. My sister, who was responsible for my education, died when I was fourteen. (My mother died only two weeks before the elections of April 1994.) As no one could continue paying for my education after my sister died, I left school to work in a factory to help my mother make ends meet. My brother had by now left home. I studied through correspondence for my Junior and Senior certificates while working at factories. At that time, I never understood why there was such a gap between the lives of the white and black people of the country. My knowledge was to be enriched by working in those factories and earning R5.00 (approximately $2.00 U.S.) per week. My hatred of oppression of any type was to be informed by our own suffering at home, my experiences in the squatter camp where I grew up, and my experiences on the factory floor. One of the most vivid pictures that comes to mind is of my mother, as a single black woman, having to move from one squatter area to another with no rights to own even the shacks that she erected. I have always felt that my only choice was to engage in the struggle against exploitation, oppression, and discrimination of any kind.

I managed to pass my Matric and finally try for a B.Sc. degree at Fort Hare University while trying to do part time jobs to pay for my fees and the maintenance of my mother, who was by now living on a very small pension. I was expelled from Fort Hare in 1973 and blacklisted as a "political instigator" so that no other university could accept me. From 1973 to 1978 I was to spend time in detention, in solitary confinement, and under restriction orders. By this time I was a political activist committed to eradication of apartheid and exploitation of any type. Within the black conscious movement were women in the forefront. Our conceptualization of gender struggles was not well formed. However, women within the organizations fought against marginalization by men. In some instances our approach was to compete with them to prove we were as capable and enduring as they were. Grudgingly, some of us were granted seats in the world of men's political activism.

I went into exile in 1978 and joined the African National Congress (ANC), its armed wing uMkhonto weSizwe (MK), and the South African Communist Party (SACP) in Lesotho. Then I also served in the military structures of MK and the political structures of the ANC and the SACP until my return to South Africa in 1991. I am on the central committee and in the Politburo of the SACP. I was put on the ANC list through the process of nominations from the branches to the national conference and was finally placed at number thirty-three out of the four hundred nominees. I have a son, Lumumba, born in 1974, studying at Rhodes University. I have recently adopted two boys who stay with relatives in my house in Johannesburg while I am in Cape Town. In Parliament, I sit on the select committee for Defense, the study group for the Reconstruction and Development Program (RDP), and on the Rules Committee.

THE ANC AND GENDER RELATIONS

The ANC is the majority party in the Government of National Unity (GNU). The party has a long tradition of support for women's rights. The recognition of gender oppression and of the need for the emancipation of women dates as far back as 1941. The ANC's pre-1941 constitution had classified women as "auxiliaries" who were to provide shelter and entertainment for delegates to its Congress, but the 1941 Constitution granted women full membership.[1] In 1945 the ANC Women's League (ANCWL) was formed, and in 1954 the Federation of South African Women (FEDSAW) was established to unite South African women against oppression. The 1955 Freedom Charter incorporated the notion of equality between men and women and called for equal pay for equal work. As is well recorded, the ANC has included women's liberation in its policies. Women have played a prominent role in the struggle for national liberation within the ANC, especially through the ANCWL. However, for the ANC, at its earlier stages, the content of the struggle for women's liberation was not only constrained by the national liberation struggle but was also subsumed by it. An understanding of the intersections among class, race, and gender was minimal. The focus until the late eighties was mainly on class and race in the theoretical and strategic analysis of South Africa. Although the threefold oppression of black women was generally emphasized, it was also implied that women's liberation would somehow be a by-product of the national liberation.

The mid-1980s saw changes in attitudes and within the ANC about gender. Understanding was perhaps facilitated by developments in the international feminist movement, especially the UN Decade for Women and its 1985 Nairobi conference as well as by the growth of women's organizations within South Africa. The developments created a favorable atmosphere for women in the movement to sensitize the cadreship—women and men—to the facts of patriarchy and patriarchal relations. For the first time in the language of the ANC appeared the notion of not only a democratic, nonracial South Africa but a nonsexist one too. The 2 May 1990 national executive committee statement on women's emancipation was both an analysis of gender oppression in the South African context as well as a critique of the ANC's shortcomings in addressing gender oppression in society as a whole and within the organization itself. It notes, "The prevalence of patriarchal attitudes in South African society permeates our own organizations. The absence of women in our organizations, especially at decision-making levels, and the absence of a strong mass women's movement has been to the detriment of our struggle."[2] The statement emphasizes that the experience of other countries has shown that "emancipation of women is not a by-product of a struggle for democracy, national liberation, or socialism." This set the tone for the ANC's commitment to ensure not only the representation of women at decision-making levels, but also the reconstruction of South Africa into a democratic, nonracial, and nonsexist society.

Advocacy by the ANC was decisive in the inclusion of nonsexism in the preamble of South Africa's transitional Constitution, in ensuring that the Constitution addressed gender inequality, and in promoting the formation of an independent Commission for Gender Equality. The ANC's Reconstruction and Development Program (RDP) tries to address gender in all spheres of reconstruction and supports affirmative action especially for the poor and rural women. This change has come about through protracted and bitter struggles waged mainly by women and gender-sensitive men, especially the then president of the ANC, Comrade O. R. Tambo.

During the process of preparation for elections, the ANC deliberately decided to adopt a quota, to approach if not yet realize proportional representation of women, in its list of candidates. As the lists were being drafted from nominations from the ANC branches, through to the regional structures and finally the national list conference, 33 percent of all the candidates had to be women. Interestingly, among the first eighty-seven nominees in the final list, there was no need for a quota, as there was a fair representation of women. The invisibility of women at the leadership level had begun to be addressed. Other political parties did not follow suit but included a few women in their nominations, and so women came to be 25 percent of parliamentarians.

The ANC went into Parliament with a policy and a program for transforming society, to create a better life for all to meet people's basic needs. The goals are clearly defined as creating a free, democratic, nonracial, and nonsexist South Africa. The six basic principles as stated in the RDP are "an integrated program, based on the people, that provides peace and security for all and builds the nation, links reconstruction and development, and deepens democracy."[3] The thread running throughout all aspects of the RDP—job creation, land reforms, housing and services, water and sanitation, energy and electrification, telecommunications, transport, environment, nutrition, health care, social security and welfare, human resource development, the economy, labor and worker rights—is the empowerment and emancipation of women.

THE ANC WOMEN PARLIAMENTARIANS

Although a significant number of women entered Parliament in 1994, when it came to the highest echelon of power—the cabinet—the idea of proportional representation disappeared. In the National Assembly there are 106 women out of 400 parliamentarians: 84 out of 252 ANC members; 1 out of 7 Democratic Party (DP) members; 10 out of 82 National Party (NP) members; 1 out of 5 Pan Africanist Congress (PAC) members; 10 out of 43 Inkatha Freedom Party (IFP) members. The Freedom Front (FF), which has 5 members, has no women, and the African Christian Democratic Party (ACDP), which has 2 members, also has no women. There are 16 women in the Senate, which has a total of 90 members. Of the 27 ministers, only 2 are women: the minister of health, Dr. Nkosazana Zuma-Dlamini, and the minister of public enterprize, Ms. Stella Sigcau, both from the ANC. Of the 11 deputy ministers, 2 are women: deputy minister of agriculture, Ms. Thoko Msane, and deputy minister of welfare, Ms. Sanki Nkondo, all from the ANC. Of the 25 chairpersons of standing committees, 6 are women and from the ANC. The speaker of the house is a woman from the ANC, Dr. Frene Ginwala. Faith Gasa of the IFP is the deputy chairperson of committees.

These numbers reflect a definite change, quantitatively and qualitatively, from the past governments and Parliament. In the last one there was one woman in the cabinet (minister of health) and one deputy minister (justice) and it seems no woman chaired any of the standing committees. In 1985 only 2.8 percent of MPs were women.

ANC women in Parliament come from different backgrounds and are relatively representative of the different strata of society. In general they tend to be women who have served in various structures of the liberation movement at various levels, in exile, in the underground, and in the mass democratic movement as a whole. Most have been in apartheid jails, endured banning orders and police harassment, and have spent long years in exile. Many of these women have demonstrated incredible levels of resilience and commitment during the years of anti-apartheid struggle.

For this essay, I talked especially in depth with seven ANC MPs:
- Lydia "mamLydia" Kompe, in her fifties, a widow with three children and seven grandchildren, is from Pietersburg. MamLydia worked in various factories in Johannesburg from 1977 to 1985, serving as shop floor steward in several trade unions. In 1986 she worked for the Transvaal Rural Community Project. This organization championed rural causes, especially those of women. She has been active in women's organizations, especially the Federation of Transvaal Women (Fedtraw) and the ANCWL. She has been harassed by police for her political activism. She has a small hut in Northern Transvaal, a flat in Hillbrow, and currently lives in the parliamentary villages in Cape Town, moving between Cape Town, Johannesburg, where her children are, and Pietersburg, where her three cattle and hut are. MamLydia sits on the land, RDP, and the agriculture, water, and forestry standing

committees.

- Ela Ghandi, divorced and in her fifties with three children in Durban. She has qualifications in social work, law, and adult education. She is a stalwart of the ANC and ANCWL, having been jailed for her political activities. She played an important role in the formation of the National Women's Organization (NOW) in the 1980s. She travels between Cape Town and Durban during sessions. She is on the standing committees for welfare, education, and justice.
- Jenny Schreiner, in her thirties, is the mother of a two-year-old son. Her partner is a musician in Johannesburg, and she and her son move between Cape Town and Johannesburg. She has a master's degree in sociology. She sees herself as a "middle-class intellectual" who, in South African terms, is white. She was active in white student's organizations in the 1970s. She was also active in the formation of mass-based women's organizations in the 1980s and in the United Democratic Front (UDF). She spent a long time in jail for her underground activities in ANC and MK in the 1980s and currently is a member of the central committee of the SACP. She sits on two select committees, Police Services and Defense, and serves as an alternate on the Correctional Service Committee and in various study groups.
- Melanie Verwoerd, in her late twenties, is the wife of the grandson of Hendrik Verwoerd, the former president of South Africa, who is known as "the architect of apartheid." She has two children, aged four years and one year. She joined the ANC in 1990 and has since been in the branch leadership of the ANC and of the ANCWL. As she says, to her pleasant surprise she was included in the national list of candidates. She currently is a member of the Western Cape regional executive committee. She is on two select committees, the Constitutional Committee and Telecommunication and Broadcasting.
- Elizabeth Thabethe is in her thirties and the mother of four children. She was, before elections, a treasurer for the Wits region of Cosatu. She has been active in the trade union movement since 1978 and has served as the gender coordinator for Cosatu in the Witwatersrand. She serves on the Finance, Trade and Industry, and the Labor Standing Committees.
- Ruth "MmeRuth" Mompati is in her sixties and has two sons and three grandchildren. She was in exile for twenty-seven years. During those years she served in UmKhonto we Sizwe (MK) and in various leadership structures of the ANC, including the national executive committee (NEC). She returned to South Africa in 1990 and was part of the earlier negotiation teams from 1990 to 1991. Before elections she was the regional chairperson of the Northern Cape. She serves on the Education and the Welfare and Surrogate Motherhood Standing Committees and in the Water Affairs Study Group.

• Girlie Pikoli, in her thirties, is the mother of three and has a degree in public administration. She was active in ANC structures in exile and returned to South Africa in 1990 to participate in both ANC and ANCWL structures. She sits on the Public Service and the Labor Standing Committees as well as in the RDP Study Group. She has recently moved with her family from Johannesburg to Cape Town.

THE WOMEN'S AGENDA OF TRANSFORMATION

Women brought no separate agenda except that transformation should not only come about in terms of class and race relations but in gender relations too. Women were committed to ensuring that a gender thread, as it is actually stipulated in the RDP document, run through the transformation process. They were committed to ensuring, through all means, that the RDP create conditions for the liberation of women. The women felt that their presence and their actions at the decision- and policy-making level would be an important driving force for the achievement of the goals set forth in the RDP and the beginning of a nonpatriarchal society. There is increasing awareness that in the struggle over the heart and soul of the RDP, women will be planting the seeds of either emancipation or entrenched patriarchal oppression.

They also felt that they were to be crucial in the transformation of not only the broad society but Parliament as a seat and epitome of patriarchy. "I expected to be directly involved in the restructuring of Parliament. I was prepared to work for the creation of a people's Parliament, a Parliament that was easily accessible to all in terms of ideas, general assistance, and direction" (Girlie Pikoli). "I expected to play a role in changing the old order into a more consultative, democratic, and transparent system" (Elizabeth Thabethe).

Most of them were not prepared to be rubber stamps on decisions of the cabinet but to be active players in those decisions. Many of them also saw themselves as bringing the agenda of gender equality directly to the cabinet and Parliament. The transitional Constitution had already laid the basis; their job was to ensure its fulfillment. In that sense they were bringing the voice of South African women into policy-making. Lydia Kompe says she knew that it was going to be very difficult for women, especially the uneducated and those from the rural areas. Despite anticipated hurdles, she saw her role as that of a watchdog, ensuring that ministers are guided by parliamentarians. She also expected to be part of a pressure group and a voice especially for rural women: "For once," she said, "these rural women would have a voice right at the top. They have a hope in me and I want to ensure that this GNU does cater for their needs."

These women were prepared to give support to and receive support from all the other ANC parliamentarians, especially the women. Ruth Mopati maintains that she knew she could rely on other women who would probably be experiencing similar tensions. They were all committed to the notion of a unified voice for the women in Parliament. This is to be achieved by what women see as one of the most important mechanisms to be set in place, the interparty women's caucus. Its establishment should not be difficult as the negotiation process had already begun to create such structures, among them the interparty subcouncil on the status of women. Outside Parliament, the Women's National Coalition had created the precedent of interparty women's groups.

A women's caucus would facilitate the inclusion of gender issues in debates about parliamentary and even cabinet structures. It would also guide the setting up of the extra-parliamentary and independent Commission for Gender Equality called for in the Constitution. Such a caucus would, further, act as the link between the women in Parliament and those located outside it for a united front against gender oppression.

In terms of structures for gender emancipation, South African women have in general tended to argue for what has become known as a package—structures at the cabinet level, in the different ministries and departments, within Parliament and in extra-parliamentary structures such as the Commission for Gender Equality and the women's movement. The women in Parliament knew that such structures had to be created, and that the driving force would be women themselves.

STRAINS EXPERIENCED BY ANC WOMEN PARLIAMENTARIANS

Parliament seems to have so far proved to be a difficult area of work for women. Many of the strains and difficulties experienced by ANC women parliamentarians relate not only to the capitalist and racial nature of the South African society, but to its patriarchal nature as well. Gender-based inequality has always shaped experience and determined access to power and resources. Worst hit have been black working-class women who, because of the intersections of race, class, and gender, are located at the bottom rung of rights and privileges. Though the strains experienced were different for white women, the common strands that run through both groups are problems of gender relations. The advantages of white women have to do with access to education and resources. The strains are at the moment experienced at various levels: gender-role conflict at home; a women-unfriendly Parliament and gender constraints; parliamentary procedures as well as structural and political factors.

Gender-Role Conflict at Home

For many women the decision to enter Parliament was neither a simple nor an easy one. The main problem was the artificial divide set up in society between the personal and the political. In addition the division of labor and roles within the family has always assigned more of this work to women than to men. Women have always been the carers and supporters of their partners, the administrators of household consumption, and the maintainers of levels of order and comfort in the home, as well as carers for the children. Men have always been defined as the head of family, responsible for the financial security of the family, and the ones to make decisions about the life of the family. How were women, some of them still toiling under the triple oppressions of class, race, and gender and the "double shifts," going to balance their political commitments with their "personal duties"? Some were single parents, others had partners or husbands who were to remain in their homes of origin. Some had activist partners; others had partners who were outside political organizations. It was not easy for some of the husbands to even consider, as a wife probably would have, moving to Cape Town, the seat of Parliament, to keep the family intact. One parliamentarian, speaking anonymously, has said, "My partner cannot accept that I have to be in Cape Town for my work and he has to care for the children. This has led to accusations both from him and my in-laws that I am irresponsible and an uncaring mother. There have been various family meetings to force me to leave Parliament."

WOMEN FIRST

1882: ALETTA JACOBS IS THE FIRST WOMAN IN THE NETHERLANDS TO ATTEMPT TO REGISTER TO VOTE; HER APPLICATION IS DENIED.

Ela Shandi, who is divorced, is of the view that it is easier for men in politics: "Men have wives at home who worry about the children and take care of the home. They do not have to worry about home and family as women do and thus they have a more fulfilling life, politically and socially."

Elizabeth Thabethe maintains that it has always been difficult to balance what is seen as personal with what is political. As a result she has always had to sacrifice her family duties, "personal needs, and fulfillment." For me also, the "personal" has always had to be sacrificed and because of that those around me, especially my son, have suffered.

All the women agree that they have always found political fulfillment at the expense of personal fulfillment. Parliament has been worse for us in that we are cut off even from the usual support base of friends and the community. Even more frustrating is a feeling of alienation from the very people we are supposed to serve and who have sent us to Parliament.

Women were faced with a difficult choice: move to Cape Town and leave the children with a partner, unwilling or even unable to care for them at home, or take the children and cope with the demands of Parliament and inadequate child care. Yet this was rarely the case with men. "Much as I care for my family and children, I am lucky in that my wife takes care of them while I am here. We have discussed the possibilities of them joining me, but I have to first ensure that my wife will find something meaningful to do in Cape Town, though at the moment she wants to care for our seventeen-month-old baby," says Duma Nkosi, a trade unionist. Some men moved with their partners or wives, while others did not find it that difficult to leave their wives back home with the children. The division of labor has always been clear for them, and so none of the social pressures, anxieties, and guilt that women experience are felt by men.

The reversal of roles within couples has created tremendous amounts of tension. Men have always believed seats of power were for them. When the woman of the house had to be the one to take that seat, this was a stressful process for both parties. While women sought support for a venture into unknown and even frightening responsibility, the men sulked, feeling left out or even undermined. In most cases, the women report that this was not openly discussed, but after the excitement of inauguration passed and the day for departure approached, joy disappeared from most houses. Unexplainable tensions, fights, explosions, threats of separation and divorce ensued. As Melanie Verwoerd has said, "I think that it is very difficult for mothers not to end up with an enormous amount of guilt feelings about their marriage and small children. And it is very difficult not to take too much notice of the comments and criticism given by society. I am, almost daily, told that I am a selfish, self-indulgent, and bad mother for not staying with my children. I have come to understand why it is so difficult for marriages to succeed when the woman is in politics, given the kind of stress this kind of career involves, especially when there are small children involved."

The men I interviewed maintain that they would have found it very difficult to adapt if their partners were in Parliament. As one male parliamentarian has said, "Though I have on weekends taken care of the children and much as I take responsibility for their upbringing, I have never had to do it on a long-term basis. My wife has always been there." Ben Martins is of the view that had the roles been changed, he would have tried to cope but would not have joined his partner in Cape Town if no political responsibilities had brought him.

A Women-Unfriendly Parliament

At an operational level Parliament is disempowering for women, especially mothers. Sittings are in the afternoon, breaking off at 7 P.M., 8 P.M., and 10 P.M. on some days. Currently the burden of child upbringing in our society is still on women. The previous governments have never organized child care. The first thing that had to be addressed then was to establish such facilities. That met with resistance mainly from men of the other political parties, as they viewed the whole province of child care as a private and personal matter for each individual. However, the Rules Committee, chaired by the speaker (a woman alert to the problem) had to create a subcommittee to investigate the setting up of a child-care facility for all those working in Parliament.

In the meantime the women are suffering. According to Jenny Schreiner, "As a parent, the frustration of this period was made worse by the absence of properly organized child-care facilities, so that each sitting began with the extra burden of finding if there were child minders, where they were, and if any progress had been made for permanent arrangements." Melanie Verwoerd adds, "Parliament and its schedule have been designed by men for men. Given that I have two small children, I find the late afternoon and evening sessions very difficult as my child care closes and my husband needs to be at work." The makeshift parliamentary facility closes at 5 P.M., while the primary school at the parliamentary residence finishes at 1 P.M. Most women therefore have to rush to the school at lunchtime—thus forfeiting their own lunch—to fetch and feed children. Most women have to leave the evening sessions to care for children. This is a pro-parenting choice that the women are not prepared to forfeit as it is crucial for the upbringing of their children. But as Jenny Schreiner concludes, "This disempowers women, as they miss out on the sessions. Even when they are there, their concentration is lost as they have to be thinking what is happening to their children left on their own." Further, having to care for children at home leaves women no time to do the necessary preparation for their work, especially the voluminous reading. "When women leave Parliament, they begin the second shift—house, family, and child care," Pikoli says.

WOMEN FIRST

1982: VIGDÍS FINNBOGADÓTTIR IS FIRST WOMAN ELECTED PRESIDENT OF ICELAND.

Lydia Kompe views the very architecture of Parliament as ominous, unfriendly, and male. The building itself, she says, "gives you the creeps. The place is cold, unfriendly, and unwelcoming. As I walk in these passages, I feel lost. It was meant to make people feel the power in the buildings themselves." She feels that it is overwhelming for those who come from the rural areas and for the uneducated. "The advanced people, especially the whites, the men, and the educated seem to fit in and walk with all the confidence in these passages. After all, they are used to sophisticated places, while we from the rural areas withdraw and feel out of place." Ruth Mompati finds the whole place overwhelming.

Elizabeth Thabethe thinks that women need to "level the playing fields, as perhaps 90 percent of the men are themselves not gender sensitive." Some women have had to lobby among themselves and among some relatively gender-sensitive men to gain positions. This has been a difficult struggle, particularly because women are not socialized to push themselves forward. The result is that women, despite their capabilities, are overlooked. In Parliament, women had to devise strategies to try to make their presence felt. Those I spoke to all agree that it was not a pleasant experience. Some decided to pull back in the face of the pressure and the struggle for power. Some men also found it difficult to push for themselves, since, at least in the ANC, there had never been position hunting. Parliament was a different phenomenon even for them, they say. However, having at least been familiar with the rules of the game in the society as a whole, most of the men soon adapted and got themselves into positions.

Parliamentary Procedures Constrain Women

Parliament has been overwhelming for all of us because of its different style from what activists were used to. Addressing rallies and meetings was easy for most men and women. Addressing Parliament was not easy for all of us. However, men soon adapted and a few women went in headlong while still others tentatively ventured in. For the intellectual women, it has not been that difficult to engage in debates, even in standing committees. Jenny Schreiner analyzes the problem: "As an intellectual, I am at home amongst papers. I have been trained how to skim read, how to critique written documents, and how to write. I am computer literate and so need no secretarial support. Even so, I feel swamped by the quantity of paperwork. How a woman who is not so familiar with English, who finds reading a strain, and who is not able to sit at a computer and write out a speech, memo, or submission copes, is not clear to me. We need to look at the varied needs of women from different backgrounds and set up different support structures." For the bulk, whose level of education is lower, it has been an uphill struggle.

Though it has been difficult for some men too, they have found mechanisms to fit in, made easy, for example, because of experience at the leadership level of the trade union, where some men learned to cope despite a low level of education. Lydia Kompe says that even parliamentary language is not accessible, as it tends to be legalistic and not the ordinary English that she is used to.

Elizabeth Thabethe feels that, though we are at a very early stage to judge, the transformation has moved too slowly. "The rules, practices, procedures, and mode of operation of this Parliament are disempowering, and the transformation process is too slow." Girlie Pikola feels that even the process of transformation is frustrating because one does not feel directly involved: "Decisions seem to be taken somewhere else outside ourselves. I don't feel that there is an attempt to ensure that parliamentarians are involved and mechanisms are set whereby people can feel they are making an input. Though there is a Rules Committee, there is no sense of them consulting us. For example, in caucuses there are no attempts to solicit ideas so that as an individual you can make a definite input." Ruth Mompati confirms the same type of disempowerment because of a lack of support.

Girlie Pikola maintains that she feels disempowered especially because she has never before worked at a leadership level. She has always had to find her own ways to make an impact: "Being a woman, in a male terrain with people unfamiliar to you, you have to make a mark as a person; and as a woman you have to make more effort because people have negative attitudes and stereotypes against women and you have at all times to be at pains to disprove these."

Structural and Political Constraints

The lack of constitutional structures to address gender issues at both the cabinet and parliamentary levels so far has been frustrating. Ministries come with bills to the Parliamentary and Portfolio Select Committees. These select committees have powers that make them an important instrument for decision making. As there is no women's ministry, there is therefore no select committee on gender, nor is there a specific budget for that.

Gender matters have had to depend so far on a few women calling for action pertaining to gender from the various ministries. This limitation is impinging on even the smallest progress that could be made with regard to gender. The lack of gender structures also means there are no proper linkages between the women in and outside Parliament that could facilitate networking, lobbying, and strengthening of the South African women's voice.

There seems to be no holistic understanding from the cabinet to the National Assembly on the notion of gender. Individual ministers throw in paragraphs in their long speeches meant to be addressing "women's problems and affirmative action" without any clear understanding of the relationship between national liberation and women's emancipation. Though the Constitution specifies this equality, neither the Cabinet nor Parliament has begun to address the main issue of patriarchy and the very patriarchal state, cabinet, Parliament, civil service, and society at large.

Parliament is a foreign terrain for everyone of the ANC. We had insufficient preparation about how Parliament operates and what to expect. As a result, each individual must find her/his way and create her/his own coping mechanisms. The ANC caucus, which could serve as an infrastructure to empower all of us, as well as offer much needed political guidance, support, and assistance, has so far been unable to do so. There have been many administrative issues to attend to and therefore the political content of the caucus has been lacking.

In addition, attitudes tend to lag behind objective or material conditions. This has been so for both women and men in Parliament. How the women perceive and project themselves has been important. On the other hand, men continue to perceive women in a particular way, try as they may not to be outrightly sexist. For instance, each time the issue of appointment of women into positions in parliamentary structures is raised, some men cry out that women want to "dominate" men. There is, it seems, a feeling of insecurity among men who find themselves and their taken-for-granted power threatened by women.

The related problem has been for some women to enter the sphere of Parliament with an acceptance of its male orientation and thus play the game according to the rules dictated by male domination instead of trying to change the whole game and its rules. To the extent that this leads to the creation of domineering, strong, competitive, unemotional people, it does not help in the restructuring of society and changing power relations.

The ANC women's decision to form a women's caucus to strengthen their hand in itself raised problems from members of the ANC. Some men felt that this was divisive, that there was no need for a caucus within a caucus. "After all, we are all comrades, and the issues facing us can be dealt with adequately within our caucus," one man said. At face value this made sense. But some women immediately pointed out that the tendency would be, as it has always been in the ANC, to deal with matters perceived to be affecting only women at the end of any agenda just as people were packing up their bags to leave the hall. Yet other women felt that while gender needed to be raised, the danger of a women's only caucus was marginalization. Besides, there were men out there who were gender-sensitive, and there was also a need to integrate gender in all aspects of our lives in Parliament. These women proposed a gender study group inclusive of all interested parties that would, like all groups, report back to the caucus, monitor gender issues, provide the needed support, and monitor all other standing committees for a gender bias. The debate is still raging.

However, the feeling is that even the ANC women's caucus has so far failed to be the support base for women. The additional problem has been that women themselves, faced with the problems of gender relations, have tended to adopt individualistic approaches to the problems. As Lydia Kompe puts it, "Some women have tended to adopt the same style as men—push, jostle, and assert themselves in whatever way possible. Some are men in skirts." This has, according to her, made those with less education and skills feel betrayed, since they had relied on their "sisters" to play a supportive role.

Elizabeth Thabethe feels that "as women in Parliament, we have so far failed to support each other, and the other pathetic thing is that women themselves undermine each other." The women's caucus is felt to have also failed to be a link between women in Parliament and women outside Parliament.

There is agreement among all that there should be not only an ANC women's caucus but also an interparty women's caucus to unite and strengthen the women's voice in Parliament and link up with the women's voice outside Parliament. The interparty women's caucus has since met and decided on terms of reference and a program for their work.

OUR NEED FOR SUPPORT

South African women have just emerged from the worst forms of oppression and exploitation. They are still scarred. They have in the past decades been isolated from other women internationally, as apartheid South Africa was correctly declared a pariah in the world. Both white and black women are victims of isolation from each other and from the international women and feminist movements. While we are transforming gender relations inside and outside Parliament, we need support. We need friends. We need sisters in and across the continent. We need to be integrated into the world community. We want to be part of the international sisterhood and the women's and feminist movements. We want to understand the politics of gender in the current epoch. We want to play a role in shaping the international agenda of women.

The United Nations Fourth World Conference on Women therefore comes at a crucial time for us. For that meeting and beyond, we extend our sisterly greetings and support to all women in their struggle for emancipation. We appeal for solidarity across the continent in terms of shared experiences of parliamentary life and governance, gender-sensitive socioeconomic transformation, and the struggle against the dichotomy between private and public life, the personal and the political.

Parliament has proved to be yet another difficult terrain for gender struggles. It is too early to tell whether its potential to take such struggles forward will come to fruition or not. As Jenny says, "The post-election South African situation has within it both the seeds of women's emancipation, which can fundamentally transform the lives of working-class women, and the seeds of entrenched patriarchy, which could be most harshly felt by the working class and poor women of our land." The transformation of the state as envisaged in the RDP provides gender activists and women in particular with the opportunity to restructure the state in a nonpatriarchal manner. In South Africa now we have both the potential and challenge to do this.

Our position as women in the current Parliament also enables us to embark on the struggle for real and not merely formal emancipation. The Constitution, the Bill of Rights, the Women's Charter, and the gender-sensitive laws cannot in themselves emancipate women. Here the link to mass-based formations in civil society and the role of women in them to give the final push to implementation of the legal changes in women's lives is vital.

MITSUI MARIKO
An Avowed Feminist
Assemblywoman
Emiko Kaya

Since she was elected a member of the Tokyo Metropolitan Assembly in April 1987, Mitsui Mariko has gained a reputation as one of the most vocal and energetic representatives and one who gives top priority to women's issues. As an avowed feminist, she has strived to examine the present conditions from an equal rights perspective and to demand that the government of Tokyo come up with effective measures to correct discriminatory practices against women. Mitsui is now serving a second term in the assembly after being reelected to office in 1989. The issues she has taken up so far include those of gender inequalities in education, the depiction of women as sex objects in the mass media, sexual harassment, problems faced by working women, and welfare programs for the aged. All of these issues have, in fact, long been raised by the women's movement but have received little attention from politicians—most of whom are male—until very recently, when women decided to try to secure seats in local as well as national legislative bodies and to tackle these issues themselves.

BACKGROUND

When Mitsui won her victory as a candidate from the Socialist Party in the election to fill a vacancy in the Tokyo Metropolitan Assembly in 1987, the mass media described her as "a 'Madonna' who magnificently transformed herself from a mere high school teacher to an assemblywoman." Mitsui, however, completely rejects this view: "A 'mere high school teacher'? No, that's not an accurate characterization. Since the early seventies I was continuously active in Women's Lib groups." After graduating from university, she worked as an "OL," or "office lady," for three years, during which she kept questioning why women are expected to pour tea as an extra duty or why they are not allowed to attend meetings or go on business trips. "Before I realized it, I found myself in and out of Ichikawa Fusae's Women's Suffrage Assembly Hall and began participating in meetings of a citizens' group that advocated making the study of home economics mandatory not just for girls but also boys."

Mitsui quit her job as an OL and became a high school teacher around the time of the International Women's Year. In 1980 Tanaka Sumiko, a legislator in the House of Councilors, was appointed vice chair of the Socialist Party. The political climate in Japan in those days, however, was far from sympathetic toward a female political leader: "I was disgusted to learn that a male politician in the Socialist Party had stated, 'If a woman is going to be a vice-chair, then I'll resign.' In those days help wanted ads imposingly read 'Men Only,' 'Restricted to female college junior commuting from their homes'. Although we pointed out the injustice of these practices, our protests were received as merely noisy complaints of aggressive women." Her involvement with the women's movement continued throughout the early 1980s. In 1985 she went to the United States to study for a year and witnessed the political processes through which women's issues were dealt with at various levels, national to local. By the time Mitsui returned to Japan she was firmly convinced of the need for women's active participation in politics. Or rather, in her words: "The activities I had been engaged in up until that time in Japan were, in fact, what is called 'politics.' My experience in the United States made me aware of this, and it seemed to me as though the Japan I found on my return had been waiting for me to make use of this experience" (Mitsui 1990a).

WOMEN FIRST

1946: WOMEN VOTE AND STAND FOR ELECTION TO THE HOUSE OF REPRESENTATIVES FOR THE FIRST TIME IN JAPAN. OF THE 79 WOMEN RUNNING FOR OFFICE, 39 ARE ELECTED.

In the fall of 1986 Doi Takako became chair of the Socialist Party. Doi was Japan's first female party leader, and her presence gave great encouragement and confidence to Japanese women, who had become increasingly aware of their potential political power. In the following year assemblywoman Mitsui Mariko made her political debut. That year a sweeping number of women candidates were elected in the regional elections held in April across the country, a phenomenon the mass media dubbed "the Madonna Whirlwind."

When Mitsui first spoke in the Tokyo Assembly in July of 1987, she did not forget to call attention to the fact that the traditional male monopoly of the political world was an aberrant phenomenon that ought to be done away with in the future:

> Please imagine the following, everyone, that all the directors sitting here on this side of the podium were women, except for one man, and that 118 of the 127 people sitting in the assembly were women and only nine were men. You would certainly think it was strange if all the members of the highest deliberative bodies with decision-making power in the government of Tokyo were women. Yet this strange phenomenon exists within the present assembly, only the situation is exactly the reverse. (Minutes of the Tokyo Metropolitan Assembly, 3 July 1987)

To make such a comment before a city assembly would have been unimaginable prior to Mitsui's appearance. Most women politicians, regardless of their political ideology, would have avoided taking such a strong feminist stand, for feminism had been viewed as somewhat too radical and dangerous, and it was thought to alienate not only most men but the majority of women, who prefer to take a moderate stand, leading to possible loss of popular votes. Political concerns of women have been accepted as long as they have remained within the realm of women's traditional gender roles, that is, those of mothers and housewives, as often expressed in such slogans as "We, as mothers who give and bring up life, demand safe food products." Outright defiance of male monopoly of politics had been very difficult.

However, the feminist movement has been growing stronger since the UN Decade for Women. Both the national and local governments (especially the government of Tokyo) can no longer ignore, at least officially, the voices of women from various sectors demanding equality of the sexes, since Japan is one of the countries that has ratified the UN Convention on the Elimination of All Forms of Discrimination against Women. It may be said that the birth of feminist assemblywoman Mitsui was made possible through the combination of many factors: her own political conviction and activities, the support of thousands of women who, like her, have been active in women's groups, and a change in the policy of Japan's Socialist Party toward greater cooperation with citizens' movements under the leadership of Doi Takako.

ISSUES TAKEN UP BY MITSUI

Since her election to the assembly Mitsui has raised several questions regarding the metropolitan government's policies with respect to such issues as gender equality in education and employment and sexual exploitation of women in advertisements, among others.

Establishing a Mechanism for Handling Cases of Sex Discrimination in Employment

In her first speech before the assembly Mitsui proposed the enactment of a "sexual equality ombudsman regulation." The Committee for

Processing Complaints about Sexual Discrimination had proved to be ineffective in resolving problems because it lacked both a legal basis for forcing companies to respond to complaints about sexual discrimination as well as the authority to enforce measures directed against eliminating discrimination. Mitsui proposed as three elements essential to an ombudsman system that its members be publicly recruited rather than appointed by the governor, be able to aid in litigation, and be able to spell out penalties (Minutes of the Tokyo Metropolitan Assembly, 3 July 1987).

She later learned that, in the assembly, proposing a member's bill requires the support of one-eighth (16.7) or more of all the assembly members, which was larger than the total number of Socialist Party members in the assembly at the time (12). In retrospect, speaking at a women's group two years later, she admitted that "proposing the ombudsman regulation as a member's bill was out of the question at the time, but I said what I had to say." She has found it very difficult to propose bills under present conditions but says: "It doesn't mean I can do nothing. I am given an equal right to speak up as the rest of the members. I have experienced firsthand the fact that the voice of one assemblyman is greater than that of many thousands of citizens. Therefore, if we want to bring up various issues pertaining to equality into the political scene in order to seek solutions, I'm convinced the most effective strategy is to send more women that women's groups can support to local and national legislative bodies" (Mitsui 1990b).

Gender Bias in Admission Quotas for High Schools
Mitsui has also questioned the metropolitan government's policies with regard to sexual equality in the field of education, using as a measuring stick the provisions called for in the preamble and Article 1 of the Convention on the Elimination of All Forms of Discrimination against Women.

> The place of learning is where equality should be carried through more than anywhere else. How on earth, then, can the Tokyo government allow public high school to discriminate against girls through the practice of setting recruitment quotas for girls? Because the so-called numbered schools [prestigious high schools that used to be boys' middle schools before the war] have a quota for girls that is about one-third that of boys, even girls who score the same as boys or higher on the entrance examinations end up not getting admitted. (Minutes of the Tokyo Metropolitan Assembly, 3 July 1987).

There have been some improvements, and since 1991 all of the thirteen numbered schools have a female enrollment of more than 42 percent. However, Mitsui notes that:

In several prefectures where sex-based quotas have been eliminated, high schools which used to be all-male in the past still have an exceedingly high number of male students, while the former all-girls' schools have mostly girls. Thus, unfortunately, the tradition of sex separation tends to be preserved. In addition, even though applications for technical and commercial programs in high school are open to both sexes, girls comprise a mere 4.6 percent of the students in the technical programs, while boys make up only 15 percent of those enrolled in commercial programs.

Sexual Exploitation in Ads and Beauty Contests

Another issue that Mitsui has been working on is that of the treatment of women as sexual commodities as witnessed in advertisements, beauty contests, and the practice of prostitution. Bringing to the assembly three posters in which a young woman's body or legs were displayed though they had no direct relation to the products being advertised, Mitsui called for a confirmation of the Tokyo Metropolitan Government's position on this matter, which is that social tolerance for the treatment of women as sexual commodities reinforces the deeply rooted tendency to view women as objects and disregards the humanity of women. She also proposed that active countermeasures be taken to eliminate such tendencies and to create a society free of sexual discrimination (Minutes No. 4 of the Special Budget Committee Meeting, 16 March 1990).

We are faced with the reality in which women's naked bodies are used for advertisement posters of many companies, and the government of Tokyo is no exception. An example was a poster for Tokyo's Bureau of Transportation which featured a woman in bikinis....Also, the subway posters showing only legs in high-heeled shoes were terrible. Our protest led to the Bureau of Citizens and Cultural Affairs issuing a warning, though it was not in writing, to all departments of the metropolitan government that in advertisement posters the female body or its parts should never be used as objects or simply to attract attention. (Mitsui 1990b)

These two posters in which the Tokyo government was directly involved were removed immediately as a result of Mitsui's questioning, although the top official concerned never acknowledged in the meeting that the posters did, in fact, treat women as mere sex objects.

Mitsui also questioned the rationale for the Miss Tokyo Contest, which has been supported by the Tokyo Metropolitan Government for more than thirty years. "There has been protest that beauty contests are an example of the commoditization of sex, and that they are like a meat market for women. What is the relevance of a woman's bust, waist or hip measurements to the social service activities and the promotion of international friendship [which are the roles Miss Tokyo is supposed to fulfill]?"

Other Issues

Other improvements for which Mitsui has worked include: (1) calling for the inclusion of sexual harassment among labor issues for which consultation is offered by the city to working women; (2) advocating extension of financial assistance to children of families headed by mothers at least until the children graduate from high school, that is, three years beyond the current limit; (3) eliminating the requirement that female, but not male, stenographers in the Tokyo Metropolitan Assembly wear uniforms; (4) including women's issues among those investigated by politicians and others taking part in city government-sponsored overseas study tours; (5) calling for a change in the architectural design of the Metropolitan Hall of Arts and Culture to create a nursery room; and (6) inviting a group of women interior designers to draw up plans for the new location of the Tokyo Women's Information Center.

> When politicians talk about their achievements in the assembly, male politicians will usually talk about having sponsored the building of a hall, a bridge, or a subway, which cost some hundreds of millions of yen. My accomplishments are totally different from those of traditional politicians, but if there existed a newspaper devoted to the cause of advancing gender equality, I'm sure I would appear on the front page. Most people, other than those who are committed to the women's movement, do not consider the kinds of things I have been doing as having much importance....Traditional politics has neglected issues pertaining to culture, social welfare, education, and equality, and spent most of our tax money on buildings and subways. However, I will stick to my position to give top priority to human rights and equality issues in politics. (Mitsui 1990b)

CONCLUSION

In February 1992 the National Federation of Feminist Legislators was established as a non-partisan network of assembly members, male and female, across the country. Not surprisingly, Mitsui was one of the main organizers. The group started with twenty members, including one male. The goal of this group is to create a society in which women's voices are reflected in politics. In order to bring this about they seek to increase to 30 percent (from the current figure of about 4 percent) the ratio of female assembly members at every level of government—prefectural, municipal, town, and village—and to promote policies to create an environment that will enable women to lead a full life ("Josei no Sekai" 1992). Membership has grown to about 130 as of July 1992. The organization has called for affirmative action programs of the type that exist in some European countries. So far, however, in Japan the concept of affirmative action has had very little support from the national or local governments, much less from private industry, although it has been recommended by advisory committees such as the Tokyo government's Council on Women's Issues as one of the most effective means to grapple with the problem of sexual inequality in present society. Mitsui has often referred to the kinds of changes that have been brought about in Norway, where not only is the prime minister a woman, but eight out of eighteen cabinet members also are women, and she has expressed strong support for the enactment of an affirmative action program in order to increase female representation in legislative bodies.

Prior to the 1992 election for the Upper House of the National Diet, the federation requested that the major political parties list the names of male and female candidates alternately, instead of listing all the male candidates' names before those of female candidates, as had always been the practice. Shortly before the election, Mitsui made the following comment: "To women who have entered late into the political world, an alternate listing of male and female candidates has great significance. With the advancement of women's status, each party finds it necessary to pay lip service to equality, but in reality it seems the male-centered ways of thinking have not changed. I feel a sense of crisis as well as anger" ("Josei Koho" 1992). The results of that election proved to be a disappointment, with the number of women elected to the Upper House reduced to thirteen, compared with twenty-two in the 1989 election, although the total number of women members in the Upper House rose from thirty-five to thirty-seven. This clearly indicates that the so-called Madonna Whirlwind that swept the political scene in the latter part of the 1980s has lost its power. And with the Japanese economy slowing down, the decade of the 1990s will further test the ability of women in Japan to break into the political world in substantial numbers and bring about long-awaited changes in the political decision-making processes. Nevertheless, as Mitsui has stated, "Women succeeded in bringing about a shift in politics from 'politics exclusively of men' to 'politics of women, too' in the 80s, and politics in the 90s should move towards 'politics of men and women'" (1990a).

W O M E N   F I R S T

1960: NAKAYAMA MASA IS APPOINTED MINISTER OF HEALTH AND WELFARE IN JAPAN, BECOMING JAPAN'S FIRST FEMALE CABINET MINISTER.

POSTSCRIPT

A great deal will have to be done if the 1990s is really to give birth to "politics of men and women." While effort in this direction has been started under the leadership of Assemblywoman Mitsui and many other female politicians like her, the difficulty of accomplishing this goal was brought sharply into focus by Mitsui's announcement in January 1993 that she was leaving the Socialist Party. The reasons she cited were: "There is no democracy within the party. We cannot engage freely in discussion and debate" and "The Socialist Party does not value the voice of women and therefore is incompatible with my efforts to try to improve the status of women" ("Togisen hikae" 1993). She spoke of some male party leaders who denigrate the concept of gender equality and engage in sexual harassment of female assembly members, and she related some of her own experiences of sexual harassment ("Mitsui shato togi" 1993). Because Mitsui not only was the most well-known member among Socialist Party-affiliated assembly members but also has gained national prominence in recent years, her decision to leave the Socialist Party and complete her term of office as an independent was seen as a serious blow to the party's image.

Following completion of her term of office as assemblywoman in June 1993, Mitsui ran, unsuccessfully, for the Lower House of the National Diet as an independent candidate in the July elections held the same year. Recognizing the difficulties facing candidates—particularly women such as herself—who are not affiliated with one of the major political parties in winning election to the National Diet under the newly instituted single-member constituency system, Mitsui has decided to concentrate her efforts for the time being on trying to get as many women as possible elected to local assemblies throughout the country by providing support and assistance to female candidates in her capacity as board member of the National Federation of Feminist Legislators.

PORTUGAL
Daring to Be Different
Maria de Lourdes Pintasilgo

I can no longer count the number of times I have been asked: "How do you explain that a country like Portugal has had a woman prime minister?"

Usually I react with a great outburst of indignation: Women in Portugal are not like the image which has been put forth to portray us! If statistics say that women are only 28 percent of the "economically active population," then what is wrong is the statistics—and the definition of being active!

What about, for instance, the 32 percent of the rural population, more than half of whom are women? Aren't they working? What about the activities carried on by so many women which are (or have been until recently) totally unpaid? What about the women writers who represent, in the last thirty years, a most astounding cultural phenomenon in Portugal, since most of them are in the forefront of literature, portraying in extremely perceptive ways the deep shifts and trends which agitate our society beneath the surface? And what about the women in technical professions—a higher percentage than in any other Western country? (In my own field, chemical engineering, we have moved from a 20 percent women's presence when I graduated a quarter of a century ago to more than 50 percent in 1981.) Of course, I could also argue the case by pointing out the enormous leap made in the law since April of 1974. The Portuguese Constitution is a unique example of the integration of the principle of equality in the basic text of a country. The sheer quantity of new legislation passed in recent years has drastically changed the identity of women, their image, and their status in society.

Statistics and laws reassure certain souls. But the question I am asked—about the general situation of women and a female prime minister—belongs to another realm. In 1979, the appointment of a woman prime minister created a strong reaction in my country. Many expressed support and solidarity, speaking of new hope, a "fresh breeze," another style and concept of politics. But many others rejected the idea in the most violent way. I will never forget the undisguised loss of control of most members of the conservative parties when, in the Parliament, I denounced the lies they had used to attack the program of my government. It went so far that some of the house-desks cracked under the fury of their fists! Neither the enthusiasm nor the rage was connected, though, with the personality of the prime minister (I think). Rather, they were responses to what was obviously still a revolutionary act, belonging to the "new tradition—of the April 25th process. Through the appointment of a woman prime minister it was clearly demonstrated that such a tradition would no longer be an exclusively male heritage. It was one of the few situations when men and women transcended their conflictual relationship and worked together in full equality toward a new future. Seen from that perspective, the fact of a woman as prime minister was a totally logical result of the participation of women on equal footing with men in the revolution.

How did we get there? Let me briefly review the paths we had covered in the preceding years.

WOMEN'S STRUGGLE AND POLITICAL CHANGE

Before the political change in 1974, the situation of Portuguese women was deeply affected by the closed, horizonless society in which we lived. War with the colonies in Africa drained us of money, dignity, hope— and people. Unrest among women had already begun to be expressed, through denunciations of the war's effect on women's lives— uncertainty about their families, the loneliness of those women left behind by men serving in Africa or who had fled elsewhere in Europe running away from the war, the weight of so many burdens carried alone, and the very fact of many women's being for the first time independent from men.

In the early 1970s, women journalists (who had managed to acquire a high status in their profession) started several newspaper-article series about women's lives and concerns. They denounced sexual discrimination but always put it into the general context of injustice in Portuguese society. It was during that period (in 1972) that the New Portuguese Letters appeared—for a moment—in the bookshops. The book was of paramount significance for all Portugal. It was, in fact, the first Portuguese public act denouncing the global system of patriarchal oppression, and it would be central to the revolutionary movement that would have its climax and triumph on April 25th. Rebellion against the political status quo took, in my country, the form of a liberation cry from women and about women:

...We will make our way back to the root of our own anguish, all
by ourselves, until we can say "Our sons are sons, they are people
and not phalluses of our males." We will call children children,
women women, and men men. We will call upon a poet to govern
The City.[1]

This is why, when the military coup of April 25, 1974, burst out,
people's power became, to a large extent, women's power. Women were
active in claiming fundamental rights for workers, in asking for better
living and housing conditions, in shaping action committees at the
neighborhood level, in denouncing the fraud that the capital owners
from Portugal and abroad were ready to make in order to "save" their
profits. Women themselves made their specific struggle a point of concern
for the whole society: Family law changed drastically, different forms of
childcare centers and old-age day-homes were created to alleviate
women's tasks, motherhood was assumed to have a social function (and
thus part of the responsibility of the whole community), measures to
attain equal work status were begun in all fields.

For almost two years, women and men were
side by side in struggle on many fronts in order to
shape a more just society. We can say that in
Portugal women's struggle has been part and
parcel of the whole process of change. It organized
itself and changed modes, patterns, scope, and
intensity according to the events and moods of
the revolution. This experience tells us that there
really is no theoretical question about priorities;
women's struggle and the global process in society
are two aspects of the same front. For the women's
movement to emerge and make a significant

W O M E N   F I R S T

1993:
TANSU
CILLER IS
THE FIRST
WOMAN
ELECTED
PRIME MINISTER
OF TURKEY.

contribution there must be some signs of a breakthrough in society.
Otherwise, a women's movement seems to represent some kind of
peculiar "sideline" goals, and its ideas can easily be taken up, mollified,
and co-opted by the establishment. On the other hand, in order for the
general political process to go beyond a mere game of superstructure,
the women's movement is vital as a link to reality, to the new needs of
a society in the process of creating itself.

But if the Portuguese women's struggle found in our Revolution
its reinforcement, it is equally true that it also found its limitations.
Women's issues had been regarded by the Right as dangerous, evil,
political stands; therefore these issues could never be discussed on their
own. Yet the limitation showed up as well in that the general enthusiasm
of the Revolution disguised deep layers of subtle discrimination against
women. As time went by and society entered the postrevolutionary
period, women discovered that—beyond the structural and legal

changes—there are concepts and values which are not so easily wiped out. Old attitudes keep coming up and shaping behavior at all levels.

The greatest limitation can be seen clearly in the question most central today to the Portuguese women's movement: When political evolution comes to a deadlock, when so-called democratic institutions get stifled (if not outright corrupt and contrary to the interests of the people), is women's struggle possible? Doesn't it become an isolated effort re-creating the pattern of earlier feminisms? Or does it in itself carry such potential that, together with other social forces, it may evoke a new turn in the sociopolitical picture as a whole?

SEX AND POLITICS

While I was thinking about writing this article, I met (separately) with several groups of adult women and young women in their late teens. I asked them, "What is the worst obstacle for Portuguese women?" Adult women gave a unanimous answer: the theme of violence built around sexual life. Young women, on the contrary, felt that they have no specific obstacle! How to juxtapose these two contradictory reactions? What do they mean? It is a fact that the changes of April 1974 brought with them all kinds of freedom. The permissiveness of society appears to be all but total in the sexual area. But adult women today are challenging the values underlying that "permissiveness." They are convinced that this is creating in younger generations the conviction that the end of taboos can be equated with full dignity for women—while their own experience as adult women has taught them that the old forms of sexual repression and abuse re-seized their lives as soon as the Revolution had ceased to mobilize the energies of the people. These women say that they still are viewed and treated primarily as objects of men's sexual lives, that violence is exercised on them, that they are required to behave according to men's modes and desires. They say that even when there is full equality between man and woman, the demands of sex according to the man's rule defines them as slaves—a feeling that cuts across all social classes and all distinctions between urban and rural women. Portuguese women feel that what is at stake is the introjection of a patriarchal model imposed on women under the label of "sexual liberation." They say that such a model is shaped by the competitive style of society and is charged with individualistic overtones which manipulate and employ the satisfaction of the "ego" in order to make the machinery of society run smoothly. (In other words, if you are too busy with yourself, you never get deeply and actively concerned with society around you; you relativize it, you see it in a mist, you imagine that you can "save" yourself alone, you become alienated through the very instrument that ought to free you.) For these women, such widespread slogans as "Women must be owners of their own bodies" are an ambiguous cry of freedom, since such ideas convey the concept of a society geared by "ownership of property" as the supreme value and sign of status.

From their experience, older Portuguese women strongly resent the path of "sexual liberation" which has been prevailing. They feel oppressed by the masculine mode of expressing sexuality as well as by values coming from alien and dominant cultures. Because they want to reinforce the cultural identity of the people to which they belong, they cannot accept a path of sexual liberation through which, in their view, foreign domination is imposed upon local lifestyles and choices.

What are women asking, then?

First of all, in a sudden transition like the one which took place in 1974 in Portugal, they plead for crystal-clear lucidity when sexual questions are analyzed. For them, sex and revolution must be seen together in the sense that the most personal experience is interwoven with the values, aspirations, and failures of the collective experience. In Portugal, sex has become for many the ultimate revolution, the other side of politics in a strange mixture of "the peace after the battle"

W O M E N   F I R S T

1990:
MARY ROBINSON IS FIRST WOMAN ELECTED PRESIDENT OF IRELAND.

and "the search for a place beyond all battles." Most of all, sex in practice has become the last bastion of the powerless revolutionaries—as well as the victory shout of the professional politicians. For the former, sex is what can be done when nothing else can; for the latter, sex is the exaltation, the paroxysm of politics. In such a situation, women not only are victims and objects but are even trapped as subjects, swept up in the same tide as men and repeating what men have always done.

Second, Portuguese women are clamoring for broader understanding of sexuality. They are very much aware of the sexual overtones of all human activity. They don't deny sexuality but are convinced that their own sexuality so far hasn't had any chance to be expressed. They cry out for the possibility of expressing a whole gamut of feelings, sensations, affections. and tenderness which they sense as inherent elements of their own sexuality. Even when these women are dismissed as "fusional" or utopian—because for them "to think of a flower is to see it and to smell its perfume"—they persist in exploring this path. They are convinced that a less Cartesian and rationalistic approach to societal questions is inextricably connected to the rediscovery of a much broader expression of human sexuality. For them, sexuality equated with mere genitality and commercialized into the consumerism of the producer-owner-buyer is to be fought as a fatal cycle of a society led by the paradigm of "progress" and by linear reasoning. For them, the shaping of a new society is interwoven with the articulation— and the living out—of new modes of women's sexuality.

This awareness and experience is the greatest strength women in

Portugal already possess. They know that they are—and can become even more—a real force in Portuguese society. They know, too, that the evolution of women in this country has a lot to do with women elsewhere.

For my part, I believe deeply that women can change society. I feel that what we must say to one another is based on encouraging each of us to be true to herself: "Now that we are equal, let us dare to be different!"

PROFILES
AND PORTRAITS

CAROL MOSELEY BRAUN
UNITED STATES

When attorney Anita Hill testified before the U.S. Senate Judiciary Committee in October 1991 and charged President George Bush's nominee to the Supreme Court, Clarence Thomas, of having sexually harassed her in the 1980s, Carol Moseley Braun was Recorder of Deeds in Cook County, Illinois. Anger at the disrespectful treatment Anita Hill was receiving from the Senate panel, anger at the vision of the demographically unrepresentative club of white men in action, and anger at their total failure to "get it" stirred Braun into historic action: She launched her own campaign for a Senate seat. Her upset win over two-term incumbent Alan Dixon (who voted to confirm Thomas) in the Democratic Party's primary election made her the first black woman to receive her party's nomination for the U.S. Senate. In the general election, she defeated Republican millionaire Representative Richard S. Williamson, making her the fourth black senator in the history of that political body and the first black woman senator ever.

Though the momentum of outside events certainly contributed to Braun's victory, her experience and credentials to stand as her party's candidate were impeccable. Born on August 16, 1947, in Chicago to Joseph J. Moseley, a police officer, and Edna A. Davie, a medical technician, Carol was the firstborn of four children. She attended Chicago's public grade schools, the University of Illinois, and the University of Chicago Law School. Upon receiving her J.D. she went to work as an assistant in the U.S. Attorney's office in the U.S. District Court of Illinois. The following year she married Michael Braun, a fellow law student. They have one child, a son named Matthew. She divorced Braun in 1986. Already involved in local politics as an avid supporter of first Congressman, and then Mayor of Chicago, Harold Washington, Braun won her own first bid for elected office in 1978, and became a member of the Illinois House of Representatives.

A passionate supporter of public education, she was the chief sponsor of every school funding bill that affected Chicago's public schools. Concerned with expanding opportunity and access for Chicago's poorest citizens, often women, Braun sponsored legislation that allowed public assistance recipients to attend school without fear of loss of benefits. She was an able and respected political leader in the Illinois legislature, becoming in 1983 assistant majority leader, the first black person and the first woman ever to serve in that capacity. After a decade of service in the state legislature, Braun was elected Cook County Recorder of Deeds, once again the first black and first woman to hold office in Cook County government. Overseeing three hundred employees and an $8 million budget, Braun was recorder until her 1992 Senate election victory.

After the historic inauguration, the Senate leadership appointed Braun to two committees in keeping with her policymaking expertise: the high-profile Banking, Housing and Urban Affairs and, what can reasonably be interpreted as an acknowledgment of the message of her candidacy and victory, the plum assignment of the Judiciary Committee, the site of the preceding year's Clarence Thomas debacle. (Currently, she remains on the Banking, Housing, and Urban Affairs Committee and serves on the Finance Committee and the Special Committee on Aging.) Announcing her arrival, Senator Braun seized an early opportunity to state for the record that her obligation to be a voice for the underrepresented was a responsibility she planned to take seriously. Braun took her stand in what would have been a routine Federal patent approval hearing for an insignia of the United Daughters of the Confederacy. The group's icon contained a representation of the Confederate flag, seen by many as a potent and offensive symbol of approval of African-American slavery.[1] In no uncertain terms Senator Braun told her colleagues that the Confederate flag "has no place in modern times, no place in this body, and no place in this society. I would like to put a stake through the heart of this dracula." Her impassioned stance had the desired result; the patent application was overwhelmingly rejected.

Braun showed herself to be unintimidated by the power of the male majority, even when she was hugely outnumbered or the men were members of her own party. Equally important, she is also unafraid of standing in solidarity with other congressional women. When Braun cast the deciding vote on major environmental legislation introduced by Senator Dianne Feinstein to protect the California desert and the bill passed, Braun embraced Feinstein in congratulations, an unusual sight in the Senate chamber.

The 1994 elections have brought sweeping changes to the composition of the U.S. Senate, transforming the Democrats into the minority party. With four more years remaining in her term, Senator Braun is dedicated to thwarting the right-wing Republican agenda as it continues to reveal itself as a social agenda that seeks to punish women, children, and minorities. The very fact of her existence stands as a challenge to those divisive forces. She will undoubtedly be a target, but they are sure to find a formidable opponent in Carol Moseley Braun, not only because she is a woman of color devoted to serving the interests of other women of color, but because in a career that has spanned more than two decades of public service and professional electoral politics, she has demonstrated herself to be a woman of power.

DAME EUGENIA CHARLES
DOMINICA

Eugenia Charles, Prime Minister, spoke in New York City in October 1994 with interviewer Levis Guy.

Levis Guy: You are a leader who has made her mark in politics, not only on the domestic scene but also on the international arena. To begin this interview I just want to note that I was told in the briefing that you are very easygoing as far as interviews are concerned.

Eugenia Charles: I have no problems with interviews. I think that you have a right to ask any question.

LG: The first question I want to ask is, Who were your early influences in politics and your career as a jurist?

EC: My influence in the things that I have already done was my father. He never forced us into education but there was an underlying theme in the house that a profession was yours if you wanted one. Not that he was a wealthy man, but I think that he spent his money on the things that interested him, and educating his children was one of them. Two sons were doctors, and when my turn came he asked what I intended to pursue. I replied nursing, and he remarked, "A nurse?" and that was all that was said. He never said yes or no.

Then there was a big case before the court in Dominica and a foreign lawyer came to argue the case. I went to court to practice my shorthand since my father insisted that I learn shorthand while still attending school. He thought it was stupid for a girl to leave school then later return to study shorthand to earn a living. I practiced my speed in court, church, and school. During the case I was indeed fascinated by this lawyer's cross examination, and my father encouraged me—not that he ever told me what to do, but he gave me the opportunity to choose. So in many ways he was my guide and mentor, a very hard-working man, a role model with very little education. I can now appreciate what he did for us. The person that I admire most now that I have grown up is Golda Meir. To me she was a remarkable woman. She gave up a lot for the politics of her country, including family life. She was down to earth and practical and I admire that very much.

I enjoyed my chosen career; I loved what I did as a lawyer, enjoyed it thoroughly. I enjoyed solving problems—not so much the court aspect, but that people came to me for advice. They'd tell me their problems and I would give them solutions. I practiced for thirty years. Before I got into government I was in the opposition for ten years and prior to that, I didn't plan to go into politics. My father was in politics before me, but he was not my model for politics. As a result of a law curtailing freedom of the press I wrote nasty letters to the newspapers criticizing the government. I believe that as I paid taxes I was entitled to freedom of speech and expression.

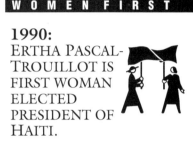

WOMEN FIRST

1990: ERTHA PASCAL-TROUILLOT IS FIRST WOMAN ELECTED PRESIDENT OF HAITI.

LG: Do you think that being a woman has helped or hindered you in politics?

EC: It has helped in a way, because as a result, it makes things more noticeable, but it has also hindered. Men at home slight women for pointing the way to new things. They try their very best to denigrate you to make it downright nasty, so that you would not stay in politics. I must say that it got to the point that one had to be very stubborn to stay in politics.

LG: Do you think that there is a difference between your ideas and those of a man?

EC: I think women, and I have noticed it, in women not only in leadership but in the civil service, and in medical professions, are more detailed than men. Men have broad ideas and expect them to be carried out, but women have ideas and stick to it and try to do every little part themselves. They are more painstaking than men in that respect.

LG: What do you think are some of the inroads and strides made by women in Caribbean politics?

EC: There are far more women in politics now than before, but women still won't go into politics because of some of the nasty comments being made. Some women did not continue because of the statements thrown at them. If you have a husband and children it can be quite annoying to be named in the press. I can say that I was lucky in the sense that I didn't have a husband and children that I have to give up. I did have a family—my parents, who had gone through a similar experience and knew what was happening and shared their experiences with me, so I didn't really care about remarks. They made it easier for me.

LG: Do you think that you have made any personal sacrifices for politics, such as family life or children?

EC: I don't know if I would have ever had a family. I can't say that

I deliberately said that I won't get married. I just think that the occasion never came for me to get married. I lived with my parents and I had a well-rounded life and I think I was too lazy to look for anyone. My family life was strong; my brothers were abroad studying, I was the youngest, and I was very close to my parents.

LG: For your contribution to politics on the domestic and international level you have earned the reputation for being decisive.

EC: As a leader you make decisions and you don't vary. Such is my personality. I listen very carefully to what is said. People think I don't listen, because I am able to make decisions quickly, but I listen and weigh the statements and I am able to come to a decision promptly, and others may think that because of this I don't listen, but as I said before when you have listened you weigh statements and make a decision. If I am wrong I am quite happy to change. I am not stubborn about that, but I don't weigh things for one hundred years. I arrive at my decisions quickly.

LG: Dominica at one point had a woman as the prime minister, a woman as Speaker of the House, another the mayor of Roseau, the capital, and a high court judge. Do you think that your leadership has enabled other women to get involved in politics?

EC: I think so, but on the other hand I don't believe that anyone made a decision based on the fact that if the prime minister is a woman, I can be a woman mayor. However, the country was ready to accept women in politics, not because I am the prime minister but because of the role I played in politics before becoming prime minister. In the ten years that I spent in the opposition there was a lot of dirty politics thrown at me. That in itself was to my advantage, because I think other women thought that if one woman could be abused like that she must be remarkable and maybe we should lend her our support. This has helped somewhat to bring other women into the political arena in the sense that if I can survive this onslaught, maybe we can survive it also, because men do not appreciate the fact that women are now in politics.

I have said this often and in many articles that are written about me, that the leader of the House of the Assembly remarked that the leader of the Opposition will not understand other people's suffering because she has never felt the pangs of childbirth. So I got up on a point of order and I replied, "Mr. Speaker, all these men should be put in a zoo because they all felt the pangs of childbirth." The public gallery was hysterical with laughter. The ruling party in turn hated me for my quick-witted reply. I think that gestures like the one I related have helped women to assert themselves and stand on their own and not tolerate unkind remarks made by men in politics.

LG: How would you characterize the importance of gender in politics?

EC: I would say there is no gender, because the problems are the same; a job is to be done. As a woman you may bring a different approach.

Gender has no influence on a decision, though as I indicated before I think women have a more detailed and painstaking approach. We tend to take a lot more advice and research into things before a decision is made. I don't deliberately say I want a woman to do a particular job. I usually say I want the best person there is to do this job and quite often it is a woman.

LG: Why do you think there are so few women heads of state?

EC: I do believe that family life does discourage a lot of women from becoming politicians. I realize that it does take up a lot of time. If you are a good wife and mother you would not want to invest in a lifestyle that takes away too much of your time with your family. Maybe that is right, although I believe that the family should be cared for by both the man and the woman giving up equal time, but it has not happened that way entirely over time.

LG: What advice would you give to women entering politics based on your experiences?

EC: That they must expect to be abused, expect resentment, even sometimes from friends. The remarks denigrate women. These remarks can be hurtful, and they must have the ability to ignore these remarks, yet turn them to their advantage by their replies.

LG: Would you consider yourself a role model for young women in Dominica and the Caribbean?

EC: I don't know. I think most women would like to have a family of their own and not consider me a role model. But if it is a role model in the sense of taking on public responsibility, then I can be a role model. This is not something that I planned. It just happened, but when it did I accepted it in my stride and I don't think I've done a bad job. There are lots of things I would have liked to accomplish, but you never get everything that you want to accomplish in life.

LG: If you could change the way women are treated in politics what would you choose?

EC: I would like men to realize that women in politics are here to stay. They are not going turn them away by being abusive, and they are certainly not going to get anywhere by making false statements about women. They must accept that women have a capability that must be utilized for the benefit of the people of the world. They should not try to turn women away merely because of petty jealousy of the way women perform their jobs.

LG: In your opinion, what is the most significant impact female leadership has brought to the international community?

EC: I believe that with the advent of more women in leadership positions more attention is being paid to the social aspect, to problems relating to women and children. It should be noted that not only women are doing this, but it is because women have become important in leadership that it is now important for other leaders of the world to ensure that these problems are addressed and solved. Social problems are the basic problems that negatively affect human life.

LG: If you can choose an event or events that have defined your political career what would that be?

EC: One of them would be a law that would have been passed in Dominica denying individuals the freedom of expression in the newspaper. I had a strong feeling that individuals should be able to express their point of view, whether or not it was agreeable to the other person. I believe that this was one of the defining incidents in my career. I wanted to ensure that Dominicans did not lose the right to express themselves freely in the press. I began to see how much more women could do in that role, not pushing themselves out primarily as women but as a force for attending to those things that women understand better than men—social problems in the home, others relating to children, which involve more women than men.

LG: What significant impact has your leadership had on the people of Dominica?

EC: I think that I have taught them that leadership cannot continue in a vacuum, that the people must work with the leadership for the benefit of the country. If that lesson is learnt then I think that I have done a good job as their prime minister.

LG: You have demonstrated that you are ready and willing to stick your neck out for the defenseless and the underprivileged, for example, Grenada in 1983 and the present Haitian crisis. Do you think that this is reflective of a woman's point of view?

EC: I think that it may be the instinctive part of womanhood. She thinks that she can teach and help people to care for themselves, to show them alternatives. Our upbringing has definitely influenced my way of thinking as a leader.

LG: In your roles as prime minister and minister of defense you have demonstrated that you make solid domestic and foreign policy decisions. In essence you have not forgotten to empower the poor, the disadvantaged, or the average citizen and to revitalize the importance of collective hard work in Dominica. How would you respond to my comments?

EC: Even before I came to politics officially the things that I was primarily interested in were young people, children, education, and caring for the elderly and the infirm. I did not think of this as social work; I thought I had the capability to serve my country. It may be because I was a woman or it may be my upbringing, but my family influence and background dictated that the best was always expected. Dominica was a relatively poor place and self-sufficiency was expected. I think self-sufficiency is the most important factor in life, taking what you have and making something beneficial of it.

VIGDÍS FINNBOGADÓTTIR
ICELAND

Vigdís Finnbogadóttir was elected to her first term as Iceland's president in 1980. The Constitution of Iceland does not grant political responsibility to the president, and she exercises only limited governmental authority, with the signing of bills passed in the Icelandic Parliament her most serious duty. However, the largely ceremonial post is not without importance. Because the president remains outside of party politics, her office represents national unity among Icelanders. "Anybody in Iceland can make an appointment to see the president," she says proudly.

President Vigdís, as she is called according to Icelandic tradition, was born to Finnbogi Rútur Thorvaldsson, a professor of civil engineering, and Sigridur Eiriksdóttir, a leader in nursing, on April 15, 1930. She attended local schools in Reykjavik up to the junior college level. In 1949 she traveled to the University of Grenoble to study French, then on to the Sorbonne for courses in literature and drama. Her interest in the theater brought her to Denmark, where she focused on theater history. She followed this with a trip to Sweden, where she studied French philology. Vigdís finally returned to the University of Iceland and graduated in English, French, and education. She married in 1954 and divorced in 1963.

Vigdís's background in French, education, and the performing arts led her down a diverse career path. After college she established herself as a teacher of French, first in a school setting and then on public television in Reykjavik. During the summer holidays she served as a guide for the Icelandic tourist bureau, where she developed and ran a training program for guides. Her continued interest in theater brought her to Grima, Iceland's first experimental theater company, of which she became a member.

In 1972 she was appointed director of the Reykjavik Theater

Company, which she headed with great success for eight years. Her status in the theater world resulted in Vigdís's hosting a well-received television series on drama for Icelandic state television. She began to give lectures on Icelandic culture at home and abroad and served as president of the Alliance Française. She became a member of the Advisory Committee on Cultural Affairs in the Nordic Countries in 1976 and chairperson in 1978.

During this busy period of involvement in cultural activities, Vigdís Finnbogadóttir kept a low political profile. But her perceived party neutrality, combined with her high visibility in theater and television and her expertise in Icelandic culture, brought her much support. Her gender also worked in her favor, for in 1975 the women of Iceland had led a general strike called "Women's Day Off," which nearly paralyzed the country. The action brought women's issues into the spotlight, and many felt it was time for a woman leader in Iceland. When she was finally persuaded to run for office, she campaigned tirelessly against three male candidates and won the four-year presidency by a slim margin in 1980.

Thus began a long and fruitful career for President Vigdís. She was re-elected in 1984 against no opponents. In 1988 she collected 92 percent of the votes against another female candidate. And she returned to office unopposed yet again, beginning her fourth term as president on August 1, 1992.

The popular president has focused on several causes while in office, among them the cultural identity of Iceland, its language, culture, and people. In her lectures and addresses around the world she often discusses how the Icelandic language has preserved her country's collective heritage by remaining close to the old Viking tongue. Her interest in preservation also extends to the natural world, and she has devoted much time and energy to the reforestation of Iceland.

Among her many accomplishments she is founder, member, and patron of the Save the Children Association of Iceland, and indeed, children are of particular interest to President Vigdís. In 1972 she became a single parent when she adopted a baby girl, Astridúr, with whom she maintains a close relationship. She has professed pleasure at being a positive female role model for young girls, noting that her own working mother, who chaired the Icelandic Nurses' Association for thirty-six years, set a positive example for Vigdís. "My message to the girls of this world is this: Get educated. Never accept a shorter education than your brothers."

She is an outspoken champion of education for all, and she is proud of her nation's image as a safe, democratic, and developed society with a well-educated populace. "I have a dream of an Icelandic information bank," she has said. "We should be in the vanguard of research in such fields as the fisheries, geology, and geothermal and hydro power—and

Nordic studies, of course, which ought to be one of our specialties."

President Vigdís has won many honorary doctorates from such institutions as the University of Grenoble, France (1985); University of Manitoba, Canada (1989); University of Nottingham, Great Britain (1990); Gakushuin University, Tokyo (1991); and University of Miami, United States (1993). She has had great success as a cultural ambassador for Iceland, bringing her country into the international spotlight on her journeys around the world. In her fourth term of office, she shows no signs of losing the respect and admiration of her fellow Icelanders, who continue to regard her as the unifying symbol of their nation.

BARBARA JORDAN
UNITED STATES

Phyllis Wheatley High School in Houston, Texas, was the site where
the teenaged Barbara Jordan found both her individual voice in the
school's debate society and her role model, Edith Spurlock Sampson, a
visiting lawyer who lectured to the students about the possibilities of
professional life. The school's name is fitting; Phyllis Wheatley, a slave,
was the first black American poet to publish a volume of poetry (1773),
ultimately winning her freedom as a result. Barbara Jordan's ability to
put together collections of words in a stirring way and speak them in a
voice "that always sounded like God" has contributed in large part to
her distinguished career as a lawyer, politician, and educator.

Jordan was born in Houston, February 21, 1936, to Benjamin
Meredith Jordan, a warehouse clerk and part-time clergyman, and Arlyne
Patten, known as a wonderful orator. Her paternal grandfather was
Charles Jordan, deacon of the Good Hope Baptist Church, and Jordan
particularly credits her maternal grandfather, John Ed Patten, with
training her to aspire to excellence and independence of thought and
action. The family's deep religious faith helped them cope with the
challenges, often brutal, of living in racially segregated Texas.

Jordan seemed destined for distinction early on. Graduating from
high school in 1952, she was voted "Girl of the Year." Her debate
coach and mentor at Texas Southern University, Tom Freeman,
encouraged her to go to law school at Boston University, where she
graduated in 1959 with one other black woman, the only women in a
class of 128. Her three years in Boston were her first outside of the
segregated south and they made a deep impression. Even though she
passed the Massachusetts bar examination, Jordan returned to her home
state determined to help bring about needed reforms. Almost
immediately she became involved in politics, working to organize the
black vote for the Kennedy-Johnson presidential election in 1960. She

was so persuasive that voter turnout in the black community was more than 80 percent that year.

In 1962 Jordan ran for the Texas House of Representatives and lost. Continuing to work in her private law practice, she laid the groundwork for the 1964 campaign. Again she was defeated. Her third attempt brought success and in 1966 she became the first black person elected to the Texas Senate since 1883 and the first black woman ever. She was hostilely greeted there with a virulent combination of racist and sexist epithets, referred to by some of her colleagues as the "mammy" and the "washerwoman." Against all odds, she proved herself to be an effective legislator, winning several significant battles: She authored the state's first minimum wage law; all Texas state business contracts must contain an antidiscrimination clause thanks to her efforts; and although she is not primarily identified as an environmentalist, most of the environmental legislation considered by the Senate during her tenure was sponsored by her.

In 1972 Jordan was elected to the U.S. House of Representatives. She was assigned to the House Judiciary Committee and was a strong advocate for expanded civil rights legislation. In August 1974 the Judiciary Committee called hearings to consider the impeachment of President Richard Nixon for his participation in the Watergate cover-up, and Jordan gained national prominenece for her staunch opposition to the abuses of power and defense of the Constitution. From her eloquence in the hearings flowed another historic opportunity. Jordan was invited to be the keynote speaker at the Democratic National Convention in 1976, the first woman or black person ever to be so honored. The enthusiasm with which her speech was greeted caused many convention participants to call for her nomination as vice president.

By the time she made the speech to the convention, she had already been diagnosed with multiple sclerosis, a progressive neurological disease characterized by speech disturbances, muscular incoordination, and weakness. She gave up her seat in Congress and took a teaching position at the University of Texas Lyndon B. Johnson School for Public Affairs. She also wrote her autobiography, *Self-Portrait,* and became a radio journalist, hosting a show called "Crisis to Crisis with Barbara Jordan." Known for her legal erudition and her devotion to students, Jordan has received more than twenty honorary degrees from institutions such as Harvard and Princeton universities. She advises on the boards of directors of numerous corporations and civic organizations and served as ethics adviser to Governor Ann Richards of Texas. Despite her illness, she travels across the country whenever she can to address students on the merits of activism and citizen involvement in her attempt to motivate a new generation to public service.

Jordan's most recent public appointment was as chair of the United States Commission on Immigration Reform under Bill Clinton. The commission's controversial recommendations included the establishment of a national database to verify the validity of Social Security numbers of immigrants and the denial of all public services to illegal immigrants other than emergency health care and school related services. The commission's report was greeted by a storm of criticism from immigrants' rights groups, a storm that Jordan has weathered with her usual grace. For her work on the presidential commission and in honor of her long and productive career in public service, on August 8, 1994, President Clinton awarded her the Presidential Medal of Freedom. This may be the highest honor awarded her to date, but it will certainly not be her last. Two centuries from now, future generations of Texas schoolchildren may well attend classes in Barbara Jordan High School and have the opportunity to ponder the towering achievements of this great Texan.

IRINA KHAKAMADA
RUSSIA

The following remarks are excerpted from an interview conducted by journalist Inna Rudenko with State Duma Deputy Irina Khakamada that first appeared in Novaya Yezhednevaya Gazeta, *December 28, 1994 (Moscow) and was translated in* FBIS, *January 23, 1995.*

Rudenko comments:

"In the new and for us as yet unaccustomed guise of a 'splendid lady' I saw a new kind of politician. Swept into the Duma not by the efforts of party ranks but by the sweeping changes of a society turned upside down, Irina Khakamada is engaged in the old, century-old but still continuing, debate among the Russian intelligentsia: What is more important, 'people' or 'institutions'? What is the source of the disease [in Russia], and what is the cure? Does it lie in external conditions, or within ourselves? In that debate she defends the independence of the individual. Yet at the same time Irina Khakamada attempts to justify the current uselessness of classical Russian literature, which focuses on the individual's spiritual search. Is that not because our classics were always on the side of the 'poor' and did not praise—something for which they are now being blamed, and at times excoriated—the merchant and the industrialist, those new rulers of the world?

"A deputy, deputy chairman of a deputies' group, and a member of the State Duma Committee on Economic Policy, Irina Khakamada is also an honorary chairman of the Liberal Youth League, president of the Liberal Women's Foundation, and chairman of the board of trustees of the Business and Children Charitable Foundation.

"'She has an adequate perception of reality,' was the principal trait of Irina Khakamada singled out by Stepan Orlov, her assistant and the director of the Liberal Youth League. She appears to combine in herself the uncombinable: a passionate appeal to people to rely solely on themselves, the freedom-loving desire to do only what she wants to do—and boring, painstaking, excruciating, and not always very clean work to create certain external patterns of life. She acknowledges that on that path there are more disappointments than not, but nevertheless she does not become disillusioned.

"Recently a Russian newspaper printed a photograph of a scowling little girl. 'This girl grew up to become a deputy,' read the caption, 'Who is she?'"

Inna Rudenko: Why does your faction call itself "liberal"? After all, the Liberal Democratic Party of Russia already exists. Wherein lies your difference, your spirit?

Irina Khakamada: The "spirits" have all been eaten already [pun on the Russian words "izyum" (raisin) and "izyuminka" (spirit)]. Thanks to Zhirinovskiy, the liberal idea has been soiled. We have made a great effort so that both here and in the West those who defend the liberal ideal do not become associated with that odious name.

IR: And what does "the liberal ideal" mean to you?

IK: To me it is not just an idea, it is a way of life. Leading a liberal life means assuming full responsibility for oneself. Since leaving state service in 1988—I was an instructor at an institute, then I joined a cooperative—I have fallen out of the system. My colleagues in my faction have followed the same path. By calling ourselves liberals we are declaring that we support a market economy and give human rights precedence over the rights of the state. A state is only as strong as its defense of human rights. That is all. In Russia one is not born liberal, one becomes liberal.

IR: You have been in the Duma for a year. What has there been more of in that year: hope or disappointment?

IK: Disappointment. With human nature. This is a dirty business...But the more disappointments like that you have, the more convinced you become that you can overcome all difficulties on your own, without relying on anyone.

IR: Are you a radical?

IK: No, I am not a radical. Maybe because I am a woman.

IR: What does that have to do with it?

IK: By their very nature women are oriented toward compromise. They are more flexible and more patient. They adapt to life better, and they can, if necessary, blend into the background. But men, like roosters, are unable to share anything. And they lose in their own hen house. Is it not women who are today saving us from civil war? Our society will be saved by the people who are able to have patience—I mean historical patience. It is like when you have a baby. It is not all joy—it keeps you up at night, and then there are the dirty diapers...Now is our time of dirty diapers. And we must not cry, or whine, or yank the baby around, so that the child does not grow up a monster. Be able to wait. And then the ugly duckling will turn into a swan.

IR: You were a businesswoman, then you suddenly left business. Why?

IK: I was not a businesswoman. Business people are people who are definitely creative, but for whom the most important thing is making money. Winning no matter what it takes. And even though the reason they win is not in order to be able to drive a Mercedes or wear Yves Saint-Laurent ties, those are the attributes of the nouveaux riches, and money is a rush for them. I never got that rush from money. And that is why I quit.

IR: But why did you go into politics?

IK: I was sick of being marginal. I wanted to realize myself as a representative of a new social group. The higher your social status, the more you can influence decisionmaking. That is why I entered the campaign.

IR: But in that case you should try to become president...

IK: No. A woman, and one with a Japanese last name at that...? There would be no way to win. And I like to win. Anyway, I think it would be easier to be president than chairman of the Central Bank. That would bore me.

IR: What grieves you the most?

IK: When I come home and see women with children standing outside my door. Unemployed, hungry women...

IR: Recently someone in the Duma asked Prime Minister Chernomyrdin: "What kind of society are we building? Gorbachev said: 'More socialism.' What do you say?" The prime minister replied: "Not socialism, and not communism..." And that was it. How would you have answered that question?

IK: Not capitalism, and not socialism, at least not the historical version that we used to preach. Generally speaking, I dislike those mossy old terms. I would put it this way: "We are building a civil society with a market economy and strong social support for the unprotected segments of the population."

Our deputies' faction has submitted to the Duma a draft law entitled "On Aid to Children," in which the amount of aid payments is based not on the minimum wage, as it is now, but instead on a minimum living standard. Immediately we were criticized by those who say we would increase government paternalism. But thinking that a market economy alone will lead to prosperity is a liberal illusion.

IR: So now you are defending not the rich but the poor?

IK: The stratification of our society is abnormally great. That is an indication that social technologies were not made an integral part of reforms.

"There is no unifying ideal!"—we hear that from the right and from the left. The search for paths to follow is assuming apocalyptic proportions. In a recent article Zhirinovskiy declared: "A tragedy has occurred in Russia; they have stolen our ideology." Yet an opponent of his who ripped into that article also wailed that "we still do not know where we are going or in what we should believe." What is that about? Down with the old ideology, and give us a new one?

Society should be guided by spiritual values, not by an ideology. Values cannot be implanted by the will of ideological leaders or spiritual pastors. Spiritual values must compete in society on a par with market-oriented values. And the role of the intelligentsia is not to create a new ideology, but rather to create new spiritual technologies, which will naturally be based on our people's interest. We need a positive picture— it is completely different forces that are playing off of our continual weeping and wailing.

IR: Is it difficult to be a female politician? And, in your opinion, what qualities should a business woman have?

IK: It is impossible to get taken seriously right at first. Such is the attitude toward women in business; after all, we are a traditional society. So the first thing is to demonstrate one's abilities and intellect quickly. Secondly, create the legend that you, a frail woman, are backed up by "tough" men. Thirdly, never turn into a manlike creature. And, most importantly, fear nothing.

IR: Is it that easy for you to stand insults and denigration?

IK: We are denigrated from the very start. It is harder to offend women—after all, they were slaves. Patricians take offense, not slaves. Just recently a certain major politician said to me: "You are still a little girl." If he had said something like that to a man, he would have had an enemy for life. But I said to myself: "Restrain yourself, and expand your potential."

IR: What do you see as your shortcomings?

IK: As a politician I have not yet learned to spin intrigue. After all, in our country intrigue wins out more often than reason. As a woman I am hurt by my 100-percent sincerity—everybody knows everything about me. But a woman should always have something mysterious and secret about her.

IR: As active as you are today, you were probably a real live wire as a child as well.

IK: No, quite the contrary. I was once reprimanded in school for "social passivity." I grew up shy and withdrawn, skinny, and ungainly. As a child I felt like an outcast. I was one of those who thinks about suicide by the age of eight. We were an odd family, always living in communal apartments with all that petty squabbling going on, my mother never looked up from her books, my father spoke Russian poorly...He was a man of unbending will—at eighty he was still playing tennis and still believed in the communist ideal. My father was a real samurai. He was strict, he never once hugged me, or kissed me, or caressed me. I was not accepted either at school or in the courtyard at home, because of the color of my skin or the shape of my eyes. But I particularly suffered at the camps I was constantly being sent to—Mama was often sick. When I was in eighth grade I accidentally got sent to Artek—that was some drill! And the food was bad, too. So several of the children, myself included, staged a little uprising. We came into the cafeteria and instead of the usual chorus—"To everyone, to everyone a good appetite!"—we sang "Everyone, everyone wants to choke!" That was such a scandal that we hid on the grounds for two days after that. But I came home with a thought that was new to me: "Does that mean that I can do whatever I want?"

IR: So, was that how it went, from a rebellious youth to speeches in parliament? Were you always such a good talker?

IK: In my first year at the Institute the geography instructor said to me: "You know the subject, so I will give you an 'A'—but this is the last time. You are very tongue-tied. Learn to talk." And so, overcoming my shyness, I began forcing myself to speak in seminars and colloquiums...After that it was easy for me to teach.

IR: What kind of books did you read as a child?

IK: At first, as a little girl, I loved to read about ants. Then, as I got older, I became interested in Tolstoy and read *War and Peace*. I thought that I was Andrey Vokonskiy, with his spiritual torments.

IR: Girls usually identify with Natasha Rostova, dreaming about her first ball. Recently you, along with many women, attended what might be called a ball: the Kremlin reception honoring the queen of England. Did you enjoy that?

IK: I do not like receptions—they bore me. But that time I got lucky. I was seated next to someone with whom I could have a normal conversation, not just chit-chat. Chit-chat is deceitful acquiescence, and I can't stand it. I prefer to have an opponent, but one who is intelligent and sincere.

ANN RICHARDS
UNITED STATES

"If you rest, you rust!" This Waco, Texas, women's group motto could just as easily be used to describe the careers of Ann Richards—the "official" career and the less visible "unofficial" one. The official career began in 1976 when Richards ran for and won a seat on the Travis County Commissioner's Court. In 1982 she was elected treasurer of the state of Texas, the first woman to hold a state office in fifty years. As treasurer she instituted computerized systems, expediting deposits of revenues and saving taxpayers millions of dollars in collected interest. She was re-elected in 1986, running unopposed. In 1988 she delivered the keynote address at the Democratic National Convention, making women everywhere proud when she stood in front of the cheering convention to declare to millions of Americans that dancer/movie star "Ginger Rogers did everything that [her more famous partner] Fred Astaire did. She just did it backwards and in high heels!"

In 1990 Richards was elected governor of the state of Texas. She presided over her state's economic recovery, formulating policies that aided in luring record numbers of new manufacturing jobs to Texas. Richards ordered audits of every state agency, streamlining spending and reducing waste. She appointed more white women and people of color to state posts than had her two predecessors combined. Richards was known as a popular leader and an effective negotiator, who at times could disarm her opposition by serving them piping hot home-baked cornbread, charming them with a colorful tale, and then hitting them with the hard facts. Under her adminstration, crime rates were reduced and educational statistics improved. She was narrowly defeated in the anti-incumbency wave that swept the nation in the November 1994 elections. Impressive as Richards's record is, it does not begin to tell her complete story. The genius of Ann Richards is that long before she sought public office she actively sought political solutions for problems she perceived in her everyday life, working to answer the needs that flowed from her family and community.

Born on September 1, 1933, Dorothy Ann Willis was the only child of Iona Warren and Cecil Willis. The children of Lakeview, Texas, including Ann, often wore clothes sewn at home with the material from feedbags. Lakeview was a working-class community, where people grew their own food and where nothing went to waste. Ann attended public schools and participated in her high school debating society, winning awards for competitions and securing a college scholarship to Baylor University. After her junior year she married her high school sweetheart, David Richards. They moved to Austin, where David attended the University of Texas Law School and Ann studied for her teaching certificate. It was in the state capital that they caught the political bug, but how they were able to give expression to their interests says more about gender constraints in the United States in the 1950s than it does about each of them as individuals. David was president of the Young Democrats; Ann was president of the Law Wives, a social club of wives of the law students. David became a civil rights lawyer; Ann stuffed envelopes at the headquarters of the National Association for the Advancement of Colored People (NAACP).

Even while she took full responsibility for homemaking and raising four children, Richards never let go of her passion for politics. She hired a babysitter for a few hours each week so that she could volunteer at the 1960 Kennedy-Johnson election campaign headquarters. When David's career took the couple to Washington, Ann went once a week to sit in the gallery of the Senate chamber and watch the debate. Back in Dallas she joined the women's adjunct organization of the local Democratic Party, the North Dallas Democratic Women. Excluded from decisionmaking and policymaking, the women nonetheless organized a network of loyal Democrats, a network that male candidates would make use of in future campaigns. In the early 1960s, Richards helped organize the Dallas Committee for Peaceful Integration, a forty-member committee that promoted racial equality and integration, radical notions in then racially segregated Texas.

Back in Austin in 1971, Richards was called on to advise Sarah Weddington in organizing her campaign for the state legislature. Weddington, the attorney who had argued the groundbreaking abortion rights case, *Roe v. Wade,* before the U.S. Supreme Court, was not considered likely to win. But by galvanizing the University of Texas community Weddington won her seat, paving the way for other female candidates. Richards worked in Weddington's office for the 1974 session, gaining invaluable insider knowledge about the Texas legislature. Richards also worked on Wilhelmina Delco's state legislature campaign with similar success. Delco was the first black woman to be elected from Travis County. It was a sign of the times that even after all of

Richards's accomplishments, it was only when David turned down the bid to run for Travis County Commissioner that Ann was approached.

As feminism came into the nation's collective consciousness in the mid 1970s and 1980s, Richards was a full participant. She served on President Jimmy Carter's Advisory Committee for Women; she lobbied members of the Texas delegation in Washington in an effort to pass the extension for the Equal Rights Amendment; and she was a member of the Texas Foundation for Women's Resources, which published the book *Women in Public Office,* a compilation of women's experiences as elected officials. When her young daughter Cecile asked "Where were the women?" at a Texas historical display, Richards responded by forming the Women's History Project, which spent four years recovering Texas's multicultural women's history. Proud of the results, Richards worked to raise money to send the new exhibit traveling throughout the state.

Richards's role as a leader was recognized when she was chosen by the Mondale for President campaign in 1984 to help advise on the selection of vice presidential candidate Geraldine Ferarro. Richards was also instrumental in forming "Leadership Texas," an organization whose purpose was to create female political networks and introduce women to government and business leaders. For the past twenty years, Richards has traveled her state talking to countless girls and women's clubs about leadership, power, and politics, taking the time to go into the details of campaigning, fundraising, media campaigning, lobbying, passing on political tools and skills to the next generation.

While there is plenty of substance to Ann Richards, there is also her marvelous style that wins admirers. She is a true Texas original: She rides a Harley-Davidson motorcycle, takes pride in being a grandmother, quotes Virginia Woolf at every opportunity—and Richard Nixon too, if ironically. While her likely occupation in coming months will be paying off campaign debts from the 1994 election, if the past is any indication of the future, retirement in any meaningful sense will not be imminent.

MARY ROBINSON
IRELAND

In any discussion of Irish president Mary Robinson, the term *symbol* invariably arises. Her election in 1990 appeared to symbolize Ireland's desire for genuine change, given her stands on such charged issues as abortion and reproductive rights, which have been anathema to other Irish leaders. And though the Irish president has no executive power and performs a purely ceremonial function, Mary Robinson has indeed used her title to promote tolerance, compassion, and national debate. She herself frequently employs symbolic gestures and language in order to promote those causes dearest to her heart: the rights of women and homosexuals; reunification of strife-ridden Ireland and its incorporation into the European community; empathy for the disenfranchised; and worldwide human rights. Her gracious manner, moral fortitude, and erudition have made her a popular figure, earning her the sobriquet "our Mary" among grateful Irish citizens.

Mary Terese Winifred Bourke was born in Ballina, County Mayo, on May 21, 1944, the only girl among five children. Her physician parents encouraged an atmosphere of independent thought and a love of learning, while her lawyer grandfather taught her that law should be a vehicle for individual justice. She showed her political bent at a young age, campaigning successfully for the right to read the Protestant *Irish Times* during six years at an exclusive Catholic boarding school. A year at a Paris finishing school was followed by attendance at Trinity College Dublin, where she garnered highest academic honors in law. In Dublin she made friends with classmates from both the Republican and the Loyalist sectors of Ulster, which fostered her personal commitment to helping her country grapple with its endemic hatreds and become more accepting of opposing points of view.

Robinson graduated with honors from Harvard Law School in 1968. Her exposure in the United States to some of the greatest turbulence of the Vietnam era impressed upon her the validity of questioning the status quo. Not given to outright protest herself, however, she subsequently used her schooling in law to effect change from within. She became the first female faculty member of the Trinity College Dublin law school in 1969 and soon began working for reproductive rights for women, a cause she continues to champion. In 1970 she married Nicholas Robinson, also a lawyer.

She has been called "a bluestocking, not a bra burner." Early in her law career there was carping about her drab personal appearance and her serious, focused demeanor. Some of her law colleagues, mostly male, were critical of her notoriety and her indifference to earning money. Seemingly impervious to their complaints, she continued to win important legal victories, including the right for women to sit on juries, laws protecting the rights of illegitimate children, the right for eighteen-year-olds to vote, and a judgment that Ireland's view of homosexuality as criminal was in violation of the European Convention of Human Rights. With her tenacity, vision, and intellectual gifts, Mary Robinson eventually came to be known as Ireland's premier constitutional lawyer. A member of many political and legal organizations before being elected to the presidency, she has, for example, served as president of CHERISH, the Irish association of single parents, since its establishment in 1973; was a member of the Irish Parliamentary Joint Committee on Marital Breakdown from 1983 to 1985; cofounded the Irish Center for European Law in 1988 and served as its director for two years; and was a member of the International Commission of Jurists, Geneva, from 1987 to 1990. With each appointment she continued to garner praise as a radical constitutional barrister known for "secular sophistication" in her devotion to civil liberties.

Robinson once stated, "A society that is without the voice and vision of a woman is not less feminine. It is less human." Her own political career began in 1971 with her successful candidacy for the national Senate from the Trinity College constituency. At twenty-five she was the youngest woman in the Senate's history. One of her early actions was to put forth Ireland's first bill to legalize contraceptives. Her two attempts to run for the Dáil, the powerful lower house of Parliament, ended in defeat. She left the Labour Party in 1985 over its endorsement of the Anglo-Irish Agreement, claiming that it excluded Protestant Unionists. In 1989 she resigned from the Senate after nearly twenty years in order to focus on her legal work, becoming a sought-after senior counsel in the growing field of European law. And then, less than a year later, it was announced that she had accepted the Labour Party's nomination to be their presidential candidate.

Observers claimed that she had very little chance of winning, and most wondered why this extremely successful woman would even want to be a national figurehead. Much was made of the fact that she received an image makeover, trading in her bland wardrobe for smart suits in bright colors. But Mary Robinson won by tirelessly traveling around the country and promising real change.

As president, Robinson has continued to champion the causes she has embraced in more than twenty-five years as a lawyer and politician. One recent goal has been to integrate Ireland into the European Community and to renounce her country's reputation for insularity and clannishness. Since Ireland approved the Maastricht Treaty in June 1992, Robinson has used her legal acumen to successfully reexamine outmoded Irish laws in the context of the new European Community standards, skillfully sidestepping generations of entrenched attitudes and bringing a refreshing openness to Ireland's political debates. She has professed the desire to become a catalyst for genuine friendship and peace between the Irish Republic and Northern Ireland. She has also encouraged empathy on her home turf, taking as a special cause the "traveling folk," Ireland's gypsies, who are roundly mistrusted and despised as outsiders.

Robinson's seemingly natural instincts for using her presidency as a symbol for healing, positive change, and inclusion extends even to her compatriots who have left Irish soil to seek their fortunes elsewhere. Almost everyone seems to know that she keeps a candle burning in the kitchen window of Áras an Uachtaráin, the elegant presidential palace in Phoenix Park, Dublin, so that the emigrants may one day find their way home. The candle may be a symbolic gesture; Mary Robinson is a politician who has proven that symbols can be powerful indeed.

MARGARET THATCHER
GREAT BRITAIN

Conservative Party leader (1975 to 1990), British prime minister (1979 to 1990), Margaret Thatcher was the first woman head of government in modern Europe and, as the winner of three successive general elections, Britain's longest continuously serving prime minister in more than 150 years.

Thatcher was born on October 13, 1925, in Grantham, England. She grew up in modest circumstances, though her father, a devout Methodist and active local politician, became mayor of Grantham in 1943. At Oxford University she read chemistry, receiving a bachelor of science degree in 1947. Political involvement began early—she became the first woman president of the Oxford University Conservative Association, the youngest parliamentary candidate when she made an unsuccessful first run at age twenty-three, and the youngest member when elected to Parliament in 1959. Prior to election she worked as an industrial research chemist; married Denis Thatcher, a wealthy businessman, in 1951; earned a law degree; gave birth to twins, Mark and Carol; and worked as a tax barrister.

Thatcher entered Parliament for Finchley, a north London Tory stronghold, and held the seat until her retirement in 1992. Her rise through the ranks was quick. She left the back benches after only two years to take a junior office in the Ministry of Pensions in Harold Macmillan's administration, held a number of shadow posts during Harold Wilson's Labour governments of the sixties, then served as education minister from 1970 to 1974, the only female member of Edward Heath's cabinet. Her relationship with Heath was impersonal, and as the head of a minor ministry, she remained outside of the inner decision-making circle. Her tenure at Education was marked most significantly by the angry public outcry that greeted her withdrawal of the government milk subsidy for primary school children, an ironic legacy since she increased department spending and expanded services.

The Heath government collapsed amidst widespread strikes and a three-day work week, and the Conservatives lost two general elections called in 1974. Heath's position as leader came under pressure, and although Thatcher was the only serious candidate to challenge him, her defeat of Heath and victory in a second round of balloting constituted a huge upset. As leader of the opposition, she sought to make a sharp break with what she saw as a Conservative drift to the political center under Heath. She advocated tight control of the money supply and reduced public expenditure in all spheres except defense and police to combat inflation; a free enterprise platform that included lower income taxes, privatization of government industries and restrictions on trade union power; and a stricter immigration policy.

In May 1979 she was elected prime minister with a strong Conservative majority and began to implement her policies. The immediate effects were a sharp increase in unemployment and fall in production as the economy tumbled into recession. By the summer of 1981 unemployment had more than doubled to reach 2.7 million, the highest since the Depression, as violent riots swept across the inner cities. Despite widespread criticism and unprecedented unpopularity, Thatcher refused to abandon her monetarist policies. The recapture of the Malvinas/Falkland Islands from Argentina in June 1982 was an important factor in turning around Thatcher's slide. When she called an election in June 1983, unemployment was continuing upward and industrial output downward, and inflation, though beginning to come under control, was falling at a lower rate than the average for European Community countries. The "Falklands factor" combined with a Labour party in disarray and a split in the opposition vote caused by the newly formed Liberal-Social Democrat Party gave the Conservatives an overwhelming majority.

Thatcher's second term continued her program. British Telecom and British Airways among others were privatized, income taxes were again lowered, and trade union reform continued. Thatcher won major showdowns with the unions, most notably defeating the miners in a bitter year-long strike. In 1986 she was sharply criticized for allowing U.S. planes to take off from Britain to bomb Libya, but as the corner began to turn on unemployment, which began dropping from a high of 13.3 percent, and inflation remained under control, the seeds were sown for another Conservative election victory in June 1987.

After a third decisive win, Thatcher felt she had the mandate to give full vent to a radical "New Right" restructuring of society. Controversial legislation included the privatization of the water and electricity industries, National Health Service reform, deregulation of radio and television, and the "poll tax," which was enacted in 1990 amid widespread demonstrations and rioting. Following another drastic income tax cut, the economy began to show signs of overheating as inflation and interest rates rose and the trade deficit grew. The unpopularity of many of the reform measures and the economic downturn registered with voters who handed the Conservatives a humiliating defeat in the 1989 European Parliament elections. Within her own party's ranks, Thatcher was an increasingly isolated figure, and in November 1990 she resigned after her leadership was challenged and colleagues advised her she did not have the support necessary to maintain it.

Thatcher's policies and political style have come to be known as *Thatcherism,* a word first coined by leftist critics, now part of nonpartisan political discourse. Thatcherism marked a move away from the postwar consensus-based politics to ideologically driven politics of "conviction." Her adminstrations abandoned Keynesian fine-tuning and a commitment to full employment and the welfare state and instituted monetarist policies developed by economists such as Milton Friedman and Friedrich von Hayek. Thatcher advocated foreign policy based on national self-interest and was so assertive critics derided her as a "little Englander." Her orientation was strongly Atlanticist, not European. She was far more comfortable with Ronald Reagan than any of her European counterparts, with whom relations were frequently marred by disputes over Britain's European Community budgetary contributions and her resistance to integration into a single Europe and membership in the Exchange Rate Mechanism. Thatcher's distinctive right-wing authoritarian populism broke with the Conservative Party's traditional upper-class leadership, whom she derided as "toffs" as she surrounded herself with ideologically attuned "meritocrat" Conservatives—ministers with business and professional experience, many of whom had come from lower-middle-class backgrounds. She demanded great loyalty and maintained tight control over her cabinet team, concentrating power and authority in a prime ministership that became unusually forceful, personalized, and interventionist.

SIMONE VEIL
FRANCE

In France "la loi Veil," the law granting French women access to legal abortion during the first ten weeks of pregnancy, has inscribed its author, Simone Veil, in French legislative history for all time. (Not to be confused with Simone Weil, the philosopher and mystic who conducted a heroic and fatal hunger strike protesting the evils of the Holocaust in 1943) Simone Jacob Veil is alive and well, at the center of power in the French cabinet, where she continues to build on a career in public service that has spanned almost forty years.

Born in 1927, Veil was one of three girls and a boy born to Andre and Yvonne Jacob in Nice, the resort on the southeastern coast of France. By the time Simone was in her early teens the Nazi-inspired racial laws were having a serious impact on her family who, while French citizens, were Jews. With the exception of Simone's oldest sister, Denise, who was away from home fighting with the Resistance, the Jacobs stayed together as long as they possibly could, despite the increasing frequency of arrests of their Jewish neighbors. As the danger of deportation heightened, Simone, her sister Madeleine, brother Jean, and parents were hidden individually by non-Jews. A teacher at the lycee Simone had attended before being forced out by the "racial laws" housed her until the day of her arrest, which came only two days after receiving her high school diploma. Simone's entire family was trapped in the roundup and summarily deported, first to Paris, then to the internment camp at Drancy. On April 13, 1944, the family was separated and Simone, Madeleine, and their mother were dispatched to the infamous Auschwitz concentration camp. Of the five Jacobs, only Simone and Madeleine survived the war.

Though the Holocaust did not claim Veil as a victim, her teenage experiences as a captive in Nazi prison camps have informed her life's work in pursuit of social justice for society's most vulnerable members.

Simone married Antoine Veil and raised three sons while also pursuing legal studies. After graduation from the prestigious Institut d'Etudes Politiques in Paris and qualifying as a magistrate in 1956, she entered public service as an atachee in the French Ministry of Justice, where she set to work on prison reform.

There have been many highlights in Veil's career, including positions at the very highest levels of French government. In 1974 President Valery Giscard D'Estaing made history when he appointed Simone Veil secretary of health, the first woman in France ever named to a cabinet position. Two years later her portfolio was doubled and she became secretary of social security in addition to her other responsibilities. In 1977 she was elected chair of the Nuclear Power Informational Council. Despite her increasing influence, some observers chose to characterize her role as an expansion of traditional female spheres of competency as society's mothers, nurses, and caretakers. One conservative critic commented that a woman could be granted responsibility for the ministry of Health because it was "technical rather than political." This comment can only be seen as ironic in light of the fact that in the face of extreme opposition from the Catholic Church, France's official national religion, and the Council of the Order of Physicians, Veil skillfully guided highly controversial contraception and abortion legislation through the National Assembly. With consummate political mastery she fashioned a compromise acceptable to both the Catholic right wing and Choisir, the women's advocacy group headed by Simone de Beauvoir.

Veil's political acumen was further demonstrated by her tenure in the European Parliament (EP), which included election to the EP in 1979, election as its president that same year, and two subsequent re-elections as a member in 1984 and 1989. In 1979 members of the European Parliament (MEPs) were elected for the first time directly by citizens of their own countries. Of this first class of directly elected MEPs in France, eighteen out of eighty-one were women, including Simone Veil. Charged with representing the citizens of the member countries, not their governments, the EP has significant informational, educational, and legitimation functions, if not binding legislative authority. For European women it presents important opportunities for gaining policy-making experience and political seasoning. Upon completion of her term as the EP's president in 1982, Veil served as chair of the Legal Affairs Committee, president of the Liberal and Democratic Reformist Group, chair of the French Committee for European Environment, and chair of the European Committee for European Cinema and Television. Characteristically, Veil seized upon each of these assignments as an opportunity to educate herself and then her fellow MEPs on vital areas of concern.

In March 1993, Veil began service in Prime Minister Edouard

Balladur's government in her most prestigious and powerful capacity to date. She operates in his cabinet in the triple role of minister of Health, Social Affairs, and Urban Affairs. It was in her critical role as overseer of France's multibillion-dollar universal health program that American First Lady Hillary Rodham Clinton consulted with Veil when constructing her own proposal. Given the wide-ranging scope of her authority, there are few social problems that do not come under her purview. France is no stranger to urban decay, AIDS, homelessness, racial and ethnic strife, and anti-immigration sentiment, to name just a few of the serious challenges before her. In an October 26, 1993, address at the United Nations, Veil made clear her unwillingness to back down from seemingly insoluble problems. Veil told the plenary session, "I do not think it possible to declare the war on drugs lost and therefore futile. On the contrary, I prefer to say that we have a war on our hands; the world is its theater and poverty its prop."

As outlined in the address, her proposal for attack on the problem is a multifaceted approach that must include not only the traditional tactics of increased punitive measures for offending countries but also strategies for prevention and treatment that account for difference by addressing the needs of specific populations. Interestingly, she suggests a role for philosophers and ethicists in an exploration of the meanings of drug use and addiction in postmodern societies. Veil's emphasis is on comprehensiveness, flexibility in the face of complexity, and the wise utilization of all available resources. Along with her ability to conceptualize sophisticated multinational solutions, Veil never loses sight of the human face of the suffering drug addict, exhorting the United Nations to take action because "it affects the very future of our societies, in the first place because the young are the main target."

> **WOMEN FIRST**
>
> **1991:** EDITH CRESSON IS FIRST WOMAN ELECTED PRIME MINISTER OF FRANCE.

Perhaps as an outgrowth of the moral authority conferred on her as a survivor of the Holocaust, combined with the evidence of her many efforts and achievements on behalf of people, Veil is beginning to be mythologized as the "conscience" of her party and her generation. Veil's adherence to principles over expediency is inherent in her longstanding commitment to women's equality, her public demonstrations of support for the State of Israel and of the right of Jews in the former Soviet Union to emigrate, her protests against any form of anti-Semitism, and her recent courageous defiance of xenophobic impulses in her own party. But assuming the mantle of "conscience" is problematic for Veil, because there is a danger in ascribing that function to an individual or to a small, separate group of society's members. Indeed, her life's work can be seen as a struggle to formalize in the political institutions in France and of Europe policies and procedures that give expression to society's highest impulses toward freedom and tolerance, not its most base.

There are many in France who hope that Veil, now sixty-seven years old and at the peak of her powers, will run for president in the next elections, breaking down that barrier in France for women as she has so many others. Her qualifications for that position are uncontested. In the depth, scope, longevity, and continuity of Veil's influence at the highest levels of French and European governance, one is hard-pressed to name many other individuals, male or female, of comparable stature. Behind the lengthy list of impressive titles is a legacy of labor and success in the areas of adoption reform, the expansion of public housing, protection of immigrant rights, promotion of public health, and, as if it could be separated from the preceding categories, the struggle for women's rights. While Veil's accomplishments demand that we recognize the mature, skilled political professional, it requires no great leap of imagination to conjure the visage of the orphaned, homeless refugee that was young Simone standing both at the heart of Veil's achievements and at her side. Fifteen hundred Jews were packed on the cattle car that carried Simone to Auschwitz fifty years ago. Among them were thirty-four of the forty-four children whom the nefarious Klaus Barbie routed from an orphanage in Izieu in perhaps the most tragic incident of the French Holocaust. Of all the children of Izieu, not one returned. It does not diminish Veil in the slightest to note that her individual success makes us realize the collective loss of the Jews of Nice, of France, and all of Europe, all the more. Although they are absent from this world, they are present at the core of Simone Veil's vision of the European Community.

Profiles and Portraits compiled and written by
Kathleen Paton, Frances Madeson, and Christopher O'Connell.

A POLITICAL TRIPLE WHAMMY

Diane Abbott

I was elected to the British Parliament in 1987. It was a triple whammy. I was working class, female, and black. Walking into the Houses of Parliament as an MP for the first time was an extraordinary moment. For months afterward I walked around in a daze. It took me years to come to terms with the scale of my achievement and with the knowledge that I had crashed through numerous glass ceilings to take my place in the oldest legislature in the Western world.

I suspect that it took me so long to take the measure of my achievement because if I had really faced up to it I would have been unnerved. The fact that I was a working-class immigrant in the highest legislative body in the United Kingdom was itself remarkable in Britain, where class origins are barriers to success as much as is race. Britain is a society still preoccupied with class. It is a society that has traditionally idolized the Queen and where people are to "know their place." You simply cannot get more out of place than being a working-class woman in Parliament.

For any woman, getting into politics is a big achievement. The British Parliament is a very masculine place. The first woman MP was elected to Parliament in 1918. Her name was Countess Constance Markievicz. She was an Irish nationalist, married to a Polish count, and she had waged her campaign from her cell in Holloway Prison, where she was being held for her activities in the cause of Sinn Fein and Irish freedom. In common with other Sinn Fein members, she never actually took her seat, as a protest against Britain's policy in Ireland. The next woman to be elected was also not English. She was American-born Viscountess Astor, who took over a seat from her husband in 1919. The total number of MPs in the House of Commons is six hundred and fifty-one. But for a long time the number of women elected was pitifully small. It didn't rise to double figures until 1929, when fourteen women were elected. For the next fifty years the number of women hovered around twenty. When I was elected, in 1987, there was a big leap to forty-one.

I was not just working class and a woman; I was black, which added another dimension to my presence in Parliament. There had been MPs of color elected before—Shapurji Saklatvala and Dadabhai Naoroji. But they had been pale-skinned Indians. The 1987 election was the very first in which men and women of African descent obtained seats in the British Parliament. That year was also the 150th anniversary of the abolition of slavery in the British Empire, which added a certain symmetry to events. There were three of us: Bernie Grant, who originated from British Guyana; Paul Boateng, whose father was Ghanian and whose mother was English; and myself, whose parents had emigrated to Britain from Jamaica in the early 1950s. We had faced a universally hostile and racist press. The media painted us as communists, black nationalists, and extremists.

I featured in the Conservative Party's national campaign against the Labour Party as the face of black extremism. But it wasn't just conservatives and right-wingers who were frightened by the notion of black people being elected. Our own party regarded us as an embarrassment. Leading members of the party refused to appear on platforms with me. We were kept at arm's length from the national campaign. I suspect the Labour Party nationally would have been a lot happier if I had conducted my entire local campaign with a paper bag over my head. The party made no effort to publicize and promote the positive aspect of their electing black MPs for the first time. Locally, we all had intensely racist campaigns waged against us. And even in our local parties there were party members who refused to come out and work for a black candidate. But despite all this, we won through.

WOMEN FIRST

1928: WOMEN AGES 21 TO 29 IN BRITAIN ARE ABLE TO VOTE FOR THE FIRST TIME, AS WOMEN'S SUFFRAGE IS REDUCED FROM AGE 30 TO 21.

So I was making a triple breakthrough. And the question that the society, the political establishment, the media, and even I myself were asking was how exactly had I got there?

It all started in a tiny village in rural Jamaica. My parents both come from the same hilly district deep in the Jamaican countryside. When sugar plantations worked by African slaves dominated the Jamaican economy, black slaves who refused to bow to the white man fled to these districts to scratch a living growing crops such as bananas, coffee, and cocoa, because it was impossible to grow sugar in this cut-off, hilly district. The blacks never got rich, but people from these districts are notoriously assertive and independent. And that was my parental legacy.

Both of my parents were enterprising and ambitious individuals. Though they were born in the same village, they emigrated to Britain separately. They were brought together by a cousin who was also living in the same part of London. They married soon afterward. My mother had just two children, myself and my younger brother, Hugh. Her first child was stillborn. When I was born, my mother wanted to send me back to my grandmother in Jamaica to be brought up. This was a common practice amongst West Indian immigrants at the time. They had a struggle to survive in Britain, and sending the children back to the Caribbean to live enabled the women to go out to work and the family to survive. But my father, perhaps because his first child had died, was adamant. I was not going to be sent back to Jamaica. I would be brought up in Britain. I am almost alone amongst my cousins in not having spent the greater part of my childhood with my grandmother. I am sure that I would have enjoyed being nurtured by that remarkable woman. But my father's decision was one of the turning points in my life. For a number of reasons I believe that had I been brought up in Jamaica and come to Britain only as an adolescent I would never have gone forward to become a member of Parliament.

My mother was a very intelligent woman, brighter than my father, although I grasped this only after they had both died. But the opportunities for poor black girls in Jamaica in the 1940s were very limited. For most girls the only option was domestic service or perhaps helping your family with agricultural work. If you were hardworking and ambitious you might obtain a clerical job in the lower reaches of the civil service. If you were exceptionally intelligent and hardworking you might become a teacher. University was out of the question, and there was a whole range of jobs that a dark-skinned Jamaican stood no chance of getting, whatever her qualifications. My mother was a teacher and then took a new opportunity that opened up in the early 1950s and sailed to England to become a nurse. At the time this was a prestigious opportunity and a path-breaking adventure.

As a child I was very close to my father and to a degree modeled myself on him. My mother was of the generation in which women sublimated their personalities into service to their families and endlessly deferred to, and massaged the egos of, their husbands. After my mother died, I realized that I actually had gotten my intelligence from her. I remember sitting by her hospital bed in the last few hours of her life when she was dying of stomach cancer and talking to an older relative who had grown up with her. He suddenly turned to me and wondered what my mother might have done if she had had my opportunities. But my father was a dominant influence in my young life. We had a close but stormy relationship. I will always remember something he told me as a child when I came home from school proud that I had come second in my class. He turned to me and said, "It isn't good enough to come second; you have always got to do better than white people." Perhaps my whole life has been ruled by that statement—and by trying to please my father.

I had a tumultuous school career. I was obviously very bright and excelled at English and painting. But I was almost too bright. Exams came so easily to me that teachers always complained that I wasn't really trying. As both a child and an adolescent I was always personally highly disorganized. I remember one set of exams when I was sixteen. I had managed to lose my exam timetable and turned up at school one morning to take my physics exam when it was actually chemistry that was scheduled for that time. I panicked. My teachers were furious and unsympathetic but reluctantly agreed to hold up the exam while I did some review. I had done no review of any kind for that subject. The entire class was held up for an hour. Then we all took the exam.

In retrospect it is impossible for me to believe that I could have taken in anything at all, so disapproving were the teachers, so frigid the atmosphere, and given my state of confusion. But I took the exam anyway and passed with straight As. Afterward I heard that my teachers were rather annoyed at this. They felt I deserved to be taught a lesson by failing. Looking back I can see that part of the hostility of my teachers to me was to do with the fact that I was the only black girl in the school. But I have to admit that black, yellow, or green I was an extremely trying little girl—always untidy, always covered in inky smudges, always late with my homework, and always up to some mischief or other.

At age seventeen, I had to decide what I was going to do when I left school. None of my immediate family had ever been to university. But reading was my passion, and in my books I noticed that time after time the heroes and heroines had been to Oxford or Cambridge. So I formed the ambition to go there too. I had no idea that it was relatively rare for working-class children to go to these universities, let alone the children of West Indian immigrants. My family would have been pleased if I had left school at sixteen and climbed up the ladder in nursing. When I told my history teacher about my ambition, she was discouraging, saying, "I don't think you are up to it." I looked at her and said firmly, "But I do and that's what matters, isn't it?" This was probably the second turning point in my life.

My education at the elite Cambridge University didn't just equip me academically. Perhaps more important, it gave me the confidence and the social skills to compete with white people at the highest level. It was also a window for me on the world of privilege. At Cambridge I mixed with young men and women who took it for granted that they would go into politics, the media, or the higher echelons of business. Cambridge formed my politics for life. I came face to face with class privilege, and ever since I have been a committed liberal and campaigner for equality.

When I left Cambridge, I pursued a twin-track existence. By day I had my paid career. I started off as an administrator but quickly went on to being a journalist. In my spare time I was a full-time activist. I started my working life as a graduate trainee in the Home Office working on policy. I then went on to work for the National Council for Civil Liberties, now called "Liberty." (This is the equivalent of the American Civil Liberties Union.) There I was the national race relations officer and worked on civil rights issues. I enjoyed the life of a lobbyist, but the glamorous world of the media beckoned. I worked as a television reporter and producer for a long and enjoyable period. And I also worked in public relations and as a freelance journalist. Looking back that variety of working experience was all very helpful to my future role as a professional politician. But my heart was always in politics.

When I came down from Cambridge, I plunged into the world of black politics. I organized. I marched. And I picketed. There wasn't a major demonstration in the late 1970s and early 1980s that I didn't participate in. But even in the atmosphere of leftist comradeship I identified sexism. Women were expected to do all the work while men took all the glory. Initially, I was cynical about mainstream political parties. But I joined the Labour Party and became more and more active until in 1982 I was elected to Westminster City Council. I was one of the first crop of black women councilors in Britain. I also campaigned ferociously for black rights in the Labour Party itself. Amidst great controversy, I helped found a black caucus.

The British Labour Party has always benefited from the votes of black and ethnic minority people. But we have always been underrepresented in the ranks of party officials and elected officials. However, in 1986, when the Labour Party was looking for candidates to stand in the 1987 general election, there were three pressures acting upon it. First, there was the high-profile campaign waged by black members like myself inside the party. Second, the party itself had turned to the left and so was more interested in issues of race and gender equality. But above all, the early 1980s had seen black and minority youth rioting on the streets of Britain, in areas like Brixton in London, Bristol and Toxteth in Liverpool. Sadly, the sight of black males rioting and looting and setting fire to buildings did more to concentrate the mind of the political establishment on black people than any amount of speeches.

So in 1986 I was being asked to run for Parliament. I went to a number of districts and went through the British equivalent of the U.S. primary process. In each case, I failed. After each failure I became more disheartened. The idea of becoming a parliamentary candidate, still less being elected, seemed more and more remote. I was just about to give up when my then secretary, Pat—a loyal and loving white woman— suggested I give it one more try.

I went up against the incumbent in the Hackney North and Stoke Newington constituency. To the surprise of everybody, particularly the incumbent, I toppled a sixty-seven-year-old white male and was selected as the candidate for a safe Labour district. I had difficulties and opposition, but I also had warm support from a variety of people, both black and white. To the surprise of many, including some black people who couldn't quite credit that a black woman could be elected to the British Parliament, I was elected at my first attempt. And this is how in 1987 I set out on my career as a British politician. Being elected seemed like the culmination of my hopes and dreams. In fact it was the beginning of my personal odyssey.

What I found when I walked through the doors of the British House of Commons that summer in 1987 were a number of difficulties specific to my class, gender, and race. The British Parliament is a ruling-class institution. It is obsessed with its own traditions and takes centuries to change. For instance, in the cloakroom where members of Parliament hang their coats, every member has a peg with his or her name by it. From every peg hangs a long loop of red ribbon. At first I was baffled as to what the red ribbon was for. Later I found out that it is to hang your sword on. Now, no one has worn a sword in the British Parliament for over a hundred years. That is about how long it takes the place to adjust to change.

A working-class person there inevitably feels like an outsider. It is partly the formality, partly the ritual, and partly the way everybody expects you to know how everything works without being told. The assumption is that if you don't come from the class of person who would know already, you shouldn't be there. It is a very hierarchial place. And this strong sense of hierarchy reinforces the class-based nature of the institution. The architecture, the pageantry, the language, the proceedings, the long hours you spend there all conspire to encourage working-class people who enter Parliament to gradually mimic and pattern themselves after the upper classes who have so firmly set their stamp on it. They may keep their accent. But their thinking becomes that of the club. And it is very much a male club.

The officers and the staff of the House are overwhelmingly male. Until recently women were confined to low-level clerical positions and waitressing. The atmosphere of the place exudes masculinity. It is full of wood paneling and leather armchairs. All around there are messengers and flunkies to wait on MPs. It all conspires to massage a specifically masculine sense of self-importance. And the British Parliament conducts itself in a peculiarly macho fashion. The assembly room is like a cockpit. The two parties sit facing each other. Their seats go up in steps like seats in a theater, and the chamber is deliberately too small. When it is full, MPs have to sit on the steps or stand, which quickly creates an excitable atmosphere. As a consequence, British parliamentary politics is theatrical, loud, adversarial, and conducted in the most noisy, macho manner imaginable. This makes Parliament an inhospitable place for women.

When I was first elected one of my young female MP colleagues was constantly asked if she was a secretary, so odd did a young woman MP in that place seem. It has been rare for young women to become MPs at all. In the past many women MPs were older women who were cast as matriarchs. Or they were the wives and daughters of male politicians, rendering them "safe" because their colleagues knew, or thought they knew, that a man was really in charge. There were occasional exceptions to the rule. One of the most famous young women MPs was Bernadette Devlin. She was elected in 1969 and was a passionate Irish nationalist. The British establishment and the press went into a complete frenzy, so extraordinary was it to them that she could take her place amongst them. She was the youngest-ever woman MP, only twenty-one years old.

It was with some trepidation that the House of Commons awaited its new black recruits. In the nineteenth century a number of Irish nationalists had been elected to the British Parliament for the first time. They created mayhem and riot. They used the procedures of the House to prolong debates indefinitely, keep the House up all night, and generally put the proceedings of the House of Commons into gridlock.

I found out some months after my election that white MPs, both in the governing Conservative Party and my own Labour Party, were anticipating with some alarm that we would be just like those nineteenth-century Irish radicals. Until we stepped through the door in the summer of 1987, you hardly saw black people in the House of Commons, even in the most menial roles. So when I was elected both I and the institution had a little adjusting to do.

There were other dimensions to my difficulties. It wasn't just a question of how I was seen by my white male colleagues. There was also the issue of how the media and the outside world saw me. Although I had all the academic and career qualifications, people were so shocked at my rise that white people and black people were quick to suggest that I was a token. And certain elements in the black community, particularly men, tried to question my black consciousness. It was sad, but some black people found it hard to believe that a black woman could make it to the top in politics without selling out. Some obviously believed that my achievements were due to "sucking up to whitey." It was a paradox that while for the white establishment I was a dangerous black nationalist, some of my own people tried to suggest that I was a sell-out. I was frequently asked whether I saw myself as predominantly representing women or predominantly representing black people. I learned to respond to my questioners by pointing out that nobody ever asked white male MPs whether they predominantly represented white people or men. It was assumed that they represented everybody. But my legitimacy was constantly called into question, even by white people who saw themselves as liberals.

My high profile was at first flattering but quickly became a burden. Most MPs spend the early years of their parliamentary career in decent obscurity. So they are able to make their mistakes in private. From the beginning I was subject to the full glare of publicity and every error received hostile attention in the media. It is also a great responsibility being seen as a role model. I quickly realized that I had to be a lot more considered and careful about my private life than I was used to. Part of it was simple things like always looking smartly turned out even if I was just going to the supermarket.

But I also realized I had to be ultra-cautious about my friends, male companions, where I was seen, what I was seen doing, and who I was photographed with. White male MPs were allowed a little frivolity. But it was soon apparent to me that what might be frivolity in someone else would have me labeled as not just a black extremist but a whore and worse. This personal scrutiny was not unique to me. All women in political life find that the media is rather more interested in what you wear than in what you say. And all women politicians are subject to much more intimate and censorious interest in their private lives than are their male counterparts. Only recently a female candidate for U.S. attorney general had to stand down because the media discovered that she had employed an illegal immigrant to look after her children. How many white male American politicians have employed illegal immigrants in their homes? Who would ever consider questioning them about who looked after their children? But these are the types of things about which women politicians are scrutinized. If you are a male politician, your wife is largely left alone. So long as she looks the part and turns up for the odd public engagement, the media isn't interested. But if you are a female politician, your partner is intensely scrutinized.

A big problem for women in public life is how to have any kind of normal personal life. Women politicians generally are more conscientious than our male counterparts. This is partly because of our earliest conditioning as nurturers and carers. But it is also because we have to work much harder than males to get any respect. This gives us very little time for ourselves. A high proportion of women MPs in Britain either enter Parliament when their families are grown up or have no children. There is an unspoken assumption that if a woman wants to get on in politics, she has to sacrifice her family life—unless, of course, like Margaret Thatcher you are fortunate enough to marry a millionaire.

In a racist, patriarchial society a white woman with power creates concern; a black woman in power generates hysteria. I have had to fight to have a semblance of a normal domestic life. My marriage broke up, partly because of the pressures of my political career. But I have a three-year-old son who is the center of my life. I have no live-in help.

And I take him to nursery every morning myself. Since he was born I have had to cut back a little on my activities, particularly travel abroad. But I have no regrets. A political career that didn't give me time for my child would not be worth having. Many older male MPs have taken me aside and told me to spend as much time with my son as possible. They say, sadly, that when their children were growing up they didn't see them and they regret it now.

I was elected during the era of Reagan and Thatcher. It was and remains a dark time for women and minorities. Our rights have been threatened and we have had to run very hard to stay in the same place. There has been progress. You can find women and minorities in high-profile positions that were unimaginable forty years ago. But for the people I live among in inner-city London, life is a struggle. Black people in Britain may have civil rights, but they have yet to obtain economic emancipation. Still I have faith. The support of other women has always been very important to me. And I am constantly amazed by what women, including black women, are able to achieve despite all the obstacles. Having a child of my own has brought it home to me that, despite feminism and the so-called "new man," keeping the family together and bringing up children remains in practice very much a female responsibility. We have to do this and run careers too.

Black people have had their setbacks. The drug-related black-on-black crime that has wrought such havoc in black communities in the United States is beginning to become apparent in Britain. But there have also been some triumphant moments for black people of the diaspora. One such was the election of Nelson Mandela as president of South Africa. All my life I have picketed, boycotted, and campaigned against apartheid. Black South Africans themselves were subjected to unimaginable brutality and economic repression. I was privileged to attend the elections in South Africa as an international observer. On election day I went into Soweto and saw the lines of black people who had been lining up since dawn to vote. I was in tears. The people of South Africa have many struggles ahead. But attending the elections was for me one of the highlights of my political career and reinforced my belief in the importance of popular struggle.

I walked a long road to be able to step over the threshold of the British House of Commons in the summer of 1987. It has not been easy since then, but I have never regretted going into politics. My darkest hours have always been illuminated by the love and support of my people. The words of Maya Angelou in the poem "I rise" have always resonated with me: "Bearing the gifts that my ancestors gave, I am the hope and the dream of the slave."

MARTIN, WHAT SHOULD I DO NOW?

Bella Abzug

It was a pickup. He was twenty-six, and I had just graduated from college. It was 1942. I had gone to visit an aunt in Florida, and I was bored. A friend said, "There's a concert in Miami City, Yehudi Menuhin playing the violin for Russian war relief." I used to study the violin, so I said okay, let's go. During intermission I noticed three guys looking at us, but I didn't pay much attention. Then, after the concert, one of these guys offered us a seat on the bus, and started talking to us. He seemed to talk in free verse, and I was thinking, oh, god, poetry. I had enough of that already, in college.

Then he insisted on meeting us the next day to go bicycle riding. My friend said, "Let's do it, he's handsome." I said, "You like him, so you go." She said, "No, you have to go." I said, "Well, I have nothing else to do, maybe it won't be so boring." So, we went. He insisted on taking me out to dinner. I said to my friend, "He talks in poetry, this guy. I don't enjoy it." Anyhow, we went out to dinner. I didn't really get to know him, because he was leaving the next day, and I was staying there for a month on vacation.

But he kept writing me, and sending me books and pictures of himself, and arranged to see me when I came back to New York. We went to another concert. In the middle of the concert he said, "We're leaving." We went up to the West Side, and it was a farewell party at his house. He was going into the army the next day. Everybody started to eye me up and down as if I was the girlfriend—and I had barely met this guy. Whereupon he took a bottle of scotch and drank the whole thing and passed out. And I was left there with everybody eyeing me as though I was the major factor in his life. Just before he passed out he said to a friend of his, "Be sure to take her home," and I thought, well thank god that's all over.

About two days later, I got a call from a Mr. Abzug, who said, "I'm

Martin's father, and we're all going to see Martin in Fort Dix. Martin would like you to come." I said to my mother, "I don't even *know* this guy, now I gotta go to Fort Dix with his family?" My mother said, "Well, how can you refuse a soldier?"

So I wound up going to Fort Dix. And I took him aside and said, "Look, what is this? Set me up here with your family, and we hardly know each other?" He said, "Will you save some room under the apple tree for me?" That was a famous song we sang in those days, "Don't sit under the apple tree with anyone else but me." "Oh," I said, "I'll be around, you know." And he went into the army, determined to fight fascism. He wrote to me about how important it was to be involved in the nation's defense. I did get a job in the defense industry. But I soon realized I was not for that world—so I went to law school, which had been my dream since I was a little kid. He came out of the army. He had eczema—which he did not tell them—and when he was in officers' training, he broke out. All of his mates went to Camp Edwards and they were later wiped out. Martin was saved by being medically discharged.

So he would come around and mope a lot, unhappy about not being able to fight fascism, and in love. Meanwhile I was in law school. I was seeing other people, but I still saw him. I never learned how to type so he used to type all my papers for me.

He had this rare sense of dignity about women. I had gone out with quite a few men—rabbinical students, rabbis, lawyers, dentists, and I always found a lack of real understanding. I was always an activist, even as a student; I would have a date and I'd sometimes send a telegram and say, sorry, I'm going to a conference, I can't show up. It used to drive them nuts. Martin wasn't threatened. Well, I fell in love with him.

We had a stormy courtship. We got along so well in forty-two years of marriage because we fought out all our differences for two years before we *got* married. And we got married when I was twenty-four, in the middle of law school. He was just four years older, but extremely mature. He was respectful of his parents but he was an equal. When he said to his mother, "Ma, I'm getting married," his mother asked to whom. (She was a real character.) He said, "To Bella." She said, "Bella? But Bella's a lawyer." (Very bourgeois woman, his mother.)

From the beginning, he did everything and anything to make possible what I was doing. If I had to work eighteen hours a day as a young labor lawyer, he would keep me company reading a book or typing in the room next to my office. On the weekends, he would always say, "You rest, I'll go do the shopping." When I went south while my first child was still quite young, he never said, "You can't go, that's ridiculous, you can get killed down there." It was in the early fifties, during the days when there were still lynchings, and in fact my life was threatened when I handled the Willie McGee case. But Martin would go to work in the morning and the men would say to him, "She's still working?" He would have fights with them about it. I was involved in the peace movement and the civil rights movement. During the 1950s witch hunt—the McCarthy period—if I represented anybody who got publicity, I'd lose a lot of other clients. He never balked. When I practiced law he said I was the greatest lawyer that ever was. When I became a member of Congress he said I was the greatest member of Congress and later he said I was the greatest stateswoman. He never felt competitive—only proud.

Oh, he loved to tweak people and say things like "Hiya sweetums" to me because that was not exactly de rigueur in front of a bunch of strong feminists. He had this enormous sense of humor. I never knew what he was going to say. One of the last appearances we did on a TV program, they were badgering him about whether he didn't feel jealous, and he'd say, "No, I've enjoyed it, it's been an adventure." They finally said, "Don't you think you're a mutant?" He sat there. I thought to myself. Oh my, these people are going to be sorry they said that. He had this disarming, sometimes slow response. Finally, sweetly, he said, "No, I'm not a mutant. I'm a Jew."

It was like having a warm fire: wherever I went over the years of struggle, there was always one place where the hearth was—Martin. I was enveloped by the warm fire of him. On the campaign trail we'd have to keep him away from people who said uncomplimentary things. And whenever there were articles written, he would always say, "I don't care what the article says. Is the *picture* beautiful, that's all I care about."

After Martin died, I got letters from all kinds of people: "I met your husband at an event, and he talked to me and made me feel that I was an important person." He was always there for our daughters. He kept saying, "I'm the lox and bagel man. I get them the things they need and Bella takes care of the emotional problems." But in fact they brought a lot of their problems to him because there were periods I wasn't there. There was a graciousness—not necessarily in the overt way—but a generosity of heart. He read a great deal, and had a tremendous love of art and culture. He wrote two books. He never showed them to me until they were published. That was his own thing. I always felt bad that he gave up a lot of his career potential to make it possible for mine to flower. He was doing free-lance writing, and I started to get involved with all sorts of cases I didn't charge people for (in those days we didn't have public interest law firms, so we were going broke all by ourselves). So he took on making the living, a schizophrenic of our times: a writer, a stockbroker.

He was a person of great order. I'm not. After he died, I couldn't dispose of his things, his clothes, his papers. But I recently painted the apartment and had to take things out of closets and shelves, and everything was highly organized. Every tax return, little monthly diaries, listings of favorite restaurants. After Martin's first heart attack he had to learn to eat differently. It made him terribly depressed. But he got over that and we learned to diet and exercise.

Of course when Martin had his first attack I was hysterical. And when he had his second attack I was hysterical. Martin was terribly male when it came to his illness, terribly unrevealing. He walked around with his first heart attack for ten days. He was the master of the kind word, but to himself, I'm not sure. He was never willing to examine that. I spent a lot of time literally forcing him to take care of himself, and watched carefully that he went to the doctor. He overcame the attacks so well it never occurred to me that he could die. I couldn't conceive of a life without him.

These past three and a half years since his loss have been the most difficult period in my life. I still have this tremendous pain. And the guilt that I wasn't there when he died. When I was called and came home immediately they had him just sitting in a chair. And I kept crying, "What did I do, why was I campaigning in Westchester, why did I run for Congress again, why wasn't I here, how stupid I was, how terrible I was, why wasn't I here to prevent this?"

WOMEN FIRST

1933:
FRANCES
PERKINS,
THE FIRST U.S.
WOMAN CABINET
MEMBER,
IS APPPOINTED
SECRETARY
OF LABOR.

People send me all these books: "How to Grieve." I haven't found any five stages, just tremendous sadness. Some friends believe he had decided this was the time to go, that he feared otherwise he might have become a burden. I watch older guys walking in the street with their wives, or somebody who can't walk or speak because of a stroke...I could have lived with that. Whether he could have, I don't know. My reputation is that of an extremely independent woman, and I am. But I was dependent, clearly, on Martin. He would embrace me in his furry chest and warm heart and protect me from the meanness one experiences in the kind of life I lead.

Part of me is angry. Part of me feels how could he do this to me, leave me? But a larger part of me still questions what I could have done better. I was in Santa Cruz recently. We had been there together in 1985 and had a wonderful time. This time I kept thinking, Why didn't we stay here, why didn't I give up everything and have Martin come here and together find peace in the sea and the sun and the beauty we both loved so much? Would he still be alive today if he stopped working? Was I so absorbed with myself that I may have missed some telltale signs?

There isn't a thing that happens that doesn't remind me of him. I talk to him. I dream of him. I dreamt not long ago that we were dancing. He was a great dancer....I still hear him saying things. When I got into problems with some of the Democratic Party leadership, I could hear him say, "You're too good for them." When I would become incensed about something, he'd say, "Bella, your standards are showing."

Now, every day, the fire has to be lit all over again. I function. I completed the campaign after Martin died because he would have expected me to. I work hard, practice law, lecture, write. I'm involved in movements, organizational work, and I travel. But there's a great loneliness. I have a lot of friends, and they've been great, but Martin and I spent our free time alone together. At the movies, theater, concerts. Just the other night I said, I'm going to do what Martin and Bella did—go to two movies in a row. But nothing substitutes. I have two wonderful daughters, very close and warm and they're always calling and spending time with me, but it's different.

Many women find freedom after their husbands die. I was on a panel recently, and one woman said, "Every time I voted my husband told me how to vote. Then he died, and I voted the way I wanted. I remarried and now my new husband is telling me how to vote!" A lot of women obviously don't have happy marriages, and they're not quite aware of it, so the death of the husband is often liberating. The women who have love marriages, we suffer for the rest of time.

It's not self-pity. Anger, guilt, a combination I guess. People say it's societal. I suppose being single is a societal issue, however you get that way. And certainly widows who live in poverty...but I'm not economically bereft. I'm emotionally bereft. The only relief I've discovered is to try to maintain the connection of life, the thoughts, the person, the strength. People say, "Don't you think it's time you had a love affair?" It doesn't relate to me. You can't allow forty-two years of greatness to evaporate by trying to "get beyond it." You have to keep the connection, so there's a natural easing of pain by communication. Which really is just memory, feeling, love, and hope that there's still a fulfillment of a joint vision. That's the only comfort I know.

What can I tell other people, that might help them, be of use? All I can say is, cherish your relationship, make sure you do whatever you possibly can to fulfill it. I had a dream recently, and in it I asked him, "Martin, Martin, what should I do now?" And he smiled that funny smile he had and disappeared in the dream.

PART THREE

WOMEN COUNT
WHY THE
NUMBERS MATTER

THE 30 PERCENT QUOTA LAW
A Turning Point for Women's Political Participation in Argentina

Gloria Bonder and Marcela Nari

This essay will describe and analyze the main results of a recent law that has revolutionized Argentinean politics and posed fresh challenges to women's political participation. We cannot focus here on women's struggle to gain the "quota law," enacted in 1991, which provides that 30 percent of all candidates standing for elections have to be women (law 24.012). But we will summarize briefly some key events in the recent history of Argentina to explain why and how Argentinean women decided to fight for a quota law and how this battle was won.

One of these events occurred under the presidency of General Juan Perón (1946 to 1955). During this period, women's participation in politics was spectacular and unusual, even at the international level. More recent events include, for example, the symbolic and cultural shock caused by the appearance of "female guerrillas" at the end of the nineteen-sixties, an unexpected image of the female in a society used to idealizing women as peaceful mothers. Through the nineteen-seventies, the gradual spread of feminist ideas in public discussion and especially in academic institutions, combined with the changing goals of the women's movements and organizations during the transition to democracy in the early nineteen-eighties, led directly and indirectly to the quota law.

Four years after the enactment of the quota law, we interviewed six women representing different political parties, and asked about their expectations, achievements, frustrations, and ideas about work yet to be done to attain the full integration of Argentinean women at all levels of political power and decision making. Their voices will be heard—anonymously—through these pages.

THE WOMEN'S BRANCH AND EVA PERÓN

The figure of Eva Perón and the experiences of the Peronist Party and, later on, its women's branch are still important influences on the political style of many Argentinean women. Peronism (1946 to 1955) represented the interests and demands of an alliance formed by old and new working sectors and a growing bourgeoisie that included women and that had emerged from domestic migrations and industrialization.

Peronism speeded up and consolidated women's social and political participation. When women's suffrage (law 13.010) was enacted in 1947, for the first time at the national level, a law gave women the right to vote and run for office. The Peronist Party was organized in sectors or "branches": the "male" or "political" branch, the "women's" branch, and the "trade unions." Since party statutes granted each of the three branches an equal share of representation, during the Peronist period women attained the highest percentage of political representation in the history of Argentina. Women held 21.7 percent of the seats in the House of Representatives in 1955 and 23.5 percent in the Senate in 1954.

Moreover, Eva Perón's power and style have helped to strengthen and legitimize women's presence in politics. She created an idealized model of the "woman politician," which, even today, influences the social and personal expectations of women politicians in Argentina. According to Marysa Navarro, "Few figures in Argentinean politics have generated so much hate and so much love as Eva Perón." To her followers, she was a generous woman who worked tirelessly to improve the living conditions of workers, women, children, and the aged. To her enemies, she was an ambitious actress, a prostitute who reached the top by using influential men, and a woman resentful of her illegitimate origins (Navarro, 1988: 101). The legends created around her (she was known as the "Lady of Hope," the "wicked woman," and, in the late nineteen-fifties, "the revolutionary") still live in the memories of many Argentinean women (Taylor, 1981), especially those who tried to recreate her legacy in the women's branch after the fall of Juan Perón's government and the banning of the party in 1955.

Eva Perón is a necessary point of reference for understanding women's experience with political power in Argentina. Whether she's followed or rejected, she continues to be a model for women's expression of their desire for political power.

WOMEN'S PARTICIPATION IN THE TRANSITION TO DEMOCRACY

One of the most difficult and cruel stages in the history of Argentina ended in December 1983. The military dictatorship in power since 1976, using the "doctrine of national security,"[1] had established state terrorism as a new and sophisticated method of social control. This policy caused the "disappearance" of some thirty thousand people, the destruction of a majority of political and social organizations and trade unions, and a split society. On the economic level, as a result of neoliberal policies influenced by the Chicago School, the country found itself burdened with an enormous foreign debt.[2] During the final stages of the dictatorship and the first years of democratic government (from 1984 to 1985), women's activities were significant to restoring and consolidating democracy. In a critical political and economic context, women participated with courage, creativity, and perseverance in the struggle to attain human rights (especially the right to one's life in the face of state terrorism), the restoration of democracy, and the economic survival of the family unit.

While the best-known example of politically active women during this period was the Mothers of Plaza de Mayo,[3] many other women's organizations were formed toward the end of the nineteen-seventies. Some of them attempted to provide day-by-day solutions to the serious economic crisis prevailing in Argentina and in all of Latin America since the end of the nineteen-seventies and especially during the nineteen-eighties. They set up soup kitchens, day nurseries, mothers' clubs, production cooperatives, community health centers, et cetera.[4] Although these practices seemed "feminine," they took on different meanings in the context of the transition to democracy and the progressive modernization of gender values. They testified, as they still do today, to women's desire to gain autonomy, to assert themselves in communities and in the family, as well as to gain full recognition of their rights as citizens. In this sense, these groups set the bases for the emergence of a new type of women's leadership. For Elizabeth Jelín, these movements implied a "struggle to achieve a more extensive citizenship which would include social recognition: a political struggle—in terms of access to the mechanisms of power—but also a cultural struggle, a search for a differentiation of identities" (Jelín, 1987: 348).

In 1983, a woman politician observed, "When the dictatorship ended, those of us who decided to enter politics realized that we had to change the [women's] movement's logic and practices and accept the rules imposed by democracy and by the internal life of political parties." All of this posed a great challenge for women, one that could not be met without pain and resistance. Undoubtedly, to fight against an oppressive regime generates a sort of mystique that facilitates internal cohesion and stimulates alternative practices that allow the breaking of "rules." "In this sense," she continued, "the rules of democracy require that women establish new links and accept leadership within the 'social contract.'" With this understanding in mind, being part of an institution became an option for most feminist activists. Some of them joined political parties; others integrated feminism with their professional lives through women's studies research and teaching, developing programs to improve women's status in governmental and nongovernmental organizations.

THE DEMOCRATIC REOPENING: FROM AN ILLUSION OF EQUALITY TO THE AWARENESS OF DISCRIMINATION

During the final years of the military dictatorship, large numbers of men and women joined political parties and participated in campaigns and in public meetings, in a climate of seeming gender equality. Many women, militants since before 1976, and the women who joined them at the beginning of the nineteen-eighties, believed that being a woman was not a limitation. The common belief held that "in politics we would be on equal footing with men." The political climate before the coup d'etat in 1976, as well as in 1983, accentuated ideological homogeneity. All "sectorial" interests were deemed to endanger the unity needed to attain the desired changes: "social" and "national liberation" during the nineteen-sixties and nineteen-seventies, and the transition to democracy during the nineteen-eighties. Only much later did a majority of women who had been members of political parties, trade unions, or the armed forces prior to the 1976 coup d'etat, admit that discrimination had existed (Feijoó and Nari, 1994). Any debate regarding gender discrimination was negligible.

WOMEN FIRST

1974: MARIA ESTELA (ISABELA) MARTINEZ DE PERÓN BECOMES THE FIRST WOMAN PRESIDENT OF ARGENTINA.

But the democratic reopening of 1983 failed to bring about substantial changes in the scope of women's participation in the legislative, executive, and judiciary sectors. This confirmed the "old" fear of women politicians that political parties would continue to treat them in the same way as before. "Only yesterday, when the political parties opened the voting registers, we were the favorites of the leaders," a politician said, referring to the campaign prior to the 1983 elections. But, she continued, "Those of us who had had some experience recognized by intuition that this was a lie, perhaps an unconscious one. We knew that much effort was still needed to make this heavy wheel turn, but we couldn't disappoint the inexperienced ones, who believed this lie" (Casas, 1985: 65).

By 1983, the percentage of women in the House of Representatives had dropped to 4.3 percent, even lower than that during the previous democratic government (between 7.8 percent and 9.1 percent in the period from 1973 to 1976)[5] (Lipszyc, 1994). This decrease was surprising, considering the percentage of women voters, party members, and militants.

Voting is compulsory in Argentina, but historically, more women than men vote. With regard to party membership during the nineteen-eighties, the percentage of women (47 percent) was slightly lower than of men (53 percent) (Braun, 1992: 573). The profile of women in political parties formed a "pyramid": broad at the foundation (membership and militancy), narrowing up toward the higher positions.

Only in some of the smaller political parties did the ratio of highly placed women exceed 20 percent. In most parties, no woman held a high position and in the largest of them, women were even by 1994 a minority of the leadership (4.3 percent in the Union Civica Radical and 9.6 percent in the Partido Justicialista) (Lipszyc, 1994).

Almost from the beginning, therefore, democratic political life showed its limitations regarding gender equality at decision-making levels. In that sense, the politicians who had thought that being a woman would not be an obstacle once democracy was restored received a shock. They realized how few they were; that they were expected to be more qualified than the men in order to compete for the same positions or to present their views; and that they had ignored the subtle codes of political life which had excluded them from the unofficial places of power where the most important decisions were made: the "small committees," the hall conversations, et cetera. For some political women, this experience was a starting point in a process. As one said: "It helped me realize that other women, as qualified as I am, have been unable to make it. I also realized that if more women had joined in the projects, proposals, and objectives I fought for, I would have needed less time to achieve my goals and would have sounded more convincing."

THE RELATIONSHIP BETWEEN WOMEN POLITICIANS AND WOMEN'S MOVEMENTS

Following the restoration of democracy, some women politicians began to participate in the women's movement, overcoming their distrust of the feminists' positions. Feminists also distrusted women politicians. But a different kind of consensus gradually gained ground, especially during a workshop on "Woman and the Political Parties" held during the Fifth National Women's Meeting (in Rosario, 1989) to lobby for affirmative action in the political area. Women continued to discuss this project and mobilize public opinion in its favor. A Forum of Women Politicians met toward the end of 1989 and, at the Fifth Meeting of Feminists from Latin America and the Caribbean, a Latin American Network of Feminist Politicians was created.

On March 8, 1991, the Argentinean section of this network[6] organized a series of activities throughout the country. The most significant of these was a simulated session of the Deliberating Council of Buenos Aires, at which feminist politicians occupied all the benches and submitted and approved municipal statutes covering all the areas of women's equality in society.

The establishment of new political interest groups and gatherings of women politicians helped to achieve consensus regarding the need to support the quota law project submitted to the Congress in 1989.

THE QUOTA LAW

The quota law (24.012), which was approved by Congress in November 1991, amends Article 60 of the Electoral Code and stipulates that "the lists of candidates must include at least 30 percent of women candidates for public office, in proportions which will make their election possible. Lists of candidates which fail to fulfill this requisite shall not be made official."

Toward the end of 1989, Senator Margarita Malharro and Representatives Norma Allegrone de Fonte and Florentina Gomez Miranda simultaneously submitted "quota law" bills to the House and the Senate.[7] While both bills initially had been promoted by lawmakers from the Union Civica Radical, the bills also obtained the immediate support of women members from other political parties.

Senator Malharro's bill was approved by the Senate on September 20, 1990, a somewhat surprising result considering the previously unfavorable climate. "That day we mobilized our colleagues, asking for their support," she said. "However, although we did not have much hope... when the bill was approved, we were stunned. What happened in the Senate was a question of luck, of opportunity." But after this unexpected victory, women from different political parties realized that, if they wanted the bill approved by the House of Representatives, they would have to coordinate their efforts and be prepared in advance.

On November 6, 1991, the law was debated in the House of Representatives. Huge numbers of women exerted strong pressure from the gallery, in the Chambers, and in the squares and streets near the Congress. Demanding, singing, talking to and even insulting male politicians during the debate, women from different social classes, with different ideologies, showed great consensus and a determination not easy to ignore.[8] As one legislator remembered the occasion, "We entered the Chamber, not knowing whether we would win or lose in the voting. We took a risk, but the mobilization of women on the day of the parliamentary debate was decisive. Among the men, many could not vote against us, either because they had promised their vote, or because they could not run the risk of 'killing' a project supported by every woman in all political and social sectors."

Prior to the parliamentary debate, Peronist Party women had organized several women's meetings to present and discuss the law, inviting male politicians as speakers. Using this strategy, they tried to induce the men to make a public commitment before mass assemblies: "We invited male political leaders who were unaccustomed to such large and spontaneous meetings. When faced by all these women, they adopted an extremely 'feminist' attitude, as would any other politician who wished to please his audience."

The interparty alliance among women was also essential for the approval of the law. Not all women favored this measure, but those who disagreed with promised not to criticize it publicly.[9] A common strategy was adopted to deal with each male representative: "We knew already which woman could speak with what man, even though each might belong to different parties. We took advantage of all existing political links, such as having worked together in the same committees, personal affinities, shared political and professional experiences, et cetera."

Without denying these facts, some affirm that the law was passed by the president's final decision. The "unofficial" story is that President Carlos Menem made a decisive phone call to the minister of the Interior at 2 a.m., ordering him to go to the House of Representatives and tell the Justicialista legislators (the majority members) to vote for the bill. Two different interpretations have attempted to explain his action. According to some opinions, the president expressed the historical commitment of Peronism to women, as well as his personal vision of the fundamental role women should play in Argentinean politics. To others, his was a demagogic strategy to obtain political advantage. Still another interpretation holds that men supported the law to show that they were "modern and democratic," assuming also that this might improve the tarnished image of politicians.

Whatever the reason, women decided pragmatically to take advantage of the situation: "Our strategy was to use this opportunity to our benefit; to make politics more accessible for women, and then to try to change politics according to our perspectives and ideals."

THE DEBATE REGARDING POSITIVE ACTION

Throughout this period, a widespread social debate brought to the surface controversial issues related to gender relationships in Argentinean society and the need for positive action to improve them. In general, public opinion was not against the quota law. But it is interesting to note that its justifications were based on at least two very different premises.

On the one hand, the law became a tool to attain equality and justice for women in the political area, thus a function of human rights and democracy. The egalitarian argument springs from liberal feminist views that seek to overcome discrimination against women in society mainly through the law and by improving access to education and empowerment. It accepts positive actions as temporary solutions to the problems of discrimination against women (Amorós, 1991).

The second argument springs from another tradition of feminist thought, one that emphasizes women as a source of moral superiority. Characteristics such as altruism, self-denial, intuition, and caring are seen as a biological "essence of femininity" or traits of a "feminine culture" which have been concealed by the patriarchal culture and which, in use, would change patriarchal institutions (Gilligan, 1982; Rich, 1978).

The first argument—based on women's demand for equality—was much more irritating than the second, since it revealed the existence of discrimination in the nation's democracy and expressed women's desire for power without any further justification. As a counterargument, some people insisted that the quota law was antidemocratic because it discriminated against political parties and the population as a whole by restricting their freedom of choice. Male politicians of both the right and the left who opposed the law insisted that, "If women and men are equal, there is no need for a quota." Hence, "The women who don't make it lack the necessary qualifications." During the parliamentary debate, one representative justified his opposition by stating that the law was "coercive, reactionary, and offensive to women who had sufficient ability to rise to the positions held by women legislators, and to all women who had made a significant contribution to this country's development" (Representative Alberto Albamonte [Union del Centro Democratico] in the House of Representatives. *Journal of Sessions,* Nov. 6, 1991).

Not unexpectedly, the claim for women's exceptional ethical and affective qualities was hailed as a refreshing contribution to politics and gained many more allies, especially among men. This was the argument men most often used in defense of this law: "This responsibility for the survival of the species makes a difference in the relationship between women and power. Men use power as an exercise; women use it to preserve life. They seek power to ensure the survival of the species. Women don't seek power because they want to manage the Central Bank.... Women's search for power has biological roots; it is their mission" (Minister of the Interior Jose Luis Manzano in the House of Representatives. *Journal of Sessions,* Nov. 6, 1991).

But, as one woman politician said, "How can one resist this proposal? It sounds like an exciting invitation, an attempt to enhance 'the best' supposed to be in women. However, behind it we detect the mechanism used to lull, to deny the real significance of our presence: to hold places of power and decision" (Sampoalesi, 1993: 10).

In this debate, a third voice could be heard, one that took issue with the debates about equality or differences and pointed to women's equal ability even to participate in corruption scandals. This voice argued: "The task of 'humanizing' politics, placing it at people's service, should be carried out by women and men together. I feel compelled to be ethical as an individual, not as a woman. I can't understand why women should be the saviors. On the other hand, I don't think that we have yet established the truth of this premise."

ENFORCEMENT OF THE LAW

When the law was implemented on March 8, 1991, the item most difficult to interpret was the one stipulating that at least 30 percent of candidates must be women, included in sufficient "proportion to have an opportunity to be elected." According to the regulating decree, these 30 percent should be placed as candidates "among the positions which each political party submits for reelection," and the lists must contain one woman candidate for every two men (*Página 12*, March 9, 1993: 2). By the time the regulating decree was issued, the quota law had also been included in the legislation of six provinces (Mendoza, Santa Fe, Santa Cruz, La Rioja, Corrientes, and Misiones) and the federal capital.

The law was first enforced during the national elections in October 1993. In spite of the regulating decree, in many districts the lists of candidates failed to comply with the law. The "women's cabinet"[10] and some women members of political parties filed immediate appeals with the election courts. In general, they were successful (*La Nación*, Aug. 8, 1993: 12). Consequently, since almost all the lists submitted at these elections complied with the law, this caused a significant *quantitative change*. The percentage of women in the House of Representatives rose from 5.4 percent in 1991 to 13.3 percent in 1993.

In 1994, a new opportunity arose to apply the quota law during the election of the delegates to the Constitutional Assembly, responsible for the reform of the national constitution. Of the 305 delegates elected to the Assembly, 81 were women. Two of them resigned, leaving 25.9 percent women (*Página 12*, May 24, 1994: 6).

The high percentage of women delegates may explain the numerous new provisions on women's rights adopted in the amended constitution. For example, the United Nations' "Convention on the Elimination of All Forms of Discrimination against Women" has acquired constitutional status in Argentina. The constitution also authorizes the Congress to promote positive action measures for women and to guarantee equal opportunities and treatment and the full enjoyment of all the rights recognized by the constitution and in international treaties (Part II, ch. 5, arts. 22 and 23). Especially regarding political rights, it guarantees women's full participation, granting men and women equal opportunity to be elected to party positions through positive measures to be adopted by the political parties and the electoral system (Part I, ch. 2, art. 37).

EVALUATING THE EXPERIENCE: GAINS, ILLUSIONS, AND FEARS

The struggle to get the quota law passed and implemented and the experience gained by women during this process gave birth to illusions, desires, and fantasies, which exert a significant symbolic and practical influence on current public discourse in Argentina. According to the women we interviewed, those who fought for the law praise the *quantitative leap* it has effected and hope that in the future it can promote *qualitative changes* in political institutions and in society. However, all agree that it is too soon to make a balanced judgment, since social change occurs slowly.

One of the basic problems of women politicians is the *admission of their desire for power:* "The majority of my colleagues feel that they have to look for excuses for doing political work. Women tend to rationalize their feelings by using *legitimate* excuses for their public activities: 'I do it to help the children, the poor, others....'" But they also expect that the younger generation will change these beliefs by expressing their desire for power with greater honesty, although younger women are still far from admitting frankly "that they *like power, deserve it, and must fight for it together with their colleagues.*"

Another problem is the *organization of alliances among women.* While women's solidarity is an effective tool that enables women to place measures that will benefit women on the agenda of political debate, some warn against unrealistic expectations that may ruin these alliances: "It seems as if we have an obligation to love each other. We should be able to say, 'We act together up to this point, but no further,' without feeling betrayed."

Despite disagreements, so-called betrayals, envy, and questions of mutual esteem and recognition, during the last decade, links have been forged among women from different political parties. Especially since the enforcement of the quota law, joint attempts have been made to promote laws on reproductive health, violence, the incorporation of women into the armed forces, and living standards.

WOMEN FIRST

1985: MARIA LIBERIA-PETERS IS THE FIRST WOMAN TO BECOME PRIME MINISTER OF THE NETHERLANDS ANTILLES.

A third very important problem is the establishment and acceptance of *leadership among women.* When the quota law was first enforced in 1991, it became obvious that few women leaders with gender awareness had the power to place other women on the lists of candidates. As one legislator said, "Many women candidates were placed on the lists because of a personal relationship with the (male) area leader, or because they supported the (male) party leader. There are still too few female leaders in a position to name candidates." Another said, "In many cases, the women elected had no previous political experience and were not committed to gender issues."

The politicians we interviewed remarked on the two major problems of women leaders. On the one hand, women need both to confront the male members of the political group and also to negotiate with them: "The men compelled to give up public office put up strong resistance. Some of them even dispute the validity of the law. Many conflicts have arisen. This is not a battle which has been won. The law is a tool which must be defended and to do so, we must create awareness among women and find a way to overcome our fear when we confront the men."

On the other hand, our sources generally agreed that, since the law preceded the creation of alliances among women politicians, it has therefore been difficult to acknowledge and appreciate other women's capabilities and to delegate power to them. The problem of fostering women's leadership, of acknowledging and assuming it, has been explained in different ways. Some attribute it to women's lack of experience in the public area. Others say the fault lies in the feminist discourse that fosters women's political participation, which is based on questioning the power of the patriarchy and on the promise of an alternative concept of power that would respond to women's needs. This notion has some profoundly paralyzing effects. For example, as one legislator put it, "We either insist on being brilliant or expect all women to be the same, simply because they are women."

Ultimately, women are learning from experience that the quota law is not a point of "arrival" but one of "departure," a permanent effort that requires great willpower, conviction, and awareness. The political work demands constant monitoring to maintain its original significance. "That is why," one legislator said, "we must make certain that women who rise to public office through this law should not betray their commitment to gender interests." The fears women politicians face every day are those of sliding back, of the manipulation of their efforts, of being trapped in structures which cannot be changed, of "not making a difference."

But women are also aware that the quota law is a progressive measure that has gone beyond strictly political ends. Perhaps its most important accomplishment has been its impact on established models of democracy, political representation systems, and gender relations. It has certainly been a useful test of "modern" Argentinean views of equality between men and women; for detecting old and new hypocrisies in political leadership; and for subtle manipulations of women's claims. Most important, it has also determined that a great social consensus exists regarding the legitimate right of women to participate in Argentinean political life.

WOMEN IN PARLIAMENTARY LIFE
1970 to 1990
Marilyn Waring

Elizabeth McCombs, Catherine Stewart, Mary Dreaver, Mary Grigg, Mabel Howard, Hilda Ross, Iriaka Ratana, Ethel McMillan, Esme Tombleson, Rona Stevenson, Whetu Tirikatene-Sullivan, Dorothy Jellicich, and Mary Batchelor were the thirteen women who preceded Colleen Dewe and me when we were elected as Members of Parliament in 1975.

I had at no time in my life contemplated being a Member of Parliament as an ambition, nor had I set about to attain such a position. I did have an obsessive interest in international politics, which was a major part of my degree in political science. I had studied New Zealand politics in those years, but despite this I could not have given you the names of all of those women. I knew Hilda Ross's name only because I came from the Waikato and Mabel Howard's name only because of the sensationalized parliamentary episode when, during a speech on consumer interests and manufacturing standards, Mabel produced a pair of bloomers to illustrate her point. Rona Stevenson's name was known to me, because like so many women in Parliament—here and overseas— she held a seat that should have moved on the swing in a general election. She held it by a handful of votes most assuredly because she was a woman. Whetu Tirikatene-Sullivan, whom I honor as the longest-serving woman Member of the New Zealand Parliament, (and another who entered the establishment with a degree in political science), was the Member for Southern Maori, having succeeded her father in 1967, when I was of an age to take an interest in the women who were breaking barriers.

As an undergraduate student in politics I remember stories that appeared in the newspaper. There was one about women Members of Parliament being turned away at the Members and Guests dining room of Bellamy's because women were not entitled to bring women guests to dine with them. I remember Mary Batchelor and Dorothy Jellicich and their efforts for admission to the billiard room. Now the billiard room is no great shakes and I'm not even sure that any women were particularly enamored of billiards. It was, however, an enormous room with very large comfortable chairs in it. It contained the sole publicly available television set for Members of Parliament and it was the only place in the whole building where you could sit undisturbed by a messenger, the telephone, or other visitors. Until the nineteen-seventies no woman Member was entitled to enter the room.

Beyond New Zealand the two key names in the press in the mid-nineteen-seventies that drew my attention were those of Bella Abzug in the United States Congress and Bernadette Devlin in the British House of Commons.

Bella Abzug was a visual memory at once, from the pages of *Time* magazine or the international pages at the newspaper with her amazing hats. But under the hat was a 100 percent voting record in the U.S. Congress on human rights. Here was the first person in Congress to call for the United States to get out of Vietnam, the first person in Congress to call for the impeachment of Nixon. I noticed this person was a woman.

Because Bernadette Devlin had entered the British House of Commons at such a young age and as a "fiery Irishwoman," New Zealanders read of her, too, on the international pages. When I was selected as a candidate, her name was mentioned with mine—and so was that of Margaret Thatcher, then Leader of the Opposition Conservative Party in Britain. But Devlin was the one whose book title was the foreboding *The Price of My Soul,* the price paid by every woman in parliamentary life.

There were other books for me to read, of and about the widows and daughters of politicians—Bandaranike, Gandhi, Bhutto, and I read everything I could lay my hands on. In those days, there wasn't much available.

The past nine years since my retirement from Parliament in 1984 have been a period of another life for me. I have not been possessed of a desire to return to Parliament, and I have pursued more constructive political activity than I had ever achieved in my parliamentary career. And I have been much healthier; perhaps in part because I have not dwelt on the past. I have not sat again in the gallery, I do not listen to the broadcasts of the House. Psychologists would say I have "blocked" the experience, and this would be true.

On reflection, perhaps the most overwhelming characteristic of my period in Parliament was an acute loneliness. I have felt it again as I have sought to prepare this lecture, not because I am thinking about it in retrospect, or because I believe it to be such an acutely lonely place for Members who are there today, but because so few who serve are left with the courage to speak truly about the experience. As a reality check

I have been reading the words of lots of other women who served in various parliaments during that period, to establish for myself that my reflections are not selective or bitter or unrepresentative. There is also the responsibility that such an address could not only give succor to those who do not wish to see women serve in equal numbers in Parliament, but I may well dissuade women of integrity and principle from ever offering themselves as parliamentary candidates.

Any woman who has stood for office, and many who have been interviewed for employment in male bastions, have known the indignity of "What if you get married?"; "Do you want to have children?"; "What about your husband?"; "How does he feel?"; and the rest of this sexist line of questioning. I am reliably informed by women candidates in both the Labour and National parties that after 1975 a regular series of questions asked "Are you a feminist?" and—if you said yes—the follow-up was "Not like Marilyn Waring?" So that too many women answered no.

Other women paid a price. Listen to this voice:

> It was a difficult campaign (1981). As a single woman I was really hammered, I was accused of being a lesbian, of living in a commune, having friends who were Trotskyites and gays, of being unstable and unable to settle to anything. 'If you elect Helen Clark' my political opponent said, 'she's for abortion on demand and your whole society will change overnight.' I was fighting on all fronts. On top of all that I could do without the living in sin label. That's the only reason I married the man I'd been living with for five years, I was really tired of being extended on the personal front as well as on political issues. Personal accusations do hurt me but over time I've got to cope with them better. When I married, a lot of the personal criticism stopped but I felt really compromised. I think legal marriage is unnecessary and I would not have formalised the relationship except for going into Parliament. I have always railed against it privately.[1]

Helen Clark speaks very frankly here, following her first term in Parliament. This is a glimpse, from a very private person, of the prices to be paid and the compromises to be made.

Whoever we are, we women come from and belong to a different culture. Unlike men, who do not believe there is anything outside or beyond patriarchy (of course there are other "cultures" in a sense of indigenous peoples, or race, or class, but they are, all of them, defined by so-called male leaders), women's lives are spent moving between patriarchy and what Jessie Bernard calls *The Female World*.[2] This is not the place to develop this thesis, but from discipline to discipline, superb works detail and document this claim.[3] So what did I find of this culture when I arrived in 1975 in the capital Wellington, as a parliamentarian?

We women numbered 4 out of 87 in Parliament, a male cabinet of 19 and 5 male parliamentary undersecretaries. All heads of government departments were men, and while there were 9 women private secretaries to Ministers, all 43 principal private secretaries were men. Thirty-one men and 8 women Members of the Parliamentary Press Gallery fed their views from central government to 37 major metropolitan and provincial daily newspapers, all edited by men. The law courts were presided over by 23 male judges and only 3 of 26 major city councils by women mayors.[4] Legislatively there had been no Juries Amendment Act, no changes in matrimonial property legislation, no domestic violence legislation, no Evidence Amendment Act for rape trials. There was no Human Rights Commission; there were no rape crisis centers, no women-run refuges, no women pilots, firefighters, or jockeys. We still had nuclear ship visits, played apartheid sport, had no Official Information Act, and much much more.

Nothing short of being metaphorically clubbed over the head could have prepared me for the Neanderthal sensibilities about women that confronted me when I entered Parliament. Clare Short, backbench British MP explains it as follows: "You realise you're feeling differently than most of them in here, you bring your womenness with you. If you didn't have it there all in a package before, you find it once you get in here, you're responding in a different way and you have a different understanding."[5]

Listen to the following. Would a male MP ever speak of "the unequal power relationships between men and women," as Margaret Shields did?[6] Or would a male parliamentarian remember history in this way:

> I believe strongly in choice. I will do all I can to retain that option for girls and women. I recall at 16 my outrage when it really dawned on me that women's suffrage had had to be fought for, that women couldn't vote because they were born women. Every cell in my body asked why, and it wasn't until much later that I found the answers. We weren't taught that at school. I had never heard of Mrs Kate Sheppard or Mrs Elizabeth McCoombs, the first women Members of Parliament or any other of the women who had helped build this country. They were invisible in our history books,

as Katherine O'Regan does?[7]

When Judy Keale was selected for Glenfield she said her major qualifications were that she was a woman and a mother.[8] The only time I recall such terms being used by men running for political office was in the contest for the selection of a candidate for the new Waipa seat in 1978.

In 1976 a tabloid newspaper had run a series of articles on my sexuality. In 1977 the Electoral Boundaries Commission, in redrawing constituencies, had managed to eliminate Raglan completely from the map, splitting it three ways. In 1978, having indicated that I would stand for the new seat of Waipa, I was challenged by three white, middle-aged, middle-class men, two of whom vigorously insisted that their key qualifications were that they were "strong family men with Christian moral values." I did win the Waipa nomination on the first ballot, and within months, one of those two was declared bankrupt and the other was left by his wife.

What does any woman find when she gets to Parliament? It's not dissimilar wherever you look. Angela Rumbold describes the House of Commons thus:

> At first the chamber of the house is a cockpit designed for men to attack each other with words, that is why the two sides are seated face to face, the whole structure of competitive debate is alien to a women's nature. When they are given the verbal equivalent of a punch on the nose their instinct is to retreat, shocked by the aggressiveness of the unsolicited attack.[9]

Women also use the House in a different way. Not for them the mindless, cliched, aggressive hectoring, but the stereotypical constant nag. I remember Mary Batchelor, year after year from the Opposition benches, introducing a private Member's bill on domestic violence and having it voted out, but finally forcing the Government to introduce its own bill. I remember Whetu Tirikatane-Sullivan, year after year from the Opposition benches introducing a Private Member's Bill on Maori language, having it voted out until, in government, the Labour Party passed the measure. I recall that it has been Helen Clark and Fran Wilde, and most recently Katherine O'Reagan, who have the courage to introduce and see through the private Member's bills on so-called conscience issues.[10]

In the New Zealand Parliament I was known as a "poor sitter." There is a ridiculous quorum rule which requires twenty Members to be present at all times during debates. Since it is then up to the Government to furnish the quorum, long mindless hours can be spent there. Any woman recognizes the inefficiency of such a practice, of doing one thing at a time. I did my best to remedy this by finding that I could read and knit and listen to debates. After finishing thirty-plus garments in nine years I considered myself the most productive Member of Parliament.

But I must also tell you about the knitting. There is a male stereotype of feminists that obviously does not include knitting. I would find during all-night sittings when I sat knitting, and in my "womanly role," that many male MPs who would never speak to me otherwise, would sit beside me and chat about their mothers' knitting, about their knitting socks in the war, and similar. There were times when I wanted to knit and not have to be polite to them. This was always secured by taking some of my favorite books of the time into the debating chamber and having them very visible on the top of my desk. The intending chatterer, spying *Female Sexual Slavery* or *Women in a Sexist Society* or *Sisterhood Is Powerful,* would beat a hasty retreat.

I don't know of any woman MP who enjoys the House, not just because the level of debate is an insult to our intelligence, but because it's a breeding ground for rank hypocrisy. Labour Member of the House of Commons Jo Richardson states:

> Yes I hate the chamber, I am not the best chamber attender. It is
> partly because I have other things to do but partly because I find it
> so macho. It's all so formalised and you get sucked into it. I just
> find it irritating and the trouble is I am irritated with myself for
> doing it. I can get up like anybody else and say 'will the Honourable
> gentleman give way', or 'I do thank the Honourable gentleman',
> but I don't thank him at all.[11]

This hypocrisy is public and audible. But there is a constant underside of sitting in the Chamber. The boys persist in their sotto voce, snide, cutting commentaries, seldom picked up by radio or television microphones. They think these are very funny. Women don't. These commentaries are overwhelmingly sexist, jeering, and demeaning of women—those on the other side of the House, or visitors in the gallery. Every one of these tests something inside you. There is no room to turn and confront. You are expected to laugh along, to "be one of the boys."

Imagine the reaction if, as a member of the Government, you were to raise a point of order, against a member of your party, for the frequent, dirty, snarling, insidious male rumblings that you are surrounded by whenever a woman on the other side of the House is speaking. Imagine the reaction in the Labour Caucus if a woman Member of Parliament from the Labour side had been the person to rise to take offense at the sexist jeers and remarks on the clothing of women cabinet ministers in Parliament recently.

You are compromised every day. I wrote in 1980:

> How creatively as a politician do I avoid being distracted from wider
> political questions by a plethora of issues which act in some cases
> to pit us against each other. How do I cope with the contradictions
> implicit in a feminist belonging to a political party. How do I explain
> that the policies of leadership, the concepts of power, what is said

in programmes, what is done, how things are done, are all offensive
to me. By remaining how much am I part of the problem?[12]

And there's yet another obvious problem, described so succinctly
by Marcia Freedman, the sole feminist in the Israeli Knesset between
1973 and 1976: "My role in politics was to place feminist issues on the
agenda and try to keep them there. It was a mission that in political
terms was doomed. Unless I turned my back on the cause that had put
me in office I was bound to fail as a politician. To succeed I would have
to fail as a feminist."[13]

But I can hear you thinking—they're not all like that. What about...?

Well, some just don't make a fuss about it. I want to pay my own
respects to Colleen Dewe, who died 1993 in Dunedin. We met at a
National Party candidates training weekend. Colleen was then, as I have
always remembered her, good-humored, relaxed, and not the least bit
self-important. And in a gesture neither threatening nor defensive she
advised her twenty-two-year-old colleague that she had "never suffered
discrimination as a woman."

I dwelled on this overnight. The next day I asked her if in all the
years of attending the annual conference of New Zealand accountants,
she had ever missed the dinner because women were excluded. Again
the tone was careful—neither threatening nor defensive. She smiled—
"Yes, I was excluded as a woman," she replied, "but I didn't suffer
from it."

Colleen was a superb constituency MP, and followed her
accountancy interest through assiduous work on the Public Expenditure
Committee. As the only other woman in the National Party Caucus,
Colleen was frequently approached by colleagues to oppose my position
on what were then known as "women's issues." It was a game she
resolutely refused to buy into. In fact, the "boys' games" were never
her method, in Parliament, the Commerce Commission, or elsewhere.

I remember her anger at the outrageous provisions of the 1977
contraception, sterilization, and abortion legislation, her support on
amendments to matrimonial property, the Juries Act. Colleen's was the
first ever successful inquiry of the Prime Minister's Department on the
representation of women on boards, tribunals, commissions, and where
others had been told it was too much work to survey the fourteen
hundred bodies and list all the names, she went head to head with
Muldoon on the issue, and won.

While many remember her Commerce Commission work post-
1978, (when she never hankered to return to Parliament—a sign of
great health rarely seen in former male MPs), I remember her work in
the chair of the Advisory Committee on Women's Affairs. At this time
she was also the New Zealand representative on the UN Commission
on the Status of Women, and the leader of the New Zealand delegation

to the 1980 UN Mid-Decade Conference on Women. I was, at that time, the only woman in the Government Caucus, but considerable lobbying was required to have me made a member of the delegation. When we arrived in Copenhagen, Colleen smiled and said: "I've instructions to keep you on a tight leash. Well, here's the end of your rope Marilyn. Just keep pulling and you won't ever reach the end. Just do what has to be done."

No—not like that either, you are insisting. What about...? Yes, well, what about the Margaret Thatchers of the world?

In 1961 as an up-and-coming politician, Margaret Thatcher attacked the Treasury's treatment of working wives, in particular married women teachers. In 1966 she urged income relief payments for women. In the early 1970s as secretary of state for education, she launched a framework for the expansion of the policy document with a commitment to nursery school education with nursery provision for 50 percent of three-year-olds and 90 percent of four-year-olds.[14] My usual response to the Thatcher question is that if you took any man, and isolated him in an institution with six hundred women for more than twenty years, he'd be a strange sort of fellow at the end of it all. What do we expect of women prisoners of patriarchal institutions?

I remember Ruth Richardson as a feminist member of the Women's Electoral Lobby (WEL) in the mid-1970s, actively involved in campaigns on reproductive freedom for women. It was her submission for WEL on the Matrimonial Property Bill that was the most radical and most influential on this major law change in 1976.

In 1980 I wrote:

> Those male politicians who fought the suffrage less than a century ago on the grounds that it would masculanise women were describing their own political lives, lives of oppression, competition, conflict. *Their mistaken assumption was that women would assume or acquire the same characteristics in the same environment.*...The task is to find a way to get there and survive without coming in any way like. Traditional women do break into the power world and use its channels to rise to high positions. A few more refuse to play the power game and will languish in the lower echelons of the power hierarchy refusing to compete with or against the legal conventional customary moral and psychological pressure brought to bear. Some women seek power as an achievement in itself.[15]

I was wrong. It requires a woman of superhuman qualities (and an extraordinary lack of personal ambition) not "to assume or acquire the same characteristics in the same environment."

"Some women say they never experienced discrimination and they may be the lucky few. However there are women who sail through the process having made a conscious decision to identify with their male colleagues and become 'one of the chaps,' albeit a feminine version," writes Helena Kennedy, describing colleagues in the English legal profession.[16] The same situation operates in politics for women to become "one of the chaps". But I consider something quite tragic has happened if they are. Listen to these voices.

"There isn't a separation between me as a person and my job. I am that same person. If you're asking 'does one never get hurt?' the answer is 'of course, I get hurt. Yes, of course, one gets hurt.'" This from Edwina Currie, former secretary of state for health in Thatcher's Conservative Government.[17] Or, "I have tended to become the political and public persona I present myself as. I've become the mask, as it were."[18] And, "I deliberately suppress a lot of my feelings in public life. I have become so controlled that I don't have many personal reactions. I wasn't like that before." This is Helen Clark, deputy leader of the Opposition Labour Party.[19]

WOMEN FIRST

1930: ALEXANDRA KOLLONTAI IS APPOINTED AMBASSADOR FROM THE SOVIET UNION TO SWEDEN, BECOMING THE FIRST WOMAN AMBASSADOR IN MODERN HISTORY.

While in office, few women can speak of the brutalizing impact of political life. Surviving takes all your emotional energy. If you were to be in touch with the truth, and to speak it, you would probably fall apart. Mary Robinson, president of Ireland, speaking in the Allen Lane Foundation lecture in February 1992, said: "Every society maintains an invisible life where attitudes and assumptions are formed. Every society is hostage to this unseen place where fear conquers reason and old attitudes remain entrenched. It is here that the chance phrases and small asides are made which say so little and reveal so much."[20]

Whatever their political party, the experience is similar. Listen to Teresa Gonnall, Conservative Member of the House of Commons:

> I think they were ageist and sexist, on and on about my age, my permed hair and my makeup. They would never make such comments about the beer bellies of male MPs. It's the same in the House. Women are judged on their appearance, even their voices are criticized by chauvinists in the press gallery. My advice to newcomers to this game is to always be on your guard with the press and never, never be your natural self....The system is merciless so you have to be calculating in order that the public doesn't get the impression that women are superficial and lightweight.[21]

Former senator and leader of the Australian Democrats Janine Haines writes: "The fact is that women often have to be tougher if not smarter than men to survive in politics. And it goes without saying that they have to be tougher as well as smarter in order to succeed."[22]

Marcia Freedman recalling the abortion hearings in the Israeli Parliament, writes:

> I came to the abortion hearings more expert than most of the expert witnesses, but the facts were hardly central to the committee's deliberations. Sex was on everyone's mind throughout the months and years of committee hearings on abortion. The committee room often filled with jokes and lurid remarks, guffaws and snickers, these meetings always loud and excited, so dismissive of women and punctuated with suggestive jokes. These meetings enraged me.[23]

I can recall at least four abortion debates in my time in Parliament. Fortunately I never had to sit on select committees on the issue. But caucus discussions were of the same theme and variations. I recall in my first term considerable concern being expressed about the number of young women (my colleagues called them "girls" and they were in "girls' homes") who would abscond just before the end of their institutional terms when, in accordance with government policy, they were to be returned to their family homes. I was not much older than these young women, and made several trips to these institutions to talk privately with them, to see what explanations they might give if I could gain their trust. It was soon obvious that the reason many ran away was because the state was about to return them to places where they were raped, beaten, or abused by fathers, uncles, brothers, or cousins. I returned to caucus to quietly raise the question of our part as an accessory to incest and other offenses. There was a stunned silence. Then one of the caucus members said: "Normal women don't think like that," and we moved to the next agenda item.

If normal women don't think like that, how do normal men parade themselves in caucus?

> In the last couple of years I have drawn back from some outright confrontations because it was just getting too difficult, too emotionally demanding to go into savage fights. It was really upsetting me and I found it profoundly depressing. Politics is conflict-ridden anyway with all the conflict from the opposing party, but when you are experiencing even more intense hatred and conflict from people who are supposed to be on your side that's an impossible situation....People get out of control in caucus, men in particular lose control entirely. They scream and shout and are personally abusive, it's really quite extraordinary. I never scream and shout, that's not my nature. I've learned to deal with their behaviour by taking notes while they are shouting and screaming

to make sure that I reply to all the points they've made. That
infuriates them. Fran Wilde takes shorthand which infuriates
them too.[24]

I laughed a great deal when I read Helen Clark's comments. Across
the building the men in my caucus tried to stop Ruth Richardson and
me from keeping notes. For one year, 1977, in my archival papers (and
in keeping with the habits learned as a political science student) I have
my complete caucus notes, the selectively edited official caucus minutes
kept by the caucus secretary (I secretly photocopied all of these), every
press statement on any subject released by any minister, and newspaper
reports of every post-caucus press conference. This will make interesting
reading when I finally have time to analyze it all, and will illustrate why our
male colleagues were paranoid and concerned about the notes we kept.

I also remember occasions when colleagues, John Banks was among
them, would have to be physically restrained from crossing the caucus
room to beat up on another National MP. And the language and lack
of self control by this mass of boys together is frequently disgusting.

Helen Clark recalls:

> It is important not to be isolated in the room when an attack is
> mounted. But sometimes you don't anticipate it and it can be quite
> a searing experience. No-one can defend you properly and you're
> out there on your own. One of the most painful experiences I had
> was before the 1983 party conference. A number of constitutional
> changes had been proposed which would have brought the Labour
> Caucus more under the control of the party and an attempt was
> made in Caucus to bind MPs to a common view against these
> reforms. I said that MPs go to the conference primarily as delegates
> from their electorates, not as MPs, so that for them to take a
> common view was inappropriate on constitutional grounds. I was
> greeted by a cacophony of sound and held down with this incredible
> jeering from people shrieking 'if you don't fucking well like it piss
> off, why do you stay in Caucus if you don't want to act like a
> member'. People screamed at me and there were some foul things
> said. I was terribly upset.[25]

Many practices in Parliament are childish and childlike. I experienced
the omnipresent boys' brand of humor delivered over the tables in Bellamy's,
the Members-only dining room, drawn together in one long line so that
they could still pretend they were all prefects at a boys' boarding school
and act in much the same way. Lunch could be a gross experience.

MP number one: "How can you legislate against rape in marriage? It
couldn't be implemented." MP number two: "That's not the point. Why
should you be able to rape your wife in the bedroom but not beat her up in

the kitchen?" MP number three: "Then beat her in the bedroom and rape her in the kitchen." Honorable Members: "Hahaha."[26]

The media duplicate the patriarchal approach. On entering Parliament I was described as a "brown-eyed honey blonde". None of my colleagues was recorded as a "balding grey-eyed potbelly".

Women who weep in Parliament are reported and labeled emotional or lacking self-control. Men who weep, and it happens not infrequently, are labeled "moving." Male anger such as that recorded by Helen Clark and myself is not "emotional," nor does it demonstrate a lack of self-control—apparently.

So what keeps you going? Clare Short explains:

> After I arrived at the Commons I became perceived as a strong feminist, probably before I used that same label about myself. It was both their reaction to me and other women's reaction to me that strengthened the very joyous sense in me of being a woman, of being different, of being there connected with lots of other women who aren't in and who ought to be here in the Commons. For me that was a lovely experience....[27]

> I got hundreds of letters and cards from women saying I was just doing the ironing and I had to stop and I'm quivering with anger and are you okay and don't worry we care about you. Not just trying to say we agree, but also there is an enormous sense of worry and concern for me to look after me which was just lovely.[28]

If Parliament was hell, the constituency was the space to recover, the opportunity to heal, to replenish, to go back one more time. Here you could help, you could be an agent to change lives, to deliver what was due, to be constructive. And you would be taught—by example or through experience. The privilege of trust invested in you by constituents and by women throughout the country is a salutary and humbling experience, and however much you feel you are drowning and fighting (metaphorically) for your own life, the cases of courage and survival challenge you to battle on for the many.

Parliament in my experience was very negative. I felt as if I spent most of my time spinning daily 360 degrees, trying to sort out the next dreadful thing, and like a human blockade, throwing myself in front of the next juggernaut to stop it happening. And you can't stop because there is always so much to do....Marcia Freedman experienced this.

> Whether it was the covert sale of arms to South Africa, abortion or violence against women, the issues I talked about to the eighth Knesset had one thing in common. Each was surrounded by a

conspiracy of silence. The walls of denial are especially thick around family concerns. Women's issues always seem to reveal shameful secrets about family life, secrets that the state has a vested interest in protecting.[29]

So the woman parliamentarian constantly beats at the conspiracy of silence. And runs an enormous risk, while we are so few, as Clare Short explains:

Everything interests me. In terms of my constituency housing is very serious, poverty is very serious. I care about disarmament and I care about South Africa. I haven't really done anything apart from being supportive about Chile and Nicaragua and Central America but I feel for them. But it's a real problem. If you're that kind of person you have to rein yourself in or you are going to splatter *yourself everywhere and be ineffective.*[30]

This essay is titled "Women in Parliamentary Life." This is quite intentional, and I should make it clear that being a woman parliamentarian does not permit any other moments of "life." Helen Clark remarks:

The real cost of this job is feeling tired all the time, being exhausted for most of the year. There's also a cost in giving up so much personal space in time and privacy. I don't read as much as I'd like to. I don't get to plays or films or music and I've lost a lot of friends simply because I don't have time for friendships anymore. The friends I've kept are those who tend to give more to me than I do to them, who are prepared to be supportive. Social occasions become very demanding. I have come to positively dislike going to parties unless I know exactly who's there and whether I can tolerate them.[31]

It does not have to be like this, but it will continue to be thus until women are represented in proportion to our population. We celebrate this year the one hundredth anniversary of women's suffrage in New Zealand, and congratulate ourselves for being the first nation-state to enfranchise all adults over twenty-one years of age. But the roll of the House of Representatives records the names of 1,127 men and only 36 women.[32] This is disgraceful, nothing to celebrate, and certainly not representative.

In this context, and in honor of the suffrage movement of one hundred years ago, the 1993 suffrage petition has been launched by Georgina Kirby, as te wero, the challenge, to all New Zealanders in this year. The petition calls for equality of and parity in gender representation in the New Zealand Parliament. I am honored, with Jocelyn Fish, to be a cosignatory with Georgina Kirby to the petition prayer.

I am familiar with the cliched arguments that contest this petition. Their echo of sentiments voiced one hundred years ago might be amusing if the subject was less serious. A typical comment that the procrastinator will make is that they think "MPs should be selected on merit." My retort is that if that were the case the score would not be 1,127 to 36. Recently Lianne Dalziel, MP for Christchurch Central, recalled Sir Robert Muldoon's saying that Parliament was no place for a woman. Speaking of its brutalizing and dehumanizing practices, Lianne remarked that it was no place for any human person.

Women in equal numbers would transform this institution in a multitude of ways. They would humanize this bastion of patriarchal power in this country. And if, in our future, we might honestly boast of a House of Representatives, Parliament might be a woman's career, in which there are moments in life that can be celebrated and enjoyed.

VOTING RIGHTS ACHIEVED
By Country

Selected Countries	Date of Right to Vote	Date of Right to Be Elected
Algeria	1962	1962
Argentina	1947	1947
Australia	1901 / 1967*	1901 / 1967*
Bangladesh	1947	1947
Bolivia	1953	1956
Brazil	1934	1934
Bulgaria	1944	1944
Cameroon	1946	1946
Canada	1917 / 1918 / 1950	1920 / 1960 / 1969
Chile	1931 / 1949	1931 / 1949
China	1949	1949
Costa Rica	1949	1949
Cuba	1934	1934
Czechoslovakia (former)	1920	1920
Denmark	1915	1915
Ecuador	1946	1946
Egypt	1956	1956
El Salvador	1961	1961
Equatorial Guinea	1963	1963
Finland	1906	1906
France	1944	1944
Gabon	1956	1956
Germany	1918	1918
Greece	1952	1952

*Where more than one date is shown, full suffrage for all adult women came only in stages.

Selected Countries	Date of Right to Vote	Date of Right to Be Elected
Hong Kong	1985	1985
Hungary	1945	1945
Iceland	1915	1915
India	1950	1950
Indonesia	1945	1945
Iraq	1980	1980
Iran	1963	1963
Ireland	1918	1918
Israel	1948	1948
Italy	1945	1945
Ivory Coast	1952	1952
Jamaica	1944	1944
Japan	1945 / 1947	1945 / 1947
Jordan	1974	1974
Kenya	1963	1963
Korea (North)	1946	1946
Korea (South)	1948	1948
Kuwait	NOT YET	NOT YET
Laos	1958	1958
Luxembourg	1919	1919
Madagascar	1959	1959
Malaysia	1957	1957
Mexico	1947	1953
Mongolia	1923 / 1924	1923 / 1924
Morocco	1963	1963
Mozambique	1975	1975
Nepal	1951	1951
Netherlands	1919	1917
New Zealand	1893	1919
Nicaragua	1955	1955
Nigeria	1957 / 1978	1957 / 1978
Norway	1907 / 1913	1907 / 1913

Selected Countries	Date of Right to Vote	Date of Right to Be Elected
Pakistan	1937	1937
Papua New Guinea	1975	1975
Peru	1950	1956
Philippines	1937	1937
Poland	1918	1918
Portugal	1931 / 1976	1931 / 1976
Puerto Rico	1929 / 1935	1929
Romania	1929 / 1946	1929 / 1946
Rwanda	1961	1961
South Africa	1930 / 1984	1930 / 1984
Spain	1931	1931
Sudan	1953 / 1965	1965
Sweden	1918 / 1921	1918 / 1921
Switzerland	1971	1971
Syria	1949	1953
Thailand	1932	1932
Togo	1956	1956
Tonga	1960	1960
Tunisia	1959	1959
Turkey	1930 / 1934	1930 / 1934
United Arab Emirates	NOT YET	NOT YET
United Kingdom	1918 / 1928	1918 / 1928
United States	1920	1788 / 1920
Uruguay	1932	1932
USSR (former)	1917	1917
Venezuela	1947	1947
Vietnam	1946	1946
Zambia	1962	1964
Zimbabwe	1957	1978

Source: Compiled from *Women and Politics Worldwide,* edited by Barbara J. Nelson and Najma Chowdhury (New Haven: Yale University Press, 1994) and *The Women's Desk Reference* (New York: Viking Penguin, 1993), pp. 806-7.

WOMEN HEADS OF STATE OR GOVERNMENT IN THE TWENTIETH CENTURY

(as of 31 December 1994)

PRESIDENTS

Philippines	Corazón Aquino	1986–1992
Sri Lanka	Chandrika Bandaranaike Kumaratunga	1994*–
Nicaragua	Violeta Chamorro	1990–
Iceland	Vigdís Finnbogadóttir	1980–
Bolivia	Lidia Gueiler	1979–1980
Haiti	Ertha Pascal–Trouillot	1991
Argentina	Isabel Martinez de Perón	1974–1976
Ireland	Mary Robinson	1990–
Yugoslavia	Milka Planinc	1982–1986

PRIME MINISTERS

Sri Lanka	Chandrika Bandaranaike Kumaratunga	1994*–
Sri Lanka	Siramovo Bandaranaike	1970–1977, 1994–
Pakistan	Benazir Bhutto	1988–1990, 1993–
Norway	Gro Harlem Brundtland	1981, 1986–89, 1990–
Canada	Kim Campbell	1993
Dominica	Eugenia Charles	1980–
Turkey	Tamsu Ciller	1993–
France	Edith Cresson	1991–1992
Burundi	Sylvie Kinigi	1993
India	Indira Gandhi	1966–1977
Israel	Golda Meir	1969–1974
Portugal	Maria de Lourdes Pintasilgo	1981–1985
Poland	Hanna Suchocka	1992–1993
United Kingdom	Margaret Thatcher	1979–1990
Rwanda	Agathe Uwilingiyimana	1993–1994
Bangladesh	Khaleda Zia Rahman	1991–

---

* Appointed Prime Minister in August 1994 and elected President in October 1994.

Source: Compiled by Division for the Advancement of Women of the United Nations Secretariat for the second issue of *The World's Women: Trends and Statistics.*[1]

FROM MOVEMENT TO GOVERNMENT
Women's Political Integration in Norway
Hege Skjeie

On May 9, 1986, a new social democratic government was formed in Norway—and a world record established. The new prime minister, Gro Harlem Brundtland, appointed a cabinet in which eight out of eighteen members were women. Since then, no Norwegian cabinet has included less than 40 percent women. Gradually, the representation of women in Parliament has reached approximately the same level. And at the recent election, Norwegian voters were presented with three different government alternatives. This time, all three candiates for prime minister were women.

Events like these have been heralded by the international media for close to a decade. The portraits of various "women's cabinets" have a worldwide distribution; this situation clearly differs from both the "lone ranger" and the "widow syndrome" images which are commonly transmitted when women occupy top political posts. Here we are instead talking about a situation where women have come to participate on close to equal footing with men in both the cabinet and Parliament, in regional political bodies, and in the leadership of the national party organizations.

To outsiders, this process of political integration might seem somewhat mysterious; even insiders have chosen to address it simply as "a political miracle." Yet the Norwegian miracle largely remains contained within the framework of party-based political institutions, where among the six largest party organizations, 39 percent of the members of the executive boards in 1994 were women. In large economic organizations, the representation of women in positions of leadership is still low (20 percent on the Executive Board of the Confederation of Trade Unions in 1994), as it is within both state bureaucracies (22 percent) and academic institutions (8 percent of university professors are women). In comparison, private business corporations continue to be almost exclusively led by men (4 percent of top executives, as of 1993, in the two hundred largest private corporations are women).

Thus, it also seems clear that the success of women's political integration can only be explained in genuinely political terms. The dramatic changes over the past twenty years in both educational levels and work force participation among Norwegian women primarily tell us that women's political influence has been achieved within a general context of changing gender roles. The fundamental changes in political recruitment, however, must be explained from the baseline of party politics. In the following, I will outline some major factors in such an explanation. In particular, I will try to show how the Norwegian feminist movement came to influence political parties, as women's demands for political representation were recognized on the basis of an argument maintaining that women had a right to be represented by their own— that is, by women.

Contrary to dominant trends in many other countries, the Norwegian feminist movement *did* advocate integration into the existing political structure as a viable strategy for empowering women. The movement had close ties to a growing feminst research milieu, which from the early nineteen-seventies both explored the foundations of a "women's culture" and combined perspectives on gender-structured social differences with a political edge stressing access and integration as strategies of power for women. From the very beginning, the feminist movement cooperated with women inside the party structure in building demands for political representation. This cooperation took many forms; most noteworthy was a series of campaigns in connection with local and national elections, financed by state authorities, and addressing voters and party leaders alike. As early as the 1971 local election, such a campaign contributed to produce a majority of women in the municipal council of the Norwegian capital, Oslo.

In connection with these campaigns, women activists built a line of political arguments that primarily maintained the following credo: Gender constitutes an important political category that needs to be fully represented in government. Regardless of partisan preferences— the argument went—women have a right to be represented by their own. Nearly a century earlier, the "common concerns of womanhood" had made up a major appeal in the fight to gain suffrage. From the nineteen-seventies onward, this appeal again became a primary one. Arguments were then phrased in terms of either "interests" or "resources." They either maintained—in line with more radical political ideologies—that the conflicting interests of men and women required a balanced representation of both parties, or they maintained—in line with more conservative political ideologies—that women's experiences would represent a valuable contribution in decision making. Both kinds of arguments stressed that actual representation by women on behalf of women was necessary: Men could not negotiate the values, or interests, of women.

To the degree that "interest" and "resource" arguments melted into more general claims of group representation, they fit with a strong tradition of social representation within Norwegian politics. While, for instance, the Storting—the Norwegian Parliament—admittedly recruits disproportionately from social elites, it does so less than most other national legislatures. The parties control the nomination of candidates to practically all important political appointments. And parties compete on a whole range of issues—which also, for a long time, have included the issue of the party's own representation profile. Most party leaders have tended to believe that voters also pay attention to the composition of the party lists in terms of representativeness—for instance, with regard to occupational background, region, or age group. Arguments about the political relevance of gender thus struck a clearly familiar note.

The result, however, was not that gender merely was added to the internal party lists as one more "relevant background criterion." Once women managed to get access to the leadership of different parties, gender achieved a prominence that made most parties adopt a set of formal regulations on the composition of political bodies. This system of gender quotas, which at present is practiced by four of the six major Norwegian parties, in fact approaches a guarantee of equal participation rights: The quota regulations simply state that each sex is to be represented by a minimum of 40 percent. They apply both to the composition of party election lists and to appointments within the national party organizations.

WOMEN FIRST

1981: GRO HARLEM BRUNDTLAND IS FIRST WOMAN TO BECOME PRIME MINISTER OF NORWAY.

Thus, the impact of feminist ideas on political parties has been witnessed in the breakthrough of what might be called a political rhetoric of difference. It was *not* individual women's rights to equal, or nondiscriminatory, treatment that constituted the major motivation for the new representation demands from the nineteen-seventies onward. Instead, it was an underscoring of gender differences that provided the crucial link to traditional principles of representation. Individual party women obviously also demanded "fair treatment" for themselves in the competition for political positions. But simultaniously they underscored the collective claim of women's right to be represented by their own. As of today, this belief is in fact shared by most Norwegian political leaders. Here men and women alike maintain that party politics now have come to reflect the negotiation of different interests of men and women politicians, and that such differences are indeed relevant to political decision making.

Today, however, some feminists contend that this "old" way of arguing for women's political participation, even when proved successful, still demonstrates continued male political dominance. This viewpoint can briefly be summarized as follows: Only to men belongs the obvious, or self-evident, right to participation. It is only women who have to justify our presence. Thus, even when present in close to equal numbers, we remain "the other"—the ones with some *special* interests or experiences. And this way, the proof will still rest with women. If we cannot demonstrate that we indeed represent something different from what men stand for, the conclusion may easily become that there is no point in our presence.

This might be a warning worth listening to. But it still overlooks some simple political facts. First, that providing justifications, or reasons, is something we ask of all political leadership; justifications are a general aspect of representative politics. Second, that new political leaderships commonly present themselves in terms of "the alternative." True enough, the justifications presented by men have rarely been stated with explicit reference to gender. It is only women's political participation that has been argued in these terms. But in collectivity, women political leaders are relative newcomers. By presenting themselves in terms of the alternative, they have thus made use of a well-known political strategy.

For the individual, however, these collective justifications will not be the only ones provided. Instead, they represent general attempts to enlarge the room, or space, where individuals participate. This way, collective justifications become practical efforts to make positive use of familiar dichotomies—to change their old implications. The splits between "masculine" and "feminine" have long contributed to the legitimation of practices that have kept women out of political life. But it is important to keep in mind that in the Norwegian context of today, they instead legitimate practices that secure the presence of women *in* political life.

EMILY'S LIST
Overcoming Barriers
to Political Participation
David Lauter

For most of its first two hundred years, the American political system effectively excluded women from full participation. The means of exclusion began with explicit legal disqualifications, buttressed by deep-rooted gender prejudice and a series of structural barriers that reduced the ability of women to compete electorally. The nation's legal bars against women's political participation began to crumble early on—with the dawn of the suffrage movement during the generation that preceded the Civil War—but did not fully collapse until after the ratification of the Nineteenth Amendment to the Constitution in 1920, guaranteeing women's right to vote. Gender prejudice persisted long after legal barriers had fallen. But the barriers built into the structure of the American political system have proven the most durable of the impediments to women seeking elective office and have required new forms of political organization to overcome.

The archetype of these new forms of organization has been EMILY's List, begun in 1985 by Ellen R. Malcolm, a political activist and heir to a substantial fortune derived from holdings in IBM Corporation. Malcolm began considering the idea of an organization devoted to raising funds for women running for office after experiencing Harriet Woods's unsuccessful campaign for the U.S. Senate from Missouri in 1982. Woods narrowly lost after essentially running out of money in the last days of the campaign, reinforcing in Malcolm's mind the importance of money in politics. After female candidates suffered several more losses in the 1984 elections, she launched EMILY's List—the acronym stands for Early Money Is Like Yeast, which, as Malcolm says, "makes the dough rise"—which in the decade since has developed into one of the most potent fund-raising forces in American politics.[1]

Malcolm's idea has since been copied by groups such as Eleanor's List, which supports women running for office in New York State, and the

WISH (Women in the Senate and House) List, which supports Republican women, but EMILY's List remains by far the largest and most influential of such organizations, becoming the largest single source of funds for Democratic candidates of either gender in the 1992 election cycle.

The idea behind EMILY's List was a relatively simple one that aims directly at the structural barriers in the American system. The group helps women raise money by identifying viable candidates early on and introducing them to a network of donors, both women and men, nationwide who provide funds. For an initial contribution of $100, which helps cover the costs of the organization, and a commitment to contribute to at least two candidates, EMILY's List members gain access to the group's analysis of candidates and key races. For candidates, EMILY's List provides access to a nationwide donor base of members— some thirty-three thousand—already committed to aiding women running for office. For members, the group provides a way of finding out about candidates they would be inclined to support but would otherwise have no knowledge of. "It's almost like hiring your own political staff. We go out and we find candidates, we make sure they're viable and have a chance of winning, we tell you all about what's going on in the race," Malcolm says.

To understand the work of EMILY's List—and the centrality of fund-raising to its efforts—it is important, first, to grasp how dramatic has been the change of the political context within which female candidates have operated. Simply put, prejudice against women in office, which for most of American history was strong enough to make female candidacies almost irrelevant, has virtually collapsed in the last two decades. With the exception of some regions of the deep South, where gender prejudice remains stronger than elsewhere, a female candidate who can overcome the structural barriers facing "outsider" candidacies— most notably fund-raising—can now run a viable race for any statewide or regional elective office. As the National Women's Political Caucus (NWPC) discovered in a comprehensive survey covering more than fifty thousand individuals who had run for office between 1972 and 1992, women incumbents are as successful in gaining reelection as are men, and female candidates for open legislative seats now win at the same rate as male candidates.[2] Indeed, pollsters and political consultants in both parties believe that in some parts of the country, gender alone actually now provides women a small but notable advantage. American history provides no comparable example of so rapid a decline of prejudice against a previously disfavored group.

The trend shows up clearly in polling data. In 1963, for example, the Gallup poll began asking Americans: "If your party nominated a woman for president, would you vote for her if she qualified for the job?" Even with the specific caveat that the woman in question be "qualified," only 55 percent of people polled said yes at that time, while

41 percent said no. That number had shifted only slightly by 1967; 57 percent said they would vote for a woman presidential candidate and 39 percent said they would not.[3] But by 1988, when the National Opinion Research Center asked the same question, the shift was dramatic: 85 percent said yes, only 12 percent no.[4] By 1993, the trend had continued—87 percent said yes and 9 percent said no. Another example can be seen in a *Los Angeles Times* poll taken in the spring of 1994. Asked if they agreed with the statement that "it is time we had a woman governor"—a statement not only of willingness to support a woman, but suggesting active preference for one—52 percent of registered voters surveyed said they agreed and only 31 percent disagreed.[5]

The West Coast, particularly California, has become the part of the country most hospitable to women running for office. Of the six U.S. senators representing the three West Coast states, three—Dianne Feinstein and Barbara Boxer of California and Patty Murray of Washington—are women. In 1992, California became the first state ever to be represented by two women in the Senate. And altogether, as of the 1992 elections, the three West Coast states had eleven women in the House of Representatives—one-sixth of the region's overall congressional delegation and nearly one-quarter of the total number of women in the House.

Elsewhere in the country, an advantage for female candidates shows up most often in Democratic Party primaries, reflecting the fact that the Democratic primary electorate is, in comparison with the population at large, disproportionately both liberal and female. Even in general elections, however, women often have a small advantage—not enough to guarantee election, of course, but enough to provide an edge in a close race.

Two major factors appear to account for the changing status of female candidates. First, the number of people who are strongly motivated to vote for female candidates outnumbers those who remain adamantly opposed to them. That vote does not break down strictly along gender lines. Older women and those who do not work outside the home continue to be more resistant than voters overall to the idea of women in office. Younger women, women who work outside the home, and younger men all tend to be more supportive of female candidacies.

In addition, at a time when voters appear strongly attracted to candidates who hold out the promise of independence from a disliked political status quo, many voters view women, per se, as more likely to bring about "change," however defined.

Some countertrends do exist. Male candidates appear to fare better against women in seeking executive, as opposed to legislative, offices. In recent campaigns for governor in some states, male candidates facing female opponents have had success by stressing attributes such as firmness or decisiveness and issues such as crime that play on voters' residual doubts about women. Those doubts are especially strong when voters consider issues involving the military, and for that reason, the presidency is likely to remain for some time the one elective office with effective barriers against a female candidacy.

Nonetheless, those areas of prejudice now have taken on the status of exceptions, not rules. The centuries-old prejudice against women holding public office has largely crumbled in the United States.

Why, then, have women not actually won election more often? One problem is simply incumbency. Because the overwhelming majority of incumbents who seek reelection win, the percentage of women in office now, and for the next decade, will continue to reflect the almost exclusively male politics of the past. But a larger reason, and the one that EMILY's List most directly aims to change, is simply that not enough women run. Since 1972, as the NWPC study showed, only 7 percent of House and Senate candidates and 6 percent of gubernatorial candidates have been women. As shown by the 1992 elections, when twenty-four new women won election to the House, doubling the number of women in that body, a large upsurge in female candidates leads directly to increased representation by women.

The small number of female candidates continues to cause the percentage of women in office in the United States to lag behind that in many other Western democracies despite the gains made in 1992. In Norway, Sweden, Denmark, and Finland, for example, women make up between 33 percent and 40 percent of the total parliamentary rosters. In Germany, just over one-fifth of the Bundestag is female, and in New Zealand, women make up 17 percent of the House of Representatives.[6]

The low number of female candidates in the United States, in turn, can be traced to a series of problems built into the structure of American politics—the sorts of problems that EMILY's List and similar groups seek to combat. As compared with most other electoral democracies, American election districts represent extremely large populations and often cover vast geographic areas. Since the 1990 census, each congressional district has contained roughly 550,000 residents, a far larger number of constituents than in most European democracies, for example. In area, too, many of the largest American congressional districts cover regions the size of entire nations elsewhere. Those realities limit the ability of candidates to campaign through direct, personal contact with voters, putting a premium on a candidate's ability to raise and effectively spend large sums of money to reach voters through the mass media—television, radio, and large mailings.

In the 1990 U.S. elections, for example, the average cost of a successful campaign in a district without an incumbent came to more than half a million dollars.[7] Spending in several hotly contested races topped the million-dollar mark. Statewide campaigns can cost far more.

Senators Feinstein and Boxer spent, respectively, $8 million and $10 million in their successful pursuit of California's Senate seats. In Texas, Ann Richards spent some $10 million in winning the governorship in 1990. Feinstein spent $12.5 million to retain her seat in 1994.

Significantly, not only do all candidates find they must spend large sums, but women appear to need to spend more, in large part to establish themselves as "credible" candidates. During the 1992 election cycle, successful male candidates running in districts without incumbents spent an average of $449,890, while successful female candidates in such districts spent an average of $636,474. Women considering running for office, therefore, must immediately come to grips with the need to raise prodigious sums. Usually lacking access to the traditional business and professional networks that allow many men to raise funds, women who consider public office often falter at precisely that point. By providing women with an alternative fund-raising network that can provide money early in their campaigns, EMILY's List directly helps to overcome that problem.

The relative weakness of American political parties reinforces the need for money. Entrenched political organizations are often seen as a force for defending the status quo, and, indeed, they often play that role. But as political organizations seek to perpetuate themselves in a changing society, they can also serve effectively to integrate new groups into the political process.

In some countries in Western Europe, for example, strong political parties, responding to the demands of newly organized women voters, have been able to make centralized decisions to rapidly boost the number of women holding office. Those decisions can be particularly effective in political systems in which voters cast ballots for a party-selected list of candidates rather than for individual candidacies in particular districts.

American parties once had that ability. "Machine" organizations in cities such as New York and Chicago played key roles in bringing successive waves of immigrants into political life. The first African-American members of Congress were also elected primarily from machine-dominated constituencies. But successive waves of political reform have largely destroyed the old machines, ushering in an era of entrepreneurial politics in which candidates largely select themselves, based to a considerable degree on their ability to raise money, while parties have almost no role in candidate selection.

Entrepreneurial politics tends inherently to favor those who are already part of the political system and to discriminate against outsiders,

W O M E N   F I R S T

1872:
SUSAN B. ANTHONY IS THE FIRST U.S. WOMAN TO REGISTER TO VOTE; SUBSEQUENTLY SHE BECOMES THE FIRST TO MARK A BALLOT, FOR WHICH SHE IS ARRESTED.

including women. Some people will give money to a political candidate on the basis of shared ideology or personal commitment, but most contributions come from interest groups hoping to secure a favorable hearing from government, and they tend overwhelmingly to follow the safe path of giving money to incumbents, not challengers. Another prime source of funds is a candidate's informal network of business or professional associates—again a source that tends to favor people who already are part of the established structure.

Finally, while members of ethnic or racial minority groups can often benefit from the effect of population concentration—running in districts where appeals to ethnic pride boost both their candidacies and their fund-raising—women by nature lack that advantage. Indeed, just the opposite occurs, as the size of the country works against the ability of a woman in one part of the country to gather help from potential supporters elsewhere. Malcolm poses the problem this way: "If you were a teacher in Des Moines, and you wanted to be represented by women in the Senate or in the House, you might not have any women running in Iowa. So how do you find out about them?" EMILY's List "literally empowered that schoolteacher in Iowa, gave her a way to try and have women represent her in our representative democracy."

At first, relatively few women took advantage of that empowerment. Through its first few election cycles, EMILY's List had only a few thousand members. But the nationally televised Senate hearings in October 1991 into charges of sexual harassment against Clarence Thomas, the Bush administration's nominee for Supreme Court justice, led to rapid growth. The sight of a panel of middle-aged, white, male senators grilling a young, black, female law professor, Anita Hill, about her charges against Thomas came to symbolize the shortage of women on Capitol Hill. For EMILY's List, as for other organizations supporting women in politics, the result was a huge upsurge in support. The organization's membership increased more than sevenfold, to some twenty-five thousand, and has continued to rise. That increase in membership, and the corresponding increase in ability to raise funds, contributed heavily to the record numbers of new women elected in 1992.

The heavy Democratic losses in the 1994 election marked a setback for EMILY's List, which provides money only to Democrats. Several incumbent Democratic women lost their seats and no Democratic challengers, regardless of gender, defeated Republican incumbents. Looked at in terms of the success of women regardless of party, however, the results were more positive. In the Senate, the election of Olympia Snowe of Maine brought the number of women to eight, up from only two at the beginning of the decade. Three of the women Senators now are Republicans. Simliarly, in the House, the election of eight new Republican women means that the women's caucus will remain the same size but will no longer be the overwhelmingly Democratic group that it was. Those results underscore a notable development of the last two election cycles: while Democrats still field more women candidates than do Republicans, the Republicans have begun to catch up. Shifts of party control, therefore, are no longer likely greatly to affect the overall number of women in elective office although such shifts do, of course, have a major impact on the ideology of the women who are elected.

Despite the losses in 1994, in that election, as in the previous one, EMILY's List played a key role in financing Demcratic candidates. In the 1992 election cycle, EMILY's List raised and spent $6.2 million, making it the largest single source of funds for congressional Democratic candidates. And the group's money is even more important than those numbers alone would indicate because of its role in early identification of candidates worthy of support. Malcolm and her staff interrogate candidates seeking the group's support (which is limited to Democrats who support abortion rights), scrutinizing their polls, their campaign plans, and their organizational abilities in an effort to weed out those whose efforts are doomed. Of the fifty-five candidates the group supported in 1992, twenty-five won election—an impressive success rate for a group that, by design, concentrates on the most competitive races.

Because of that sort of record, EMILY's List has developed a reputation for being able to pick candidates who have a chance of winning. As a result, winning the group's imprimatur now serves to open the doors of other liberal organizations as well—magnifying the ability to channel funds to those women who appear on the list.

Inevitably, as EMILY's List has become larger and more successful, the group's activities have generated more controversy. One controversy has embroiled EMILY's List in a long-running fight with supporters of campaign-finance reform. The argument involves the technique EMILY's List uses to raise and disburse its funds—a practice known to campaign-finance experts as "bundling."

Under current federal law, an organization cannot directly give a candidate more than $5,000. That limitation severely restricts, for example, the amount that corporate and union political action committees can give a candidate. EMILY's List gets around that restriction by asking its members to send contribution checks made out directly to the candidate or candidates they wish to support. The group then takes the checks, "bundles" them together, and forwards them to the relevant campaign as individual contributions rather than as one donation from EMILY's List.

As the reformers point out, widespread use of that practice would effectively allow almost any group to get around the campaign-finance limits. General Motors, for example, can set up a political action committee to give money to favored candidates, but by doing so is limited to giving only $5,000. A group of one hundred General Motors executives, by contrast, easily could give the same candidate $100,000 by bundling together $100,000 in individual contributions. Charles Keating, the politically active head of a savings and loan company, did precisely that during the late nineteen-eighties, bundling together checks from business associates and delivering them to key members of the Senate Banking Committee. When Keating's savings and loan empire collapsed, his role as a fund-raiser became the center of a scandal that ended the political career of at least one senator, California's Alan Cranston, and endangered several others.

To prevent future Keatings, reformers have pushed for new limits on bundling. EMILY's List has become the chief opponent of that move, rallying support from House Democrats, particularly women, to block any bill that would put the group out of business.

"I think EMILY's List is campaign-finance reform, because we've showed the schoolteacher in Iowa how she can participate," Malcolm argues. "I'm not writing out her check. She's writing out her check. She's making that decision. But it's a way of involving her in the process. The special-interest money always finds a way to get into the system, and if you don't have a way to offset it with small contributors, women are left out."

So far, EMILY's List appears to have prevailed in that fight. A second battle has proven more difficult to end, pitting EMILY's List against activists who attack the group for being too wed to the political status quo.

The target here is the group's insistence on supporting only candidates who appear likely to win. Critics complain that that approach translates into an unwillingness to back candidates who are radical, offbeat, or too nontraditional. EMILY's List, for example, did not initially provide funds to Carol Moseley Braun when she challenged incumbent Senator Alan J. Dixon in the 1992 Democratic primary in Illinois. Only when Braun began to gain on Dixon in the closing phase of the primary campaign did the group send funds her way. Similarly, in a bitter three-way Democratic primary battle that same year in New York, EMILY's List chose to back one of two women running—former vice presidential candidate Geraldine Ferraro, rather than splitting its funds between Ferraro and the other woman in the race, New York City comptroller Elizabeth Holtzman. That decision drew bitter complaints from Holtzman's supporters.

Malcolm defends the process, arguing that to do otherwise would fritter away contributions, rather than allowing the group to concentrate its funds in the most effective manner. When women first began running for office in significant numbers in the late nineteen-seventies, "We were so excited that any woman was out there running that we'd support every woman who ran, regardless of whether she had a chance. We were taking this little tiny pot of money and disbursing it so widely that nobody had enough money to win anything," she recalls. "So we said

'Look, we've got to make sure that our money goes where it's going to make a difference, and we've got to support women who have a realistic chance of winning races.'"

"The political world knows that if we find a candidate who is viable and get involved, that we're going to deliver. So the women now have new credibility in the political establishment."

PART FOUR

WOMEN HOLD UP
HALF THE SKY

GUATEMALA
A Story of
Tragedy and Promise
Rigoberta Menchú

The history of my life is not just a personal story; rather, it is part of the history of Guatemala, a history of tragedy and, at the same time, a story of promise.

It has been difficult for me as an indigenous woman to find the confidence to speak publicly, particularly since we were raised to believe that the only role for women is to maintain a household and to bear children. If you broke with this role, you were seen as abandoning tradition and you would lose the respect of the people.

We were born into poverty. I am from a very remote village called Chimel, nine hours' walk from Uspantán. We lived on roots and greens, and often our only hope for going to the market in Uspantán and returning with a handful of chile for the household or with some other necessity was our ability to find mushrooms and greens which we could sell in the market. When we were growing up we would go to plantations to harvest cotton, coffee, and sugarcane. This is how we spent our childhood.

Yesterday marked thirteen years since my father and thirty-eight others were burned alive in the Spanish Embassy on January 31, 1980, in Guatemala City. The flames left their bodies in ashes. Papa was a man who struggled for twenty-two years for land and for a document proving that he owned the land. During those twenty-two years of struggle, he was imprisoned a number of times and, once, kidnapped and tortured. My mother, who was a remarkable woman and a midwife since she was sixteen years old, was kidnapped, tortured, and assassinated. We weren't able to bury her and to this day she doesn't have a grave.

One of my brothers was also tortured and assassinated. He, too, was burned alive. Another brother, his three children, and his wife were also killed. They were all shot.

It has hurt me to repeat and relive that story again and again in public. But that's what people listened to. Personal testimony is something which must be shared with moral courage and dignity by those who have been victims. It is a right and also a responsibility that transcends the indignation you feel when the value of human life is not respected.

Often we forget our history, but sometimes our history is all we were left with. It is what we have lived and what we have seen during these years of war. The widows and mothers of Guatemala will never forget this history. This book allows our stories to be heard, our stories as women who have suffered, yes, but also as women who are struggling for change. One gains a sense of the lives of Guatemalan women, a sense of our work, and a sense of what we have learned. One becomes aware of our pain but also of our dreams, our hopes of accomplishing something in our lives, and our hopes for a new Guatemala.

BEING INDIGENOUS

We indigenous make up the majority in Guatemala and comprise twenty-two of the twenty-three language groups. Our people could often speak two or three languages and could weave highly sophisticated designs, but for so long we have suffered because we would not give up our culture. We have been ridiculed and treated as folklore. The government remembered the indigenous when it needed us for publicity purposes and when it wanted to display the indigenous as "colorful" relics from the past. We were treated like ruins, not living people with rights and a future. It has been a long path for us to articulate our own struggle and reality. Over the past ten or twelve years, many of us have learned Spanish, learned to read and write, learned something about the experiences of other peoples in Guatemala and have gained a voice and dignity before the world.

We insist that Guatemala become a nation where indigenous and *ladino* people, women and men, can all participate in society. We need a country that is multicultural, that is to say, a country which respects the diversity of peoples. Racism—the cultivation of fear between *ladinos* and indigenous people—is one of the most deeply rooted problems we face. Will Guatemala be a country which annihilates the indigenous culture or will it be a country where the indigenous have the same rights to control our development as other peoples? National unity cannot be built on eliminating differences but must be based on the reality that we are a country of twenty-three different groups. We need to build a national movement which goes much further in addressing the question of what is "national identity" and what is cultural diversity. We don't all need to think the same and live the same way to be able to respect one another. How are we going to build a future for our people? I believe one important aspect is to instill pride in our people: pride in our roots, in our culture, and in all that it signifies. But not only this. We have to accompany this pride with a comprehensive awareness of our problems and of who our allies are. Our future depends on our awareness, our organization, and our ability to unite our struggles.

BEING WOMEN

More often than not, we are desperately poor. For those with five or six children or for those who are widows, the primary struggle is to survive. If a mother doesn't have a place to leave her child, how can she look for a job? How can she become better educated? How can she become more involved in changing her community and in changing her country?

In the last decade women have contributed tremendously to the struggle for justice. Thirteen years ago, for example, perhaps the only well-known woman was Mamá Maquín, a *campesina* leader killed in the Panzós uprising, and later two women, both of whom were named Maria Anaya. They had led important struggles and later both died in the Spanish Embassy massacre. However, women as leaders were always something exceptional.

WOMEN FIRST

1982: ROSARIO IBARRA DE PIEDRA IS THE FIRST WOMAN TO RUN FOR PRESIDENT OF MEXICO.

In more recent years the participation of women has increased dramatically. In just a few years, the National Coordination of Widows of Guatemala (CONAVIGUA), an all-women organization, has grown to eleven thousand to thirteen thousand members. It has not been easy for women such as Rosalina Tuyuc of CONAVIGUA or Justina Toj of the Council of Ethnic Communities—Runujel Junan (CERJ) to become important national figures. But as persons who represent the marginalized, the indigenous, and women, they unite a number of social groups in the same cause. Because of their impact in denouncing injustice and human rights abuses against the members of their organizations, they—particularly Rosalina—have been under strident attack by the military which accuses them of being guerrillas. Their leadership, as well as the leadership of many other *compañeras* in popular organizations in Guatemala, is proof of the advances of women in the movement.

The barriers to women's full participation in society have not been eliminated, however. Even in the national liberation movements and progressive struggles for democracy throughout Latin America, progress has been insufficient. And, too often, there is an attitude of resignation when there has been little change.

Thirty years of war have given us the moral and political authority to demand *peace*. The struggle for peace has cost us so much thus far, and it is going to cost us even more to forge a lasting peace. If the immense problems of Latin America and Guatemala are still unresolved, how can we speak of peace or speak of the future? Peace requires meaningful change, defending rights, and building a better world. We need changes that are not just formal, not just empty words, but rather which involve real participation by the people and in which the indigenous people and our popular organizations are part of the national decision-making process. This gets at the heart of what the struggle for civil society is—a struggle for the participation of all the people, not just the military and the small wealthy class. We want to participate in the economy, in the political system, in the decisions that make our destiny. We want to be in the Congress, we want to be in the government, and we want to participate like any other citizens and make our contribution to the history of Guatemala.

In many respects these past years have raised incredible hopes for women, the poor, the oppressed, and above all for those women who are indigenous. For the first time we have achieved something: We have been heard. We are respected. At times, being heard is enough for us because as a rule we have been the object of study but we weren't listened to. Now, we are no longer the objects of study. We are the ones making history.

THE DANCE OF LIFE
Women and Human Rights in Chile
Marjorie Agosín

During the seventeen years of military dictatorship in Chile, women formed the country's most visible human rights groups.[1] In times of severe repression and censorship, many women dared to enter a forbidden zone: the streets. From this space—which was previously considered a male domain—these women demanded justice and truth concerning the fate of their loved ones who were missing due to state-sanctioned terrorism.

It is a paradox that, during the periods of worst repression in the nineteen-seventies and nineteen-eighties, Latin American women took on new roles. Accustomed to living in the confined spaces of the home and other historically female places such as markets, schools, and hospitals, through public protest women broke out of their physical isolation to transform their traditional, apolitical, passive role.

Women's language is intimate and personal, a discourse full of nurturing elements. Nevertheless, under the dictatorship in Chile, as under other dictatorships in Latin America, woman transformed their language to address the political repression taking place in the country. They went out into the streets to make their voices heard, because that is where individuals become visible, movements are born, history unfolds, and authority is exercised. Women transformed the "masculine" streets through the use of uniquely female symbols, such as the handkerchiefs embroidered with the names of missing children used by the Mothers of Plaza de Mayo in Argentina. As Adriana Valdés points out, the mothers thus decontextualized and reinterpreted the language of the street.[2] The mothers' traditional role in society legitimized their search for an answer to the disappearance of their children. The women's unique strategy in denouncing the violations of human rights served as an opening to the public space of the street and to history. Through activities charged with a profound cultural symbolism, such as marching every Thursday afternoon in a plaza in Buenos Aires, the Mothers of Plaza de Mayo occupied the public space that was previously denied to them as women.

The authoritarian ideology paradoxically permitted them to create a collective female space and a uniquely female set of images. The women filled the physical, historical, public space with a plethora of messages: the photographs of the faces of young people tied to their mothers' chests; the white embroidered kerchiefs, bobbing on the women's heads in beat with their steps. Through this strategy, the Mothers of Plaza de Mayo created for themselves as well as for those who observed them different images and ways to unmask the oppressive military regime. They did this through and from a woman's perspective.

In the case of Chilean women, the strategy of unmasking the oppressors has also been powerful. One of these strategies has been the symbolic transformation of the *cueca,* the national dance of Chile, into the *cueca sola*—the *cueca* of solitude.

WOMEN FIRST

1979: LIDIA GEILER IS FIRST WOMAN ELECTED PRESIDENT OF BOLIVIA.

On March 8, 1983, various groups of Chilean woman who were fighting against Pinochet's fascism met to celebrate International Women's Day. Signs and banners filled the Caupolicán Theater, located in the center of Santiago. A large sign proclaimed, "Democracy in the country and in the home," underscoring that the personal is political and that domestic violence is profoundly linked to the violence in the country as a whole.

The most memorable event that afternoon was the performance of the cueca sola, an important symbol created during Pinochet's dictatorship. Although Chile is now a democracy, women continue to dance the cueca sola at public demonstrations to demand justice from the government.

The cueca symbolizes the different stages of a romantic interlude between a man and a woman. As the guitar and harp intone the melody and hands joyously clap the rhythms, the man lifts his head, raises his large kerchief, and smiles. As they dance face to face a few steps apart, the couple's movements unfold around an imaginary circle.[3]

The cueca sola is danced alone by a female member of the Association of the Detained and Disappeared. The performance suggests a strategy of revealing oneself before the oppressive power as well as appropriating the language of the body in a public space. The audience is quite familiar with the cueca, since it is the national dance, and appreciates the irony of the fact that it represents the same nation that has deprived the dancer of her children.

The cueca sola has become an important metaphor for Chilean women confronting human rights violations. Popular culture has noted and incorporated these acts of remembrance in honor of the missing, where members of the Association of the Detained and Disappeared perform a dance of loneliness and lost love in front of an emotional crowd.[4] International music stars have been inspired to write songs about this ritual, including Sting's "They Dance Alone" and Holly Near's "Hay una Mujer Desaparecida."

Judith Lynne Hanna, in her book *Dance, Sex and Gender,* notes that women's dances are an affirmation of their identity. Addressing the importance of female dance at the beginning of the twentieth century, she writes:

> Through modern dance and its affirmation of the female body, women choose to be agent rather than object. Constrained economically as well as physically by male-imposed dress styles that distorted the body and hampered natural movement, by restricting education, and by health practices that prevented them from breathing fresh air and eating a sensible diet, some innovative women displayed their strength and their displeasure with traditional roles by breaking the rules of the rigidly codified traditional ballet. They extended the boundaries of dance with revolutionary movement vocabularies, grammars, composition techniques, themes, and costumes. Women offered new dance systems and images alongside the danse d'ecole developed by men. Showing their new choreography onstage invited audience admiration, empathy, and contact, perhaps relieving some women's male-imposed feelings of social and physical insignificance.
>
> The dance medium also permitted women to control and sublimate their sexuality, which had been dominated by men. To get ahead in an uncharted avant-garde, some women needed a nunlike dedication; other middle- and upper-class respectable women in dance had love affairs in and out of marriage to show their new sense of social/sexual equality.[5]

A woman who dances alone evokes in the cueca's rhythm the memory of the man who is absent, and the dance changes from a pleasurable experience to a well of pain and memory. The woman's kerchief reminds the spectator of the shrouds that cover a dead body. The woman's steps take on a certain power as she moves alone through an empty stage.

As the country's official national dance, the cueca is full of a vast symbolism and history. The women attempt to transform and decentralize this "official" status by inverting its historical and political connection with freedom. The cueca sola thus becomes subversive and is reborn as a metaphor of repression and a symbol of women who fight for human rights. The dance comes to represent a denunciation of a society that makes the bodies of victims of political violence disappear, denying them a proper burial and a space to occupy, even underground, and silencing their mourners.

Through the cueca sola, the dancers tell a story with their solitary feet—the story of the mutilated body of the loved one. Through their movements and the guitar music, the women also recreate the pleasure of dancing with the missing person. When the women step onto the dance floor, they invoke the dead and perform a dance of life for them.

Each act of forced disappearance is a metaphor for all clandestine acts. The cueca sola implies a defiance of these illegal acts, but it also represents a social event where rhythms and movements take place that wouldn't be permitted anywhere else.[6] As in the women's demonstrations in the streets, with the cueca sola, women take control of public spaces and languages prohibited to their gender and, in turn, reinterpret and reinvent official forms of discourse.

The women's commitment to historical and political truth is linked to their personal set of ethics. In dancing the national dance in this way, the group's members denounce the government's actions on the public space of the dance floor. By dancing the national dance of Chile alone, the women begin to emerge as historical beings with an identity of their own, defying the tradition of couples dancing together. The cueca sola breaks the protocol of the dominant culture where women are prohibited from dancing by themselves and, symbolically, with their missing, dead loved ones.

In 1983, the Association of the Detained and Disappeared formed a folklore group, where women collectively sing and compose songs about their lives as women alone.[7] Most cuecas deal with love and the eternal struggle of a man to win a woman's love. In the cueca sola, the woman is the one who searches for the affection of the missing man, who also symbolizes the mutilated and divided country.

Violeta Parra (1918–1967), one of the best-known folklore figures in Chile and throughout Latin America, is remembered and invoked by the women who write and perform the cueca sola. Parra sang two types of melodies that later became cuecas and that appealed to God and humanity to alleviate the pains of daily life.[8]

The members of the Association of the Detained and Disappeared sing cuecas to God, pleading for guidance in their search for the bodies of their loved ones. The women sing in the style of Violeta Parra, imitating her distinctive, rustic voice and guitar. When they sing as a group, they use harps, guitars, and clapping. The cueca's rhythms are important; in the case of the cueca sola, singers echo, "Where are they?"

Different cuecas solas are sung at demonstrations and memorial services, among them "Te He Buscado Tanto Tiempo" (I have searched for you for so long). The song's theme is the search for a missing person, and the lyrics describe a long journey through the country and an accusation of the guilty.

I have searched for you for so long
I can't find you
I have lost, I have cried out
and no one wants to listen to me.[9]

The powerful chorus reveals the position the family members find themselves in as they search:

I demand the truth
I will search heaven and earth
without tiring of my search
and I will give my whole life
and I will give my whole life
to know where they are.[10]

The last verse of the "Song of Hope" reflects the collective search, the common consciousness in all of the dancers and in all of the women:

Give me your hand, Maria
take my hand, Rosaura
give her your hand, Raquel
let's affirm our hope.[11]

One of the group's members, referring to the sense of hope that the women share, tells us the following:

> This hope is based on the strength that the struggle for life gives us. It may be that many of our family members have not survived the atrocities to which they were subjected, but according to the testimony of people who were with them, many could have remained in hidden places, and we still might be able to rescue them.[12]

The dance represents an affirmation of life and a negation of death. In the cueca sola, the pleasure of dancing goes beyond the exploration of the music and the movements. Dance, and in particular this dance remembrance, permits the body to free itself from all bonds. Through the cueca sola and its movements full of soft and delicate cadences, the women are representing the free body, the body that hasn't been tortured, the body that is full of life. For this reason, the folklore group is called Song for Life. It is a life committed to politics and searching, as well as to meeting with women and hearing their individual stories. The disappearance of a loved one becomes part of the country's history, and the concept of homeland assumes a female identity; one of the slogans of the women who fight for human rights is "freedom is the name of a woman."

The cueca sola recalls the past, the company of a partner, pleasure, desire, and the sensuality of dancing with a loved one. The dance also reflects the pain of missing a loved one:

At one time my life was blessed
my peaceful life filled my days
but misfortune entered my life
my life lost what I loved the most.
At one time my life was blessed.

I constantly ask myself
where are they keeping you
and no one answers me
and you don't come back.[13]

According to Leslie Godfrid, the vision and passion that the dance inspires can be powerful in promoting social transformation.[14] As a form of resistance and denunciation of the illegal actions of dictatorship, the cueca sola reflects this transformational quality.

The creation of *arpilleras* by the families of the detained and disappeared during the years of military dictatorship also represents a form of resistance.[15] Arpilleras are small textile collages made from rags that depict daily life. During Pinochet's dictatorship, women whose relatives were kidnapped anonymously embroidered arpilleras that recounted their personal suffering as well as the nation's pain. In 1983, the women who created the arpilleras went a step further and, in addition to using their hands to embroider, they presented their whole bodies in public protest. The bodies of the persecuted came to life in the bodies of the women who invoked them with their hands, feet, and kerchiefs in the air.

Watching a woman dance the cueca sola has a great impact, because her steps reflect the daily trajectory of a murky, national history. We again observe the incredible transformational power of the women who, from within the dominant culture and through this inherently masculine, national dance, created a new, alternative cultural space. The women are truly alone, without men or a country, because this same country has taken away their men, their sons, their husbands, as reflected in the following cueca sola:

Ladies and gentlemen
I am going to tell a story
of all I have suffered
and I keep it in my memory.

It is a very sad story

that I would rather not tell you
what happened in my country
where life isn't worth anything.

Children were left without parents
and mothers abandoned
life has been destroyed
the injustice doesn't end.

How sad it is for the children
when their father is missing
they are only left with
their mother's protection.

I want this to end
and that they be punished
for the crime they have committed
with "the disappeared."

And with this I say goodbye
a small piece of crystal
and those who have committed this crime
must pay with their lives.[16]

Dancing the cueca sola is, then, a way for women to overcome the silence and to remember the dead. With the movement of their bodies, they recount what has happened to them, using their roles as mothers and wives to interpret the male language of the street and of history through a female set of images.

The cueca sola, and its relationship to resistance and denunciation, is a powerful phenomenon of Chilean popular culture. Many Chilean women have been abused, through torture or domestic violence. The women who dance the cueca sola use their bodies and the sensuality of their movements to tell their stories to a captive and compassionate audience, transforming the country's traditional dance into a call for freedom. Women appropriate the symbolism of the cueca as they dance for independence, and through this strategy they dedicate their free, whole bodies to the cause.

Long is the absence
and throughout the land
I ask for conscience.[17]

With its powerful and moving symbolism, the cueca sola has become one of the most creative and effective forms of protesting human rights violations in Chile. For this reason, the women say as they approach the stage:

> We have created this cueca as testimony of what we are living
> and to fight so that a woman will never again have to dance the
> cueca sola.

Translated by Janice Molloy

WOMEN, INFORMATION, AND THE FUTURE
The Women of Kenya and the Green Belt Movement

Wangari Maathai

What is there to say about women that has not yet been said by now? As for information, I live in a world where the battle for freedom of information and expression is still being fought. The politicians still decide what is good and safe for us to read and, so far, the Bible is one publication that has successfully evaded and, indeed, impressed the censors hands down.

So I do read the Bible, which is a book full of wisdom and with a message for all seasons. Hosea 4:16, for example, says, "My people perish for lack of knowledge," which is the salt of the earth. In the Garden of Eden, moreover, we find that the tree at the center of the garden is the tree of knowledge; but Eve is warned that if she partakes of it, she will be like God.

Without trying to be a theologian, which I am not, I find these references to knowledge very inspiring. I quote them often because I want to emphasize the importance of acquiring knowledge and using it for the common good. We read these quotations in the Bible to remind ourselves that what we need is *correct* information so that we can make the right decisions and take appropriate actions. We urge people not to escape from knowledge by clinging to supernatural powers in the hope that these powers can be subjected to the will of human beings. For we must all seek knowledge and information from the tree of life in the center of our garden, our garden being our intellect, our heritage, libraries, laboratories, and, indeed, even good old Mother Nature herself. For that is exactly what Eve did: She took action to seek knowledge, never mind what man had to say about that!

On the personal and professional levels, I have spent most of my life collecting information and processing it through the work I do. I am currently working with the Green Belt Movement (GBM). This has been a long journey; I first collected information in the humble but rich countryside of my childhood. Then I moved to the classrooms, libraries, and laboratories, never cutting my link with the countryside no matter what advances I made in the classrooms.

My formal educational background is in the biological sciences, which I studied at the Mount Scholastica College in Atchison, Kansas. I then proceeded to the University of Pittsburgh, Pennsylvania, where I earned my master's degree under a wonderful man called Professor Charles Ralph, the man who introduced me to the embryology and microanatomy of the pineal body of birds. This research gave me some techniques in the preparation of tissues for microscopic observations and aroused a special interest in anatomy, embryology, and histology. It was this specialization that led R.R. Hofmann of the University of Giessen to recruit me for the University of Nairobi in Kenya. To improve this knowledge and to be introduced into electron microscopy I went to the University of Munich in Germany and spent almost two years in beautiful Bavaria in the company of the late Professor Walter. The experiences I gathered during these years of formal education greatly influenced my perception of the world and the values which shape my life.

When I returned to the University of Nairobi I pursued a Ph.D. program in the same field and became confirmed as a permanent staff member on the Faculty of Veterinary Medicine. This was in the early 1970s and it seemed as though, besides being an African wife and mother, I was destined to be a University of Nairobi professor to help produce graduates in veterinary medicine who would feed the nation and the eastern region of Africa with livestock products. At that time the livestock industry in Kenya was the best in the eastern region. I thought that from then on it would be smooth sailing to old age and eternity. Was I wrong!

As part of the academic discipline at the university I took up research on the life cycle of a parasite that is responsible for east coast fever, a fatal cattle disease along the east coast of Africa. Part of the life cycle of the parasite is spent in the salivary glands of brown-ear ticks. I collected hundreds of these ticks, removed their salivary glands, cut them up for microscopic observation, and produced thousands of slides. Unfortunately, my life in the university was cut short and I have never been able to complete that study. Others have continued to study both the tick and the parasite, and progress is still being made. However, a cure for the disease has not yet been found. Neither has the life cycle of the parasite been fully unraveled.

While I was collecting ticks I was inspired to recognize environmental degradation in my country. I observed that the animals from whose bodies I picked the ticks were thin and clearly suffering from hunger. There was little grass and other fodder, and during the dry season much of the grass was dry. The people, too, looked undernourished and poor. The vegetation in the field was scanty and it was quite clear that the soils in the fields were poor, the yields low, and famine almost guaranteed.

This information was hitting me from all angles. It was coming from various observations as I collected specimens for my research on the brown-ear tick. It was coming from informal exchanges with women, from seminars organized by the National Council of Women of Kenya, from the press, from the newly formed United Nations Environment Programme, and from a group of diligent European and American environmental activists.

From these encounters I realized that the real threat to the cattle industry was not the brown-ear tick but the deteriorating environment around me. I also recognized that not only the livestock industry, but I, my children, my students, my fellow citizens, and my entire country, were threatened by the deteriorating environment. It would appear that the cumulative knowledge I had acquired through various experiences made it possible for me to make the linkages between the symptoms of environmental degradation which I was observing and the causes of such degradation. What are some of those causes? They are now well known (deforestation, devegetation, unsustainable agriculture, soil loss, pollution).

Several years later, when I joined the National Council of Women of Kenya, I attended seminars about women and the problems they face. At one seminar I was struck by the research data indicating that children from the fertile Central Kenya Province were suffering from diseases associated with malnutrition. Women, the researcher reported, were using agricultural residues to cook and were, therefore, opting for foodstuffs that required little energy to cook. These turned out to be processed foods like bread, maize flour, rice, and tea, all of which are rich in carbohydrates but wanting in vitamins, proteins, and minerals.

W O M E N   F I R S T

1982:
EUGENIA
CHARLES,
DOMINICA,
IS THE FIRST
WOMAN TO
BECOME
PRIME
MINISTER
IN THE
CARIBBEAN.

As we now well know, this changed diet was also a symptom of environmental degradation. So was the rampant poverty in urban and rural areas. The privileged among us could choose to sit in an ivory tower and, like the historical Marie Antoinette, wonder how so many people can be so poor and seem unwilling to do something to change their situation. Marie Antoinette was probably uninformed. But most of us are and we know that such people are trapped in a vicious cycle from which they cannot escape.

Let us revisit the National Council of Women of Kenya. Its leadership was the privileged few; most of us were well educated and successful in our business, professional, or religious lives. We were preoccupied with giving each other company and moral support in whatever sphere we were involved in. We were also concerned with the social and economic status of the bulk of our membership, which was based in the rural areas. We were concerned with water, school fees, clothing, and wondered what we could do to ease the burden of those less privileged than ourselves. After all, that is where our mothers and our sisters were, and are, still living. It was not charity, therefore, or a guilty conscience that spurred us on; indeed, we felt that it was as much our duty as theirs.

At this time, despite the culture of development aid and an influx of experts from the developed countries, I had come to know that it is better to teach people to fish rather than to donate fish to them. Therefore, through the National Council of Women of Kenya we decided to encourage women to plant trees so that they could meet many of the needs they were expressing at the meetings. The idea of planting trees with rural women was the right idea at the right time.

Hence, in 1977, the Green Belt Movement was born. Over the years, GBM has identified a long list of both short- and long-term objectives. However, the overall objective is to raise the awareness of ordinary citizens on the need to care for the environment so that it, too, may take care of them. We do this by educating them on the linkage between their own survival and that of the environment in which they live, helping them meet their needs and thereby promoting sustainable development.

The main activity is the planting of tree seedlings that women raise and share with neighbors. To date over ten million seedlings have been planted. But I think that the real success of the movement lies in having demystified the forestry profession and created an accepted category of foresters without diplomas! That has been done by giving the women information on afforestation, tree planting, and maintenance, and by making connections between trees and food, fodder, shade, and the beauty of the natural environment.

In the beginning, we were not fully aware of the impact this activity would have on the women in particular and the entire society in general. In the end, the tree has turned out to be a great sign of hope and a source of inspiration. It was a new idea, though, because tree planting was a profession for foresters with diplomas, almost all of whom were men. But the women made a success of it.

The women of the Green Belt Movement took up tree planting to meet their needs for firewood, cash, building and fencing materials, fruits, shade, and an aesthetic countryside. In the process they learned about the causes and the symptoms of environmental degradation. They have begun to appreciate that they, rather than their government, ought to be the custodians of the environment, and ought to consider the rights of future generations to a healthy environment that will also help them meet their needs. The women of the Green Belt Movement are foresters without diplomas and this gives them a great sense of accomplishment. As we all know, information and success are empowering tools and these women continue to experience both. The communities in which they live have also been positively affected by this experience.

It has taken sixteen years to develop the many objectives we now pursue and we have encountered many obstacles. These obstacles have been identified as bottlenecks of development, and we argue that unless they are tackled, development will not be realized in our part of the world. Among them are corruption and the abuse of human rights. To counter these bottlenecks we must create a strong and free civil society and form a national government that is democratic, accountable, and responsible to the people who vote for its leaders in free and fair elections. These are some of the issues to which we have devoted much time and energy because we believe that they are important now and for the future.

We in the Green Belt Movement have never decided to become political, to fight for a more open and democratic civil society, or to become human rights activists. We just found ourselves confronting injustices against ourselves, our members, and the environment. In the beginning our concern was personal. Then it extended first to the workplace, then to national issues, and finally to work on the international level.

As for myself, I do not know when it actually started. Perhaps before birth. But I remember finding myself asserting my right to be myself. I thought I saw nothing wrong with being a woman, a graduate, and a professional; and I claimed the rights to have an opinion on all manner of issues, to fall in love, to marry, to raise children, and to remain a completely sane woman. But many people did see something wrong. And because I insisted and persisted, I became labeled an activist, a controversial figure, a radical, a rebel. But I still insist that none of that is really me. I am Wangari. I do not need an adjective. It became clear to me that I was breaking new ground. I was absolutely certain that it was OK for women to pioneer on the basis of the information at their disposal.

Twenty years ago, few men and women in my country shared that view. I now believe that the few who did were either too jealous to be sympathetic or too scared to be publicly associated with such sentiments. The public opinion was that the woman's place was at the bottom and that there must have been something seriously wrong with a woman who aspired to reach for the stars. Many men wanted to see such women publicly humiliated to teach all women a lesson. In addition, women who were not sympathetic were comforted to know that they were not alone under the stifling oppression of men. That is the only way I have been able to understand the reactions I got from both men and women. Today it is a very different story because many women believe that asserting my rights was a great inspiration and encouraged them to do the same in their own worlds. At that time it seemed I was almost alone. Today we are a multitude.

Our struggle for human rights and a more democratic, responsible, and accountable governance is best exemplified by our efforts to save Uhuru (Freedom) Park in downtown Nairobi. Our government, like many in the region, was a one-party dictatorship led by greedy and corrupt leaders who used national resources as their own personal property. So the president of our country decided to take over the only remaining public park in town to build a sixty-two-story skyscraper and beside it a four-story statue of himself! He intended to borrow money on the international market on behalf of the Kenyan people and have the Kenyan government guarantee the repayment of the loans. This was going to be yet another white elephant in Africa for the prestige and ego of one man. This happened as recently as 1990.

WOMEN FIRST

**1992:
BETTY
BOOTHROYD
IS FIRST
WOMAN
CHOSEN TO
BE SPEAKER OF
THE HOUSE OF
COMMONS IN
GREAT BRITAIN.**

When we raised the alarm we were abused and ridiculed at a parliamentary session and reminded that as African women we ought to have known that when men spoke, women should be agreeably silent.

Well, this time around, the women spoke; they disseminated information to the relevant bodies and friends and exposed the greed and corruption of a government that was interested in creating such a grandiose monolith.

The women of the Green Belt Movement and the Kenyan people received support from environmental and human rights activists around the world. Fortunately, the donors listened. Financial arrangements were canceled and the project stalled. We believe it may never be built. The park continues to be a haven for ordinary people in the middle of busy Nairobi. This experience was greatly empowering, not only to women, but also to all who were fighting for the democratization of our governing system and for an end to violations of human rights. Once again people saw the power of information in the hands of a small group of determined women.

Another example of the struggle for human rights and the determination of women came in 1992 when mothers of political prisoners walked to Uhuru Park and staged a peaceful hunger strike demanding the release of their sons. Their sons had been jailed because they had agitated for democratization and an end to the dictatorship of a one-party political system. By this time they were being illegally held because the government had already conceded to a change in the constitution and allowed the formation of many political parties. The strike was initially planned to last three days. The sight of mothers on a hunger strike and sleeping out in the open in a corner of the park, soon to be dubbed Freedom Corner, attracted huge crowds of citizens who already supported calls for an end to dictatorship and one-party government. Many visitors, including leaders of churches and political parties, came to the park to support the mothers and their demands. In very moving and telling accounts, survivors of torture and detention without trial narrated their stories for the first time. People sang, prayed, and held all-night vigils. We shared information, learning and drawing strength from one another.

The government knew that knowledge in the "wrong" hands was a dangerous thing. It reacted to the few and peaceful women by sending hordes of police to attack and beat them with batons and the butts of guns and to blind them with tear gas spray. It was a scene reminiscent of violent attacks against black people by state police during the civil rights marches of the 1960s in the United States and more recently in South Africa. The women felt abused and infuriated. In desperation some of them stripped to expose their nakedness, a tradition used to express utmost disgust, anger, and frustration. This expression of abhorrence is supposed to place a curse on the attackers. The women who were not taken to hospital were evacuated from the park and driven to their respective homes by night under police guard. Yet, without any previous consultation, the women returned to the city and regrouped in the basement of the nearby All Saints Cathedral of the Anglican Church.

Several weeks later, the government sent more than five hundred heavily armed army men to surround the cathedral. The siege lasted for about one week. When negotiations between the bishop and the government were over, the soldiers moved out of the church compound, the bishop blessed the church to drive the devil away, and the women were barred from receiving visitors. The women were, therefore, effectively isolated from the rest of the world. Yet they continued their campaign in silence. They also published and distributed information about their jailed sons. The government tried to woo them and to corrupt them to accept compromises. Nevertheless, most of the women held fast to their ideals.

Almost one year after the mothers staged the strike, fifty-one sons (only one was retained by this time) were released and the women held a thanksgiving service in the same cathedral. Many sons, including many who had suffered in jail in previous years, joined the mothers to celebrate their victory and the release of their sons.

We are now putting up a monument in the crypt where the women lived for almost one year. This monument will honor those mothers for standing up for the rights of their sons and all those who had been jailed for following their conscience. The monument will also remind future generations of the courage of women in the struggle against dictatorship and corrupt leaders and inspire future generations to stand up for justice and the rule of law.

I have shared with you several experiences of my life as an informed woman living in a world in which information is hidden from the ordinary by the economically and politically powerful. In my personal and professional life I have tried to use the information at my disposal to reach out to my fellow citizens, to empower them so that they can liberate themselves and improve their quality of life. What we do with information is the challenge to which each of us must rise. I am greatly encouraged by the knowledge that we are not alone in this struggle; we are, indeed, a multitude.

PART FIVE

TOMORROW'S PROMISE

SULTANA'S DREAM

Rokeya Sakhawat Hossain

"Sultana's Dream," published in 1905 in a Madras-based English periodial, The Indian Ladies' Magazine, *is one of the earliest "self-consciously feminist"[1] utopian stories written in English by a woman. It is certainly the first such story to be written by an Indian woman. Its author, Begum Rokeya Sakhawat Hossain (1880-1932), is the first and foremost feminist of Bengali Muslim society. One hesitates to use a term that is not context-free, and* feminism *does mean different things to different people, yet it is the term that automatically occurs to many who read Rokeya's work now. At the time she wrote this story, she had already attracted considerable attention as an essayist, having pubished several articles in Bangla dealing exclusively with the subordination and oppression of Bengali women, especially Bengali Muslim women.*

The text of "Sultana's Dream" presented here is closely based on the text included in the collected works of Rokeya, Rokeya Racanavali, *published in 1973 by the Bangla Academy of Dhaka. That text retains the style of Rokeya's early-twentieth-century Bangla-influenced English. For clarity to readers of this volume, capitalization, spelling, and punctuation have been standardized according to present-day U.S. conventions.[2]*

—Roushan Jahan

One evening I was lounging in an easy chair in my bedroom and thinking lazily of the condition of Indian womanhood. I am not sure whether I dozed off or not. But, as far as I remember, I was wide awake. I saw the moonlit sky sparkling with thousands of diamondlike stars, very distinctly.

All of a sudden a lady stood before me; how she came in, I do not know. I took her for my friend, Sister Sara.

"Good morning," said Sister Sara. I smiled inwardly as I knew it was not morning, but starry night. However, I replied to her, saying, "How do you do?"

"I am all right, thank you. Will you please come out and have a look at our garden?"

I looked again at the moon through the open window, and thought there was no harm in going out at that time. The menservants outside were fast asleep just then, and I could have a pleasant walk with Sister Sara.

I used to have my walks with Sister Sara, when we were at Darjeeling. Many a time did we walk hand in hand and talk lightheartedly in the botanical gardens there. I fancied Sister Sara had probably come to take me to some such garden, and I readily accepted her offer and went out with her.

When walking I found to my surprise that it was a fine morning. The town was fully awake and the streets alive with bustling crowds. I was feeling very shy, thinking I was walking in the street in broad daylight, but there was not a single man visible.

Some of the passersby made jokes at me. Though I could not understand their language, yet I felt sure they were joking. I asked my friend, "What do they say?"

"The women say you look very mannish."

"Mannish?" said I. "What do they mean by that?"

"They mean that you are shy and timid like men."

"Shy and timid like men?" It was really a joke. I became very nervous when I found that my companion was not Sister Sara, but a stranger. Oh, what a fool had I been to mistake this lady for my dear old friend Sister Sara.

She felt my fingers tremble in her hand, as we were walking hand in hand.

"What is the matter, dear, dear?" she said affectionately.

"I feel somewhat awkward," I said, in a rather apologizing tone, " as being a purdahnishin woman I am not accustomed to walking about unveiled."

"You need not be afraid of coming across a man here. This is Ladyland, free from sin and harm. Virtue herself reigns here."

By and by I was enjoying the scenery. Really it was very grand. I mistook a patch of green grass for a velvet cushion. Felling as if I were walking on a soft carpet, I looked down and found the path covered with moss and flowers.

"How nice it is," said I.

"Do you like it?" asked Sister Sara. (I continued calling her "Sister Sara," and she kept calling me by my name.)

"Yes, very much; but I do not like to tread on the tender and sweet flowers."

"Never mind, dear Sultana. Your treading will not harm them; they are street flowers."

"The whole place looks like a garden," said I admiringly. "You have arranged every plant so skillfully."

"Your Calcutta could become a nicer garden than this, if only your countrymen wanted to make it so."

"They would think it useless to give so much attention to horticulture, while they have so many other things to do."

"They could not find a better excuse," said she with [a] smile. I became very curious to know where the men were. I met more than a hundred women while walking there, but not a single man.

"Where are the men?" I asked her.

"In their proper places, where they ought to be."

"Pray let me know what you mean by 'their proper places.'"

"Oh, I see my mistake, you cannot know our customs, as you were never here before. We shut our men indoors."

"Just as we are kept in the zenana?"

"Exactly so."

"How funny." I burst into a laugh. Sister Sara laughed too.

"But, dear Sultana, how unfair it is to shut in the harmless women and let loose the men."

"Why? It is not safe for us to come out of the zenana, as we are naturally weak."

"Yes, it is not safe so long as there are men about the streets, nor is it so when a wild animal enters a marketplace."

"Of course not."

"Suppose some lunatics escape from the asylum and begin to do all sorts of mischief to men, horses, and other creatures: in that case what will your countrymen do?"

"They will try to capture them and put them back into their asylum."

"Thank you! And you do not think it wise to keep sane people inside an asylum and let loose the insane?"

"Of course not!" said I, laughing lightly.

"As a matter of fact, in your country this very thing is done! Men, who do or at least are capable of doing no end of mischief, are let loose and the innocent women shut up in the zenana! How can you trust those untrained men out of doors?"

"We have no hand or voice in the management of our social affairs. In India man is lord and master. He has taken to himself all powers and privileges and shut up the women in the zenana."

"Why do you allow yourselves to be shut up?"

"Because it cannot be helped as they are stronger than women."

"A lion is stronger than a man, but it does not enable him to dominate the human race. You have neglected the duty you owe to yourselves, and you have lost your natural rights by shutting your eyes to your own interests."

"But my dear Sister Sara, if we do everything by ourselves, what will the men do then?"

"They should not do anything, excuse me; they are fit for nothing. Only catch them and put them into the zenana."

"But would it be very easy to catch and put them inside the four walls?" said I. "And even if this were done, would all their business—political and commercial—also go with them into the zenana?"

Sister Sara made no reply. She only smiled sweetly. Perhaps she thought it was useless to argue with one who was no better than a frog in a well.

By this time we reached Sister Sara's house. It was situated in a beautiful heart-shaped garden. It was a bungalow with a corrugated iron roof. It was cooler and nicer than any of our rich buildings. I cannot describe how neat and nicely furnished and how tastefully decorated it was.

We sat side by side. She brought out of the parlor a piece of embroidery work and began putting on a fresh design.

"Do you know knitting and needlework?"

"Yes: We have nothing else to do in our zenana."

"But we do not trust our zenana members with embroidery!" she said laughing, "as a man has not patience enough to pass thread through a needlehole even!"

WOMEN FIRST

1991: KHALEDA ZIA RAHMAN IS THE FIRST WOMAN TO BECOME PRIME MINISTER OF BANGLADESH.

"Have you done all this work yourself?" I asked her, pointing to the various pieces of embroidered teapoy cloths.

"Yes."

"How can you find time to do all these ? You have to do the office work as well? Have you not?"

"Yes. I do not stick to the laboratory all day long. I finish my work in two hours."

"In two hours! How do you manage? In our land the officers, magistrates, for instance, work seven hours daily."

"I have seen some of them doing their work. Do you think they work all the seven hours?"

"Certainly they do!"

"No, dear Sultana, they do not. They dawdle away their time in smoking. Some smoke two or three choroots during the offfice time. They talk much about their work, but do little. Suppose one choroot takes half an hour to burn off, and a man smokes twelve choroots daily; then, you see, he wastes six hours every day in sheer smoking."

We talked on various subjects; and I learned that they were not subject to any kind of epidemic disease, nor did they suffer from mosquito bites as we do. I was very much astonished to hear that in Ladyland no one died in youth except by rare accident.

"Will you care to see our kitchen?" she asked me.

"With pleasure," said I, and we went to see it. Of course the men had been asked to clear off when I was going there. The kitchen was situated in a beautiful vegetable garden. Every creeper, every tomato plant, was itself an ornament. I found no smoke, nor any chimney either in the kitchen—it was clean and bright; the windows were decorated with flower garlands. There was no sign of coal or fire.

"How do you cook?" I asked.

"With solar heat," she said, at the same time showing me the pipe, through which passed the concentrated sunlight and heat. And she cooked something then and there to show me the process.

"How did you manage to gather and store up the sun heat?" I asked her in amazement.

"Let me tell you a little of our past history, then. Thirty years ago, when our present Queen was thirteen years old, she inherited the throne. She was Queen in name only, the Prime Minister really ruling the country.

"Our good Queen liked science very much. She circulated an order that all the women in her country should be educated. Accordingly a number of girls' schools were founded and supported by the Government. Education was spread far and wide among women. And early marriage also was stopped. No woman was to be allowed to marry before she was twenty-one. I must tell you that, before this change, we had been kept in strict purdah."

"How the tables are turned," I interposed with a laugh.

"But the seclusion is the same," she said. "In a few years we had separate universities, where no men were admitted.

"In the capital, where our Queen lives, there are two universities. One of these invented a wonderful balloon, to which they attached a number of pipes. By means of this captive balloon, which they managed to keep afloat above the cloudland, they could draw as much water from the atmosphere as they pleased. As the water was incessantly being drawn by the university people, no cloud gathered and the ingenious Lady Principal stopped rain and storms thereby."

"Really! Now I understand why there is no mud here!" said I. But I could not understand how it was possible to accumulate water in the pipes. She explained to me how it was done; but I was unable to understand her, as my scientific knowledge was very limited. However, she went on:

"When the other university came to know of this, they became exceedingly jealous and tried to do something more extraordinary still. They invented an instrument by which they could collect as much sun heat as they wanted. And they kept the heat stored up to be distributed among others as required.

"While the women were engaged in scientific researches, the men of this country were busy increasing their military power. When they came to know that the female universities were able to draw water from the atmosphere and collect heat from the sun, they only laughed at the members of the universities and called the whole thing 'a sentimental nightmare!'"

"Your achievements are very wonderful indeed! But tell me how you managed to put the men of your country into the zenana. Did you entrap them first?"

"No."

"It is not likely that they would surrender their free and open air life of their own accord and confine themselves within the four walls of the zenana! They must have been overpowered.'

"Yes, they have been!"

"By whom?—by some lady warriors, I suppose?"

"No, not by arms."

"Yes, it cannot be so. Men's arms are stronger than women's. Then?"

"By brain."

"Even their brains are bigger and heavier than women's. Are they not?"

"Yes, but what of that? An elephant also has got a bigger and heavier brain than a man has. Yet man can enchain elephants and employ them, according to his own wishes."

"Well said, but tell me, please, how it all actually happened. I am dying to know it!"

"Women's brains are somewhat quicker than men's. Ten years ago, when the military officers called our scientific discoveries 'a sentimental nightmare,' some of the young ladies wanted to say something in reply to those remarks. But both the Lady Principals restrained them and said they should reply not by word but by deed, if ever they got the opportunity. And they had not long to wait for that opportunity."

"How marvelous!" I heartily clapped my hands.

"And now the proud gentlemen are dreaming sentimental dreams themselves.

"Soon afterward certain persons came from a neighboring country and took shelter in ours. They were in trouble, having committed some political offense. The King, who cared more for power than for good government, asked our kindhearted Queen to hand them over to his officers. She refused, as it was against her principle to turn out refugees. For this refusal the king declared war against our country.

"Our military officers sprang to their feet at once and marched out to meet the enemy.

"The enemy, however, was too strong for them. Our soldiers fought bravely, no doubt. But in spite of all their bravery the foreign army advanced step by step to invade our country.

"Nearly all the men had gone out to fight; even a boy of sixteen was not left home. Most of our warriors were killed, the rest driven back, and the enemy came within twenty-five miles of the capital.

"A meeting of a number of wise ladies was held at the Queen's palace to advise [as] to what should be done to save the land.

"Some proposed to fight like soldiers; others objected and said that women were not trained to fight with swords and guns, nor were they accustomed to fighting with any weapons. A third party regretfully remarked that they were hopelessly weak of body.

"'If you cannot save your country for lack of physical strength,' said the Queen, 'try to do so by brain power.'"

"There was a dead silence for a few minutes. Her Royal Highness said again, 'I must commit suicide if the land and my honor are lost.'

"Then the Lady Principal of the second university (who had collected sun heat), who had been silently thinking during the consultation, remarked that they were all but lost; and there was little hope left for them. There was, however, one plan [that] she would like to try, and this would be her first and last effort; if she failed in this, there would be nothing left but to commit suicide. All present solemnly vowed that they would never allow themselves to be enslaved, no matter what happened.

"The Queen thanked them heartily, and asked the Lady Principal to try her plan.

"The Lady Principal rose again and said, 'Before we go out the men must enter the zenanas. I make this prayer for the sake of purdah.' 'Yes, of course,' replied Her Royal Highness.

"On the following day the Queen called upon all men to retire into zenanas for the sake of honor and liberty.

"Wounded and tired as they were, they took that order rather for a boon! They bowed low and entered the zenanas without uttering a single word of protest. They were sure that there was no hope for this country at all.

"Then the Lady Principal with her two thousand students marched to the battlefield, and arriving there directed all the rays of the concentrated sunlight and heat toward the enemy.

"The heat and light were too much for them to bear. They all ran away panic-stricken, not knowing in their bewilderment how to counteract that scorching heat. When they fled away leaving their guns and other ammunitions of war, they were burned down by means of the same sun heat.

"Since then no one has tried to invade our country any more."

"And since then, your countrymen never tried to come out of the zenana?"

"Yes, they wanted to be free. Some of the Police Commissioners and District Magistrates sent word to the Queen to the effect that the Military Officers certainly deserved to be imprisoned for their failure; but they [had] never neglected their duty and therefore they should not be punished, and they prayed to be restored to their respective offices.

"Her Royal Highness sent them a circular letter, intimating to them that if their services should ever be needed they would be sent for, and that in the meanwhile they should remain where they were.

"Now that they are accustomed to the purdah system and have ceased to grumble at their seclusion, we call the system *mardana* instead of zenana."

"But how do you manage," I asked Sister Sara, "to do without the police or magistrates in case of theft or murder?"

"Since the mardana system has been established, there has been no more crime or sin; therefore we do not require a policeman to find out a culprit, nor do we want a magistrate to try a criminal case."

"That is very good, indeed. I suppose if there were any dishonest person, you could very easily chastise her. As you gained a decisive victory without shedding a single drop of blood, you could drive off crime and criminals too without much difficulty!"

"Now, dear Sultana, will you sit here or come to my parlor?" she asked me.

"Your kitchen is not inferior to a queen's boudoir!" I replied with a pleasant smile, "but we must leave it now; for the gentlemen may be cursing me for keeping them away from their duties in the kitchen so long." We both laughed heartily.

"How my friends at home will be amused and amazed, when I go back and tell them that in the far-off Ladyland, ladies rule over the country and control all social matters, while gentlemen are kept in the mardanas to mind babies, to cook, and to do all sorts of domestic work; and that cooking is so easy a thing that it is simply a pleasure to cook!"

"Yes, tell them about all that you see here."

"Please let me know how you carry on land cultivation and how you plow the land and do other hard manual work."

"Our fields are tilled by means of electricity, which supplies motive power for other hard work as well, and we employ it for our aerial conveyances too. We have no railroad nor any paved streets here."

"Therefore neither street nor railway accidents occur here," said I. "Do not you ever suffer from want of rainwater?" I asked.

"Never since the 'water balloon' has been set up. You see; the big balloon and pipes attached thereto. By their aid we can draw as much rainwater as we require. Nor do we ever suffer from flood or thunderstorms. We are all very busy making nature yield as much as she can. We do not find time to quarrel with one another as we never sit idle. Our noble Queen is exceedingly fond of botany; it is her ambition to convert the whole country into one grand garden."

"The idea is excellent. What is your chief food?"

"Fruits."

"How do you keep your country cool in hot weather? We regard the rainfall in summer as a blessing from heaven."

"When the heat becomes unbearable, we sprinkle the ground with plentiful showers drawn from the artificial fountains. And in cold weather we keep our rooms warm with sun heat."

She showed me her bathroom, the roof of which was removable. She could enjoy a shower [or] bath whenever she liked, by simply removing the roof (which was like the lid of a box) and turning on the tap of the shower pipe.

"You are a lucky people!" ejaculated I. "You know no want. What is your religion, may I ask?"

"Our religion is based on Love and Truth. It is our religious duty to love one another and to be absolutely truthful. If any person lies, she or he is…"

"Punished with death?"

"No, not with death. We do not take pleasure in killing a creature of God—especially a human being. The liar is asked to leave this land for good and never to come to it again."

"Is an offender never forgiven?"

"Yes, if that person repents sincerely."

"Are you not allowed to see any man, except your own relations?"

"No one except sacred relations."

"Our circle of sacred relations is very limited, even first cousins are not sacred."

"But ours is very large; a distant cousin is as sacred as a brother."

"That is very good. I see Purity itself reigns over your land. I should like to see the good Queen, who is so sagacious and farsighted and who has made all these rules."

"All right," said Sister Sara.

Then she screwed a couple of seats onto a square piece of plank. To this plank she attached two smooth and well-polished balls. When I asked her what the balls were for, she said they were hydrogen balls and they were used to overcome the force of gravity. The balls were of different capacities, to be used according to the different weights desired to be overcome. She then fastened to the air-car two winglike blades, which, she said, were worked by electricity. After we were comfortably seated she touched a knob and the blades began to whirl, moving faster and faster every moment. At first we were raised to the height of about six or seven feet and then off we flew. And before I could realize that we had commenced moving, we reached the garden of the Queen.

My friend lowered the air-car by reversing the action of the machine, and when the car touched the ground the machine was stopped and we got out.

I had seen from the air-car the Queen walking on a garden path with her little daughter (who was four years old) and her maids of honor.

"Halloo! you here!" cried the Queen, addressing Sister Sara. I was introduced to Her Royal Highness and was received by her cordially without any ceremony.

I was very much delighted to make her acquaintance. In [the] course of the conversation I had with her, the Queen told me that she had no objection to permitting her subjects to trade with other countries. "But," she continued, "no trade was possible with countries where the women were kept in the zenanas and so unable to come and trade with us. Men, we find, are rather of lower morals and so we do not like dealing with them. We do not covet other people's land, we do not fight for a piece of diamond though it may be a thousandfold brighter than the Koh-i-Noor,[3] nor do we grudge a ruler his Peacock Throne.[4] We dive deep into the ocean of knowledge and try to find out the precious gems [that] Nature has kept in store for us. We enjoy Nature's gifts as much as we can."

After taking leave of the Queen, I visited the famous universities, and was shown over some of their factories, laboratories, and observatories.

After visiting the above places of interest, we got again into the air-car, but as soon as it began moving I somehow slipped down and the fall startled me out of my dream. And on opening my eyes, I found myself in my own bedroom still lounging in the easy chair!

SHE WHO WOULD BE KING

Ama Ata Aidoo

An encounter that took place in the kitchen of a university guest house. Half a century earlier, in 1976.

He-of-twenty-five-years-old: "So what did you say you will be when you grow up?"

She-of-ten-years-old: "The president."

"The what?"

"The president?"

"The president?"

"Yes."

"Of what?"

"This country."

"W–H–A–T–?–!–!"

"Why not?"

"You are mad."

"I'm not."

"Yes, you are."

"No."

"Well, you can't."

"Yes, I can."

"You are mad."

"I am not."

"Anyway, you can never be the president of this country."

"Why not?"

"Listen, I don't think the men of this country will ever let a woman be their president."

"No? We shall see."

And now, the year is 2026. The month, May. The day, the twenty-fifth. The old woman is eighty-six years old. Her daughter the lawyer, whose story this should have been, turned fifty-nine six months ago. Her granddaughter, whose story it turns out to be, will be thirty-six at year's end.

The Old Queen, as the family calls her behind her back, is lying in the adjustable chair in the corner. The members of her family think that she is old beyond joy and sorrow. So they have arrived at an unspoken agreement. That the only way she can jubilate with them over this most welcome but still unbelievable piece of news is for others to fuss over her. So they keep fiddling around with the contraption, rearranging now her pillows, now the headrest....Then before she can open her mouth to say she is fine, someone comes to raise—or did he lower?—the footrest.

But the plain truth is that she really is quite comfortable. In fact, if anybody had ever told her that a day would come when she would feel this much at peace with herself and the world, she would have laughed in her face. Her life has been very difficult, and full of surprises that were not always pleasant. She could never plan her life. So time had often taken her into some awkward places. But then this is not supposed to be her story...

Her daughter is Adjoa Moji, professor and dean of the law faculty. Her students call her Professor AdjMoj, affectionately, behind her back. She is in the house but not in the family room. The Old Queen cannot see her. But she can feel her.

They are, at least, four generations of the family in the room, as well as representatives of several different branches of it. Actually, it is not a room as such. It is really the square open space linking the four sides of the house, roofed with glass, and a huge skylight created in the process. So that as you approach from the garage, you are pleasantly surprised to find yourself entering a classical clan courtyard, which is also a lounge in the European style.

The house itself, built with a loan from the university, is rather small. However, its design is so original that it has become a subject of intense discussions among the professor's friends and colleagues, as well as members of the general public. Suddenly, everybody is an expert on architecture. Of course, those who don't like the professor, or envy her and her family, say that the thing looks and feels like a hothouse.

The television set is in the center of the room facing west. Its screen is as wide as that for a small lecture theater. This is 2026, so of course, it's high definition. But since this is 2026, the Anane household's screen is neither the biggest nor the highest-defined around. In this neighborhood near the university campus, people are not the poorest in the country. But they are also not the richest. In fact, in the real "cash-dey" sections of this city, some homes have television sets with screens that are almost as wide as those that used to be in the old cinema houses in the city center. As soon as the sun goes down, the skies in such areas are lit by the glare from the television sets. Yet this is only a state capital. They say that in the capital city of the Confederation of African States, there are many more such neighborhoods. Those who have been there claim that, in fact, even if the city council were to stop providing streetlight at night, the total glow from television sets would be enough to light the streets.

Of course, the first name that everybody had originally thought of for the union was the United States of Africa. But then everybody had also agreed that that would not do. People would want to abbreviate it. And when they did, it would be "U.S.A." And of course, everybody knew Uncle Sam wouldn't like that. So the formal abbreviation in English is "C.A.S." But one trait that survived with the Africans who survived the unspeakable twentieth century is their cynicism and the capacity to laugh at themselves. So they have already decided to call the union "The CASE."

The capital city has taken all of the last twenty-five years to recover from the previous thirty years of civil war.

It isn't Africa's capital alone that went through a rough time. The entire continent went through hell in the last forty years of the twentieth century and the first ten years of this century. She had been in hell of one kind or another for exactly five hundred years. But those last fifty were something special. Manmade but accidental, manmade and deliberate, home-grown, imported, natural. Name it. If it was a calamity, Africa suffered it.

At the height of the AIDS epidemic, priests from different religions had had to set up camp in the cemeteries from eight o'clock in the morning and did not leave until late at night. To cheer themselves up, everybody joked that burials had become the hottest nine-to-five job in town with no pay for overtime.

Then there was The Drought. At its worst, those who were paranoid had said that white folks were fiddling with the planet.

"They are fixing Africa to face the sun permanently."

"...to deprive us of rains."

"They are trying to fry us."

"...part of the Great Plot to wipe us off the surface of the earth. So they will be free to take our continent completely. Instead of just holding on to it by devious and vicious means, as they've been doing the last five centuries..."

The real tragedy was that in those days you could find plenty of support for such fears. And very little to discount them with. However, others had talked then of the thirty-year drought cycle. Most of them knew nothing for certain. They were only doing some wishful thinking. But a few had been geographers, weather people, and sundry other such experts. Anyway, to our general relief, those who belonged to the latter, more optimistic group seemed to have been proven right.

Almost on the dot of January 1, 2010, the rains started. From the Cape to Cairo, it rained, and rained and rained. The Nile, the Niger, the Congo, the Zambezi, and all our rivers swelled and overflowed their banks. And so did the great lakes: Chad, the Volta, Victoria, and Kariba had filled up again. Even the Sahara and the Kalahari began to green up. Of course, that wasn't going to last.

The deserts were not going to become rain forests. But the illusion that they might stay green, as they were at the beginning of time, was not bad for our spirits. Hope had been long in coming. Now it was here, and we held onto it, every which way we could.

The Old Queen knows that, at this very minute, AdjMoj is in her bedroom, dancing before her dressing mirror. That is, if the high jumps, wide arm throws, and kicking she does when she is happy can be called that. How well she knows this child of hers!

Her mother is right. AdjMoj is dancing. What else can she do? On a day and in an hour like this? She can hear her grandmother, a long time ago in the village, muttering to herself whenever something nice happened, or she heard a piece of good news: *"Tarkwa ewu ntsem muo!"* Oh yes, it must be unfortunate to die early in Tarkwa, or anywhere else for that matter. She has remembered the saying because she has lived long enough to see this day. And not just her. Even Mama has lived long enough to see this day.

The main news has come on. And sure enough, Afi-Yaa has been elected the first president of the newly formed Confederation of African States.

An encounter that took place in another part of town, the evening of this same day of May 25, 2026.

He-of-seventy-years-old: "Did you watch the news?"

His son, in his forties: "Who didn't?"

"Hmmm…"

"She is only thirty-six! And they say her grandmother is eighty-six, tight like a wire, and lucid like the edge of a razor blade."

"But is a razor blade really lucid?"

"Eh…hm…well, it's sharp."

"So her grandmother is eighty-six, and sharp like a razor."

"Anyway, that's it. We are going to have her for the next fifty years!"

"Why do you think that?"

"This is Africa, isn't it? No one resigns here. Certainly not heads of governments or any outfits for that matter. And they never allow themselves to get voted out of power. Not if they can help it. No, they are either thrown out in coups, or they sit on people's heads until they rot with old age. And those who wait in the wings as deputies or the opposition are no better. Sometimes they even manage to be worse."

"That was quite a speech. But wake up. These are the twenty-twenties, not the nineteen-seventies. In any case, it was I who lived through all that. Not you. So, wake up.…And she is a woman."

"What difference does that make?"

"Should be a lot. Those were power-hungry old men...."

"...and power-hungry young men."

"Okay. Well, she is a young woman, and she doesn't seem to be hungry for anything. Least of all power."

"No? We shall see."

"Hm...that's what her mother said to me a long time ago."

"Her mother?"

"Yes. I know her."

"You know her mother? That professor?"

"Yes. Or rather, I knew her then."

"How?...Where?...When?...H–O–W–?"

"It's a long story....And why are you so surprised?"

"Well...well..."

"Well, what? You know something? Some things clearly do not change. She is a university professor who has built a cottage that is supposed to be the most interesting house in town. And I am only a manufacturer, a businessman—"

"With lots of money and the biggest house in town!"

"No, we didn't leave our prejudices and other pettiness in the twentieth century. What a pity!"

"Please, Father, I didn't mean it that way. Stop being so sensitive about being rich and tell me about you and this girl's mother."

"OK. You just said, 'No? We shall see.' That's exactly what the mother said to me one day, when I told her that the men of this land would never let a woman be president."

"She wanted to be president of this country?"

"Yes. Or at least, that's what she told me when she was ten years old, and this was a country."

"Now her daughter is the president of Africa!"

"The first president of Africa."

"Good Lord."

WOMEN FIRST

1995: TWO WOMEN RUN FOR PRESIDENT AND 8 FOR VICE PRESIDENT IN PERU, THE FIRST TIME WOMEN HAVE BEEN CANDIDATES FOR THESE OFFICES.

"Don't swear. The Ancients have said that it's the same thing if a horse doesn't go to the battlefront, but its tail does."

"Good Lord."

"Didn't I ask you not to swear? Wanting to be corrected at your age like a little boy! And remember, 'that girl' is your president....In fact, as my workers at the site would insist, 'Old contri chief be president, all-Africa chief no be president: e be king. So as for this woman, e be she-king.'...My son, you better look for a more decent way of referring to her, even in private."

"Good L-o-r-d."

NOTES

INTRODUCTION pp. 1–9

1 The campaign took its slogan from the name of a nineteenth-century U.S. cattle trail, an important thoroughfare from after the Civil War until the expansion of the railroads.

2 "Women and children first" is perhaps best remembered as a phrase used in rescue operations when ships were in peril of sinking and women and children were put onto the life rafts first.

Part One
NOT FOR WANT OF TRYING pp. 13–26

1 In Tasmania the methods of election for the two houses are the reverse of what applies in other states and more women have been elected to their lower house than to their upper house as a result. New Zealand's unicameral parliament is currently made up of single member electorates in which women have been reasonably well represented in the past few decades compared with their sisters in other English speaking parliaments. A different electoral system will be in place for the next election in that country however and it will be interesting to see how this will affect the number of women elected.

2 Inter-Parliamentary Union fact sheet 1994.

3 New Zealand Parliamentary Debates 1891.

4 New Zealand Parliamentary Debates 1893.

5 South Australian Parliamentary Debates, July 1894 column 815.

6 Australian Parliamentary Debates, House of Representatives, 23 April 1902 p. 1937.

7 South Australian Parliamentary Debates, 11 Dec 1894 column 2777.

8 Australian Parliamentary Debates, The Senate, 13 Dec 1983, p. 701.

9 Australian Parliamentary Debates, House of Representatives, Vol 176, 1943, p. 182.

10 *The News* (Adelaide South Australia) 7 Nov 1983.

11 *The Australian* 8 Feb 1990.

THE IMPACT OF GERMAN UNIFICATION ON WOMEN pp. 27-40

1 The Convention is a document that spells out the human rights of women in the public and private spheres and in all areas of life; it also includes strategies to achieve these rights through legislation; the institutionalization of policy-making for women in governments and political administrations; and through mechanisms such as affirmative action. As a human rights instrument, it has contributed to the expansion of the definition of human rights in general. Ratification of this document by a member state of the United Nations obliges the government of that country to guarantee its female population the enjoyment of their human rights and, at regular intervals, to report to the Committee on the progress made in these areas. Thus, the Convention is a recognized and important agent for the de jure and de facto improvement of women's situation worldwide. Article 7 of the Convention on the Elimination of All Forms of Discrimination against Women stipulates equal access for women in politics while Article 4 provides for temporary measures to advance de facto equality in all areas of women's lives. Article 2 provides for the establishment of political institutions for women's policies. Implementing these articles through an increase in female politicians and through the creation of institutions for women's policies certainly can make a difference for women, as the Scandinavian countries, and, I argue, the example of Germany at a very critical moment in its political development, has shown. Nations who have signed the CEDAW document may elect representatives to the Committee to serve for fixed terms. Though they are appointed by their governments, they are "independent" in the sense that their concerns are those of CEDAW.

A CONVERSATION WITH WU QING pp. 41–57

1 Bing Xin is a writer who gained prominence during the 1911 May Fourth Movement. She is Wu Qing's mother.

2 China has three tiers of People's Congresses: The District Congresses in urban areas and the County Congresses in rural areas constitute the first tier. The Municipal and Provincial Congresses, respectively, form the second level. The National People's Congress is at the top.

3 In the past, political parties (the Communist Party and small democratic parties) and mass organizations (trade unions and the All-China Women's Federation) put forward candidates. Upper level Party or administrative units also issued guidelines to constituencies requiring them to nominate candidates of a certain type to abide by the constitution.

4 The districts are divided into constituencies that encompass small shops, factories, offices, schools, universities, and residential streets. All registered residents 18 years and older may vote or stand for election.

5 BFSU has 4,000 voters who elect one deputy.

6 Deputies to the NPC are elected by the deputies to the mid-level (Municipal and Provincial People's) Congresses.

7 Deputies to the Provincial Congresses are elected by the deputies to the County Congresses.

8 District and county government officials report to the district and county deputies, respectively, on economic, financial, health, educational, security, and other affairs. Typically, there have been little discussion and criticism of these reports. Many deputies feel that being informed about the government's workings is the extent of their function. Furthermore, deputies nominated by their local Party or administrative leadership in recognition of their work think it would be unseemly to use their position to criticize the government.

POLITICAL WOMEN AND WOMEN'S POLITICS IN INDIA pp. 59–72

1 Arvind N. Das, "Dynasty: A South Asian Soap Opera," in *Seminar* 425, (January 1995), pp. 46–48.

2 Known as the Rani Sati Sarva Sangh, the organization sought to revive the cult of widow immolation *(sati)* through building temples to the goddess of sati and monuments to individual satis, leading sati processions and producing leaflets, booklets, audio cassettes, posters, etc., on sati.

3 Significantly, Madhya Pradesh is one of the states in which the women's movement is weakest; this was also the case with the pre-independence women's movement. Though there are strong women's organizations, such as the Chhattisgarh Mine Workers' Women's Organisation and the Bhopal Women Gas Victims Organisation, these are class-based and minority groups (the former is a tribal organization, the latter is primarily Muslim) and lack the middle-class support that women's groups have elsewhere.

4 *Hindutva* is used to describe the political ideology of a Hindu nation that is espoused by the Bharatiya Janata Party, the Vishwa Hindu Parishad, and the Rashtriya Swayamsevak Sangh and can be distinguished from the systems of belief and practice of Hinduism.

5 The left parties are an exception here: in general it is respectable to be an active member. However, this applies only to the top echelons of the party hierarchy, the politburos, members of Parliament, and party intellectuals, who are largely drawn from the upper middle class. The rest, party cadres and branch organizers, are generally regarded as lumpenised.

6 Uma Bharati, for example, was accused of having an affair with Govind Acharya, one of the Bharatiya Janata Party's chief ideologues, and the party made clear to her that as a woman and low caste her position was contingent on subservience to their dictate. See Rajendra Yadav, editorial in *Hans* March 1993; translated in *Bulletin of Concerned Asian Scholars* 25, No. 4 (Oct.–Dec. 1993), p. 52.

7 For example, SEWA encouraged its members to open their own bank accounts and taught them how to manage them. Most of their members had been unable to control their own incomes until then, and having their own bank accounts not only helped them to make household ends meet, it also gave them some bargaining power with their husbands. Interview with Ela Bhatt, June 22, 1978.

8 See R. Kumar, *A History of Doing: An Illustrated Account of Movements for Women's Rights and Feminism in India, 1800–1990,* Kali for Women, New Delhi, and Verso, London and New York, 1993, pp. 54–70.

9 These words were actually spoken by the hero of his novel Char Adhyaya, cited by Tanika Sarkar, "Politics and Women in Bengal: The Conditions and Meaning of Participation," *Indian Economic and Social History Review* 21, No.1 (Jan.–March 1984), p. 92.

10 Gail Omvedt, "Two Steps Forward One Step Back: The Political Empowerment of Women," unpubl. paper, p. 3.

11 See also Mary Fainsod Katzenstein, "Organising against Violence: Strategies of the Indian Women's Movement," *Pacific Affairs* 62, No. 1 (Spring 1989), pp. 53–71.

12 *The Times of India,* July 29–August 7, 1980.

13 Known as The Muslim Women's (Protection of Rights on Divorce) Bill, the bill was enacted on February 25, 1986. While removing the right of divorced Muslim women to maintenance from their husbands, as this was held to be un-Islamic according to an interpretation of the Muslim law book the *Shariat,* the bill made the Muslim charitable trusts, the *Waqf,* responsible for maintenance.

14 Socialism in India ranges from liberal democratic to center-right to radical left, but these latter generally prefix revolutionary to socialist. In this essay the references are only to the former two.

15 For an account of these groups see Tanika Sarkar, "Women's Agency within Authoritarian Communalism: The Rashtrasevika Samiti and Ram Janmabhoomi," in Gyanendra Pande, ed., *Hindus and Others,* Viking/Penguin, Delhi 1993; Paola Bacchetta, "All Our Goddesses Are Armed: Religion, Resistance, and Revenge in the Life of a Militant Hindu Nationalist Woman," and Amrita Basu, "Feminism Inverted: The Real Women and Gendered Imagery of Hindu Nationalism," both in *Bulletin of Concerned Asian Scholars* 25, No. 4 (Oct.–Dec. 1993).
16 Radha Kumar, op cit., p. 155.
17 Parties such as the CPI-M in West Bengal, the Telegu Desam in Andhra Pradesh, and the left coalition in Kerala all protested.
18 Gail Omvedt, op cit., pp. 7–8.
19 Ibid. See entire paper.
20 Informally known by the name of its author, the Mandal Commission Report lay forgotten until 1990. The Janata Dal's decision to implement it was widely seen as a desperate attempt to garner popular support when it became clear that a midterm poll would have to be called as the government could not last out its term.
21 When reservation of government jobs for low castes was introduced in the 1960s, most of the jobs were of the lowest order, and many were job categories already filled chiefly by low castes (such as sweeping, delivering, caretaking).

BLAGA DIMITROVA pp. 73–78

1 A weekly for literature, social life, fashion, and housekeeping, published between 1921 and 1944, edited by Hristo Cholchev; it had a circulation of 14,000.
2 "Lonely Woman on the Road" is one of Blaga Dimitrova's best-known poems.

Part Two
FROM PRISON CELL TO PARLIAMENT pp. 103–117

1 Cock, J. 1991. *Colonels and Cadres: War and Gender in South Africa.* Cape Town: Oxford University Press.
2 ANC National Exectuive Committee Statement on Women's Emancipation. 2 May 1990. Johannesburg.
3 The Reconstruction and Development Program, ANC, 1994.

PORTUGAL: DARING TO BE DIFFERENT pp. 127–132

1 *New Portuguese Letters* (U.S. ed., Garden City, N.Y.: Doubleday, 1974), p. 70.

PROFILES AND PORTRAITS pp. 133–164

1 In the U.S. Civil War, fought over the issue of abolition of slavery, the Southern states that were slaveholding broke away and formed the Confederacy. The Daughters of the Confederacy is an organization of women representing those original breakaway states.

Part Three
THE 30 PERCENT QUOTA LAW pp. 183–193

1 According to this ideology, which took a foothold in the armed forces of various countries in Latin America in the nineteen-sixties, domestic social conflicts were considered to have sprung from an international communist conspiracy and therefore to be suppressed.
2 Since 1930, the democratic system in Argentina has been interrupted by a succession of military coups d'etats. However, the last one (from 1976 to 1983) was especially ill-fated because of the government's open commitment to repression, torture, and assassination.

3 In April 1977, at the height of the military dictatorship, fourteen women met on Plaza de Mayo (in front of the presidential palace in Buenos Aires, the Plaza de Mayo is the nerve center of Argentinean politics) to deliver a letter to President Jorge Rafael Videla. The women demanded that their children, who had "disappeared," be "returned alive." Gradually, other mothers joined this group and started to hold secret meetings in homes and coffee houses to organize the world-famous "rounds," held each Thursday on Plaza de Mayo. The participants were persecuted for their activities and many were detained and/or disappeared. Since 1982, with the weakening of the military government, the Mothers of the Plaza de Mayo have gained national and international recognition and many have joined their movement.

4 The most significant features of the crisis were: an acute recession, reduction of the social benefits provided by the state, and increased unemployment among male workers. In this context, women of all ages were pushed into the formal and informal labor markets to compensate for the reduction in real family income and the declining living standards (Geldstein, 1992; Ibarlucía and others, 1990).

5 The historical low point for the number of women in the House was 0.5 percent in 1963 and 1964.

6 The Argentine Network of Feminist Politicians was officially established at the end of 1991 (Lubertino Beltrán, 1992: 37-39).

7 A few months earlier, the First Meeting of Women from the Union Civica Radical, held in Santiago del Estero, had discussed the strategies to be used for promoting a national quota law which would provide for a minimum representation for women. Almost all the committees favored this measure and authorized their legislators to advance such projects.

8 This "gender alliance" brings to memory a meeting held on another square on October 17, 1945, one of the key dates in modern Argentinean history. On that day, men and women from the underprivileged classes gathered in great numbers on Plaza de Mayo to plead for the freedom and reinstatement of General Perón, who had been removed from the government. A short time later, Perón won the presidential election.

9 The only exception were the women from the Union del Centro Democratico (center right party) who definitely opposed the law.

10 In 1993 the president appointed nine women as a Shadow Cabinet, responsible for advising him on positive action measures for women and for working with the ministers to develop equality policies in different areas.

WOMEN IN PARLIAMENTARY LIFE pp. 195–208

1 Virginia Myers, *Head and Shoulders* (Penguin Books, Auckland, 1986), pp. 158–59.

2 The Free Press (New York, 1981).

3 See, for example, Bouthaina Shaaban, *Both Right and Left Handed: Arab Women Talk about Their Lives* (Indiana University Press, Bloomington, 1991); Fatima Mernissi, *The Veil and the Male Elite: A Feminist Interpretation of Women's Rights in Islam* (Addison-Wesley, Reading, Mass., 1991); Gerda Lerner, *The Creation of Patriarchy* (Oxford University Press, New York, 1986); Robin Morgan, *Sisterhood Is Global: The International Women's Movement Anthology* (Anchor Press/Doubleday, Garden City, New York, 1984); Marilyn Waring, *Counting for Nothing: What Men Value and What Women Are Worth* (Allen & Unwin/Port Nicholson Press, Wellington, 1988).

4 Marilyn Waring, *Women, Politics and Power: Essays* (Allen & Unwin/Port Nicholson Press, Wellington, 1985), p. 48.

5 Lesley Abdela, *Women with X Appeal: Women Politicians in Britain* (Optima, London, 1989), p. 14.

6 *Dominion*, 26 May 1989.

7 Katherine O'Regan, "The Thread is Politics", in *Beyond Expectations: Fourteen Women Write about Their Lives*. Edited by Margaret Clark (Allen & Unwin/Port Nicholson Press, Wellington, 1986), p. 153.

8 *Broadsheet*, September 1984.

9 Abdela, *Women with X Appeal,* p. 23.

10 On abortion, adoption, and sexual orientation.

11 Abdela, *Women with X Appeal,* p. 103.

12 Waring, *Women Politics and Power,* p. 12.

13 Marcia Freedman, *Exile in the Promised Land: A Memoir* (Firebrand Books, Ithaca, N.Y., l990), p. 97.

14 Abdela, *Women with X Appeal,* p. 200.

15 Waring, *Women Politics and Power,* p. 32.

16 Helena Kennedy, *Eve Was Framed: Women and British Justice* (Chatto & Windus, London, 1992).

17 Abdela, *Women with X Appeal,* p. 164.

18 Myers, *Head and Shoulders,* p. 13.

19 Ibid., p.164.

20 Kennedy, *Eve Was Framed,* pp. 63–64.

21 Abdela, *Women with X Appeal,* p. 93.

22 Janine Haines, *From Suffrage to Sufferance: A Hundred Years of Women in Politics* (Allen & Unwin, North Sydney, 1992).

23 Freedman, *Exile in the Promised Land,* p. 96.

24 Myers, *Head and Shoulders,* p. 167.

25 Ibid.

26 Waring, *Women, Politics and Power,* p. 56.

27 Abdela, *Women with X Appeal,* p. 26.

28 Ibid., p. 19.

29 Freedman, *Exile in the Promised Land,* p. 101.

30 Abdela, *Women with X Appeal,* p. 27.

31 Myers, *Head and Shoulders,* p. 171.

32 The roll of the House of Representatives after the 1993 general election was 1,139 men and 45 women.

WOMEN HEADS OF STATE OR GOVERNMENT IN THE TWENTIETH CENTURY pp. 212

1 Editor's note: For further information on statistical trends and indicators, please see *The World's Women,* volumes 1 and 2. *The World's Women 1970–1990: Trends and Statistics* is the most comprehensive and authoritative analysis of global statistics and indicators on the status of women. A second issue of the book, with updated statistics, and new topics, published in August 1995 serves as a main official background document for the Fourth World Conference on Women in Beijing. The volume contains chapters on population, families, and households; population and environment; health; education; work and power. It highlights new and innovative statistics on such subjects as women in the media, women refugees, women in international migration, and violence against women. As 1995 is the fiftieth anniversary of the United Nations, it also presents an overview of the participation of women throughout the history of the development of the world's predominant international organization.

The second volume of the publication updates the statistics on women's participation in public life previously documented in volume 1. Specifically, it includes country data from several sources on women's representation in national legislative bodies, and their representation in decision-making posts in government. (Decision-making posts include ministers, deputy and assistant ministers, and government directors.)

EMILY'S LIST pp. 217–225

1 Author's interview with Ellen Malcolm.
2 National Women's Political Caucus, Washington, September 1994. *Los Angeles Times,* September 8, 1994, p. 1.
3 Gallup Organization, national surveys, August 15–20, 1963, April 19–24, 1967.
4 National Opinion Research Center, General Social Surveys, 1988 and 1993.
5 *Los Angeles Times* Poll, March 1994. *Los Angeles Times,* March 31, 1994, p. 1.
6 Inter-Parliamentary Union, "Distribution of Seats between Men and Women in National Parliaments," Geneva, June 1993. *Los Angeles Times,* "Women and Power," June 29, 1993.
7 Data compiled by Dwight Morris, editor for special investigations, *Los Angeles Times.* See also Morris and Sara Fritz, *Gold-Plated Politics: Running for Congress in the 1990s.* Washington: Congressional Quarterly Press, 1992.

Part Four
THE DANCE OF LIFE pp. 233–240

1 For more information about women and human rights groups in Latin America, see Jean Jaquette, *Women's Protest Movements in Latin America,* Unwin Hyman, 1989.
2 See Adriana Valdés's article, "Mujeres entre culturas." *Revista de crítica cultural.* 1, año 1 mayo 1989), p. 34.
3 This description of the Chilean *cueca* was given by Rodríguez Arancibia, *La cueca chilena—coreografía y significado de esta danza,* Servicio Nacional de Turismo, Santiago de Chile, 1945, p. 42. The most complete book about the *cueca* was written by Pablo Garrido, Editorial Universidad, Santiago, Chile, 1980.
4 The Association of the Detained and Disappeared was created in Chile in 1974 by the Vicaria de Solidaridad to investigate the fate of the detained and missing. For more information about this group's work, see the reports by the Vicaria de Solidaridad for 1978 to 1984. This information is available through Vicaria de Solidaridad, Plaza de Armas 444 2do piso, Santiago, Chile.
5 From Judith Lynne Hanna, *Dance, Sex and Gender,* University of Chicago Press, 1988, p. 132.
6 Leslie Godfrid, "Women Dancing Bach." In *Postmodernism, Feminism and Cultural Politics.* Henry A. Simoux, ed. State University of New York Press, 1990, p. 178.
7 For more information about the folklore group created by this association, see *Canto por la vida,* Agrupación de Detenidos y Desaparecidos, Vicaria de Solidaridad, Santiago de Chile, 1987.
8 For more information about Violeta Parra, see Agosín and Dolz, *Violeta Parra–Santa de pura greda,* Editorial Planeta, 1988.
9 From *Canto por la vida,* "Te he buscado tanto tiempo," p. 29. This cueca was composed by Richard Rojas.
10 *Canto por la vida,* p. 29.
11 *Canto por la vida,* "Canción de la esperanza," p. 23.
12 *Canto por la vida,* p. 23.
13 "La cueca sola," collective song in *Canto por la vida,* p. 7.
14 See "Women Dancing Bach," p. 184.
15 For more information about the history of the Chilean *arpillera* movement, see Marjorie Agosín, *Scraps of Life,* Red Sea Press, New Jersey, 1987.
16 *Canto por la vida,* "Una historia," p. 35.
17 From the introduction to *Canto por la vida.*

Part Five
SULTANA'S DREAM pp. 251–260

1 Ann J. Lane's introduction to Charlotte Perkins Gilman, *Herland* (New York: Pantheon Books, 1979 [1915]), p.xix.

2 This headnote is an excerpt from Roushan Jahan's "'Sultana's Dream': Purdah Reversed," in *"Sultana's Dream" and Selections from The Secluded Ones* by Rokeya Sakhawat Hossain, edited and translated by Roushan Jahan, with an Afterword by Hanna Papanek (New York: The Feminist Press at CUNY, 1988). The text of "Sultana's Dream" that follows is reprinted from the same source.

3 The Koh-i-Noor ("mountain of light") is the name of a large and exceptionally brilliant diamond in the possession of the Mughal rulers of India, currently part of the British Crown Jewels. To Indians, it is a symbol of great wealth.

4 The Peacock Throne is a famous jewel-encrusted throne built for the Mughal Emperor Shah Jahan, also known for the Taj Mahal. It was carried away from Delhi by the Persian invader Nadir Shah. Its current location is the cause of much speculation. Many think that one of the thrones displayed in the Istanbul Museum is the Peacock Throne. It is a longstanding symbol of royal power and splendor to Indians.

BIBLIOGRAPHY

MITSUI MARIKO pp 119–126

"Josei Koho Heru Fuman" (Discontented with the Decrease in the Number of Women Candidates); *Asahi Shimbun* (Asahi newspaper), 22 July 1992.

"Josei no Seikai She'a Mokuhyo 30%" (Women's share in the political world aiming at 30 percent), *Asahi Shimbun* (Asahi newspaper), 4 February 1992.

Minutes of the Tokyo Metropolitan Assembly, 3 July 1987.

Minutes of the Tokyo Metropolitan Assembly, 8 December 1988.

Minutes No. 4 of the Special Budget Committee Meeting of the Tokyo Metropolitan Assembly, 16 March 1990.

Mitsui, Mariko. 1990a. "Hey Mister Businessmen There Are No Mrs. Sazaes: So, Whatchya Gonna Do?", *Asahi Journal*, 30 March. Translated from the Japanese by Miya E. Gardner.

———. 1990b. "Josei ga Seiji ni Noridashita Hi" (The day women launched into politics). *Nihon Fujin Mondai Konwakai Kaiho* (Bulletin of the Japan Women's Forum), no. 49 (March):58–68.

"Mitsui shato togi ga rinto todoke" (Socialist party metropolitan assembly member Mitsui gives notice she is quitting the party), *Asahi Shimbun* (Asahi newspaper), 14 January 1993.

"Togisen hikae tohombu konmei" (Party headquarters in turmoil in face of upcoming election for metropolitan assembly), *Asahi Shimbun* (Asahi newspaper), 14 January 1993.

PROFILES AND PORTRAITS pp 133–164

Atlanta Constitution. August 8, 1994.

Bair, Deirdre. *Simone De Beauvoir: A Biography.* New York: Summit Books, 1990.

Brown, Karen. "A President with a Purpose." *Kansas City Star.* August 29, 1993.

Carroll, Joe. "The Changing Face of Ireland: Mary Robinson." *Europe.* February 1993.

Collier's Encyclopedia. New York: Macmillan, 1991.

Congressional Quarterly. January 16, 1993.

Derbyshire, J. Denis, and Ian Derbyshire. *Politics in Britain: From Callaghan to Thatcher.* W & R Chambers, 1990.

Duchen, Claire. *Feminism in France: From May '68 to Mitterand.* London: Routledge & Kegan Paul, 1986.

Duffy, M. "Symbol of the New Ireland." *Time.* June 29, 1992.

The Economist. "Vote in Fear." September 1, 1990.

Essence. October 1992.

Gutman, Israel, ed. *Encyclopedia of the Holocaust.* New York: Macmillan, 1990.

Hine, Darlene Clark. *Black Women in America.* Brooklyn: Carlson, 1993.

Ivins, Molly. "Other Voices." *Atlanta Constitution.* August 13, 1994.

Jarbore, Jan. "Ann's Plans." *Texas Monthly.* July 1992.

Jonsdottir, Rannveig. Interview with Vigdís Finnbogadóttir. Translated by Anna Yates. *19 Juni* (the annual publication of the Icelandic Women's Rights Association). 1987.

Lewis, Anthony. "A Different President." *The New York Times.* January 15, 1993.

Lodge, Herman. *The European Parliament and the European Community.* New York: St. Martin's Press, 1978.

McCafferty, N. "Ireland." *Ms.* May 1992.

McCarthy, Justine. "Politics and the Presidency." *The Independent* (London). May 29, 1993.

Moritz, C., ed. "Mary Robinson" and "Vigdís Finnbogadóttir." *Current Biography.* New York: H.W. Wilson, 1987.

The New Yorker. "President Vigdís." March 29, 1989.

Newsweek. "Mixing It Up." May 18, 1992.

Ogden, Chris. *Maggie: An Intimate Portrait of a Woman in Power.* New York: Simon and Schuster, 1990.

O'Shea, Stephen. "Simone Veil—Vive la Conscience." *Mirabella.* June 1994.

The Oxford Companion to Politics of the World. New York: Oxford University Press, 1993.

Penniman, Howard R., ed. *The French National Assembly Elections of 1978.* Washington, D.C.: American Enterprise Institute, 1980.

Richards, Ann. "Remarks by Governor Ann Richards to the Governor's Commission for Women." July 26, 1993.

_____. "Remarks by Governor Ann Richards at the Elizabeth Sutherland Carpenter Lectureship Featuring First Lady Hillary Rodham Clinton." April 6, 1993.

_____. "Remarks by Governor Ann Richards from Texas Chair, Democratic National Convention." Convention Proceedings, 1992.

_____. "Remarks by Governor Ann Richards for the Commencement Exercises of Smith College Northampton, Massachusetts." May 17, 1992.

_____. "Remarks by Governor Ann Richards before East Texas State University Women's Enrichment Series." November 12, 1991.

Richards, Ann, with Peter Knobler. *Straight from the Heart.* New York: Simon and Schuster, 1989.

Riordan, Theresa, and Sue Kichhoff. "Women on the Hill: Can They Make a Difference?" *Ms.* January/February 1995.

Robinson, Mary. Address on being presented with the Special Humanitarian Award by CARE. Washington, D.C. May 14, 1993.

_____. Address accepting the 1993 International Human Rights Award of the International League for Human Rights. New York, N.Y. May 17, 1993.

_____. "We the Peoples of the United Nations...Renewing That Determination." Address to the Harvard Colloquium, John F. Kennedy School of Government, Boston, Mass. *The Irish Times.* March 11, 1994.

Salem, Dorothy C. *African-American Women: A Biographical Dictionary.* New York: Garland, 1993.

Scandinavian Review. "Cultivating the National Garden." Autumn 1994.

Smith, Jessie Carnie, ed. *Notable Black American Women.* Detroit: Gale Research, 1992.

Stetson, Dorothy McBride. *Women's Rights in France.* Westport, Conn.: Greenwood, 1987.

Time. "A Shock to the System," April 15, 1991; "Thunder on the Right," September 30, 1991.

Uglow, Jennifer S. *The International Dictionary of Women's Biography.* New York: Continuum, 1982.

Veil, Simone. "Address by Her Excellency Simone Veil Minister of State, Minister of Social Affairs, Health and Urban Affairs." Address given October 26, 1993, before the 48th Session of the United Nations General Assembly.

Weitz, Margaret Collins. *Femmes: Recent Writings on French Women.* Boston: G. K. Hall, 1985.

Who's Who of American Women: 18th Edition 1993–1994. New Jersey: Reed Reference.

Woodworth, Paddy. "What the Arts Mean to Me: An Interview with Mary Robinson." *The Irish Times.* June 24, 1991.

Zucotti, Susan. *The Holocaust, the French and the Jews.* New York: Basic Books, 1993.

THE 30 PERCENT QUOTA LAW pp. 183–193

Amorós, Celia. *Hacia una Crítica de la Razón Patriarcal.* Barcelona: Anthropos, 1991.

Barrig, Maruja. "The Difficult Equilibrium between Bread and Roses: Women's Organizations and the Transitions from Dictatorship in Perú." In Jane Jaquette, comp. *The Women's Movement in Latin America: Feminism and the Transition to Democracy.* Boston: Unwin Hyman, 1989.

Bianchi, Susana, y Norma Sanchís. *El Partido Perónista Femenino.* Buenos Aires: Ceal, 1988.

Bonder, Gloria. "Las organizaciones de las mujeres en la Argentina y la transición a la democracia." In *Femmes et Contre-Pouvoirs.* Quebec: Editorial Boreal, 1987.

Braun, María. "Actitudes políticas de las mujeres en el Cono Sur." *Desarrollo Económico* 31, no. 124 (Jan.–March 1992).

Briones Veláustegui, Marena. "Redescubriendo el significado del poder." *Feminaria* 7 (1991).

Casas, Nelly. "Las listas de candidatos y las grandes ausencias." In *Compromiso Ser Mujer.* Buenos Aires: Peña Lillo, 1985, p. 65 (originally published in *Tiempo Argentino,* Sept. 10, 1983).

Chaney, Elsa. *Supermadre: La Mujer Dentro de la Politica de America Latina.* Mexico: Fondo de Cultura Economica, 1983.

Dos Santos, Mario. "La acción colectiva desafiada." *Iniciativas para el Desarrollo de Espacios Solidarios* 4 (Buenos Aires, s/f).

Elshtain, Jean B. "Mothers against the Authoritarian State." Speech presented at XV Congreso Mundial de la Asociación Internacional de Ciencias Políticas, Buenos Aires, 1991.

Feijoó, María del Carmen. "The Challenge of Constructing Civilian Peace: Women and Democracy in Argentina." In Jane Jaquette, comp. *The Women's Movement in Latin America,* op. cit.

Feijoó, María del Carmen, y Marcela Nari. "La modernización de la sociedad argentina: La participación socio-política de las mujeres durante el período 1950-1990." Informe Final Proyecto Investigación Anual, CONICET, 1994.

Geldstein, Rosa. "Aumentan los hogares sostenidos por mujeres." *Boletín del SIDEMA* 6 (CENEP, December 1992).

Gilligan, Carol. *In a Different Voice: Psychological Theory and Women's Development.* Cambridge, Mass.: Harvard University Press, 1982.

González Gass, Gabriela. "Después de la cuota, qué?" In *Cuota Mínima de Participación de Mujeres: El Debate en la Argentina.* Buenos Aires: Fundación Friedrich Ebert, 1992.

Ibarlucía, Blanca, Norma Sanchís, y Virginia Haurie, comp. *Argentina: Mujeres y Varones en la Crisis.* Buenos Aires: Ediciones Imago Mundi, 1990.

Jelín, Elizabeth. "Ciudadanía e identidad: Una reflexión final." In Elizabeth Jelín, comp. *Ciudadanía e Identidad: Las Mujeres en los Movimientos Sociales Latino-Americanos.* Geneva: UNRISD (Instituto de Investigaciones de las Naciones Unidas para el Desarrollo Social), 1987.

Laclau, Ernesto. *Política e Ideología en la Teoría Marxista: Capitalismo, Fascismo, y Populismo.* Madrid: Siglo XXI, 1986.

Lipszyc, Cecilia. "Podemos las mujeres transformar el sistema de poder?" In *Feminaria* 11 (1993).

Lipszyc, Cecilia. "Participación en el poder y facultades de decisión en los niveles económico, político, judicial y administrativo nacional." Informe Final Nacional, IV Conferencia Mundial sobre la Mujer, Buenos Aires, 1994.

Lubertino Beltrán, María José. "Historia de la Ley de Cuotas." In *Cuota Mínima de Participación de Mujeres,* op. cit.

MacKinnon, Catherine. "Feminism, Marxism, Method, and State: Towards Feminist Jurisprudence." *Signs* 8, no. 4 (1983).

Marx, Jutta. "Acerca del poder, la dominación y la violencia." *Feminaria* 5 (1990).

_____. *Mujeres y Partidos Políticos. De una Masiva Participación a una Escasa Representación. Un Estudio de Caso.* Buenos Aires: Legasa, 1992.

Marx, Jutta, y Ana Sampaolesi. "Elecciones internas bajo el cupo: la primera aplicación de la ley de cuotas en la Capital Federal." *Feminaria* 11 (1993).

Meyer, Birgit. "Las mujeres al poder!? Sobre la política del intervencionismo para cambiar la política." *Feminaria* 1 (1988).

Murmis, Miguel, y Juan Carlos Portantiero. *Estudios sobre los Orígenes del Peronismo.* Buenos Aires: Siglo XXI, 1987.

Navarro, Marysa. "Evita el peronismo y el feminismo." In Míguez, José, y F. Turner. *Racionalisdad del Peronismo.* Buenos Aires: Planeta, 1988.

Reynoso, Nené. "Ley de cupo: una prioridad del movimiento de mujeres." *Feminaria* 8 (1992).

Rich, Adrienne. *Nacida de Mujer.* Barcelona: Noguer, 1978.

Rossi, Laura. "Cómo pensar a las Madres de Plaza de Mayo?" *Fin de Siglo* 4 (Buenos Aires, October 1987).

Sampoalesi, Ana. "Desvelos en el quehacer político." *Feminaria* 11 (1993).

Schmukler, Beatriz. "Women in Social Democratization in the 1980s in Argentina." Speech presented at XV Congreso Mundial de la Asociación Internacional de Ciencias Políticas, Buenos Aires, 1991.

Taylor, Julie. *Evita Perón. Los Mitos de una Mujer.* Buenos Aires: Editorial Belgrano, 1981.

NOTES ON
CONTRIBUTORS

Alida Brill is a feminist activist and social critic who writes about women, culture, and politics. She is the coauthor of the award-winning book *Dimensions of Tolerance: What Americans Believe about Civil Liberties*. Brill has served on a variety of feminist boards of directors and committees and for several years was the program officer at the Russell Sage Foundation where she directed a national program of research on gender and institutions. She lectures widely on the problems of power and gender in America, especially as they relate to sexual and reproductive choice. The author of numerous essays, articles, and books, she most recently published *Nobody's Business: The Paradox of Privacy*.

❖ ❖ ❖

Diane Abbott currently serves in the British Parliament as a Labour Party MP. In 1987 she became the first black woman to be elected to the British Parliament. Abbott was the recipient of the Minister's Medal of Appreciation for her services to the island of Jamaica.

Bella Abzug is a former U.S. congresswoman and an attorney. Abzug cofounded Women Strike for Peace, the Women USA Fund, and the Women's Environment and Development Organization, of which she is currently cochairperson. Abzug headed the National Commission on the Observance of International Women's Year.

Marjorie Agosín is a poet, fiction writer, literary critic, and human rights activist. She has published seven collections of poetry, including *Happiness* (White Pine Press, 1993), *Dear Anne Frank* (bilingual, Azul Edition, 1994) and *A Cross and a Star: Memoirs of a Jewish Girl in Chile* (University of New Mexico Press, 1995). Agosín lived in Chile until 1973 and now teaches Spanish at Wellesley College in Massachusetts.

Ama Ata Aidoo is a prize-winning novelist, poet, and playwright from Ghana. In 1982 and 1983 she served as minister of education in Ghana and has taught in Ghana, Kenya, and the United States. Aidoo was the first recipient of the UNESCO-PEN Women's Committee Fellowship and received the Best Book in the Africa Division of the Commonwealth Writers' Prize in 1992 for her novel *Changes*. She currently teaches at Brandeis University.

Hanan Mikhail Ashwari is official spokesperson for the Palestinian delegation to the Middle East peace talks. Formerly a professor of English at Bir Zeit University (West Bank), she writes fiction and poetry and is currently working on her autobiography.

Ilana Bet-El is a historian and a lecturer at Tel Aviv University. She served in the United Nations as the Israeli representative to the Third Committee of the General Assembly. Bet-El is also cofounder and director of the Trento Group on Film and History. She has written numerous historical papers; *Experience into Identity: British Conscripts 1916–1918* (forthcoming); and "Real Men and Unknown Soldiers: British Men, Concepts of Masculinity and the Great War" in B. Melman, ed., *Gender in War and Peace* (forthcoming). She is currently taking up a senior position with UNPROFOR in Macedonia.

Ulrike Bode works as a freelance translator and editor in New York City. She cotranslated *Anarchism: Left, Right, and Green* (1994) and *China for Women* (1995) into English. She has begun graduate work in anthropology.

Gloria Bonder is secretary of state on women's issues and public policies in the Ministry of Education, Argentina, and the general coordinator of the National Program for Women's Educational Equal Opportunity in the Ministry of Culture and Education. Dr. Bonder is a psychologist and founder and former director of the first Center for Women's Studies in Argentina.

Isabel Crook, a Canadian, was born and raised in China. In 1947 she went to the Chinese Liberated Areas to study the Communist land reform. She taught English for over thirty years at the Beijing Foreign Studies University where she co-initiated the Women's Studies Forum in the mid-1980s. Together with her husband, David Crook, she has published *Revolution in A Chinese Village* (1959), *The First Years of Yangyi Commune* (1966), and *Ten Mile Inn: Mass Movement in a Chinese Village* (1979). She is completing a comprehensive study on a Chinese village.

Blaga Nikolova Dimitrova, former vice president of Bulgaria, is a poet and translator of poetry from the Slav languages, ancient Greek, French, and German. She is a recipient of the Lundqvist Prize of Sweden and the PEN Club Prize of Poland, and her books have been published in the United States, Great Britain, Russia, France, Germany, Poland, Hungary, Czechoslovakia, Belgium, Sweden, Denmark, Vietnam, Slovenia, and Croatia. Dimitrova is a member of the board of the "Clubs for Democracy" Federation and the Open Society Fund and president of the Free Poetic Society.

Rabab Hadi is cofounder of the Union of Palestinian Women's Associations in North America.

Janine Haines is an educator, author, and politician. Haines began her political career in 1977 after being chosen by the South Australian Parliament to fill a Senate casual vacancy and went on to be elected to three consecutive terms. In 1986 she was elected federal parliamentary leader of the Australian Democrats. Recently, Haines has focused on her writing. She was a member of the commonwealth election observer delegation to South Africa in 1994.

Rokeya Sakhawat Hossain (1880–1932) was born in what is now Bangladesh to a Muslim family. She wrote fiction and was a journalist and an activist against the tradition of purdah. Hossain established the Sakhawat Memorial Girls' School and founded the Bengali Muslim Women's Association.

Emiko Kaya has taught Japanese in the United States and currently teaches English at Tokyo Metropolitan Ueno Senior High School. In addition to contributing chapters to *Onna no me de miru: koza joseigaku 4 (Seeing through Women's Eyes: Lectures on Women's Studies,* vol. 4) and *Josei shakaigaku o mezashite (Toward a Sociology of Women),* she has translated into Japanese Susan J. Pharr's *Political Women in Japan* and the chapter by Carolyn W. Sherif, "Bias in Psychology," in *The Prism of Sex,* Julia A. Sherman and Evelyn Torton Beck, eds. She is also a cotranslator of Lillian B. Rubin's *Intimate Strangers.*

Radha Kumar, historian and political activist, is a distinguished scholar who has been extensively published. She has been the director of the Helsinki Citizens' Assembly, International Secretariat, Prague, and is associated with the Indian Forum for Women and Politics. She is currently an SSRC-MacArthur Fellow at the Institute of War and Peace Studies at Columbia University in New York City.

David Lauter is National Political Editor for the *Los Angeles Times* and has written about politics since 1979. Lauter has received several journalism awards, including the *Los Angeles Times* Editorial Award for sustained excellence in 1992.

Liu Dongxiao is a graduate student in law at Peking University and an active member of the China-Canada Young Women's Project, a bilateral initiative aimed at increasing the participation of young women in the 1995 UN Fourth World Conference on Women.

Wangari Maathai is the founder and coordinator of the Green Belt Movement. Educated in Kenya, the United States, and Germany, she was formerly associate professor of anatomy at the University of Nairobi, Kenya. Maathai received the Right Livelihood award for her endeavors through the Green Belt Movement to improve environmental conditions.

Rigoberta Menchú is a political activist and writer from Guatemala who received the Nobel Peace Prize in 1992.

Gertrude Mongella is secretary-general of the United Nations Fourth World Conference on Women. For many years a teacher and then a school inspector, her career in public life began in 1975 when she became a member of the East African Legislative Assembly. She has been minister of state responsible for women's affairs, minster of lands, natural resources, and tourism, and minister without portfolio in the president's office of Tanzania. Gertrude Mongella has also represented Tanzania on the UN's Commission on the Status of Women, at CEDAW hearings, and as a member of the Board of Trustees of INSTRAW.

Thenjiwe Mtintso was elected to the South African Parliament in 1994 following her service as gender department convenor, South African Communist Party. A member of several black organizations in South Africa in the 1970s, Mtintso was exiled from 1978 until 1991.

Marcela Nari, a historian, is currently a researcher in Women's History for the Interdisciplinary Women's Studies Group, Department of Philosophy and Literature, University of Buenos Aires.

Maria de Lourdes Pintasilgo became the first woman prime minister of Portugal in 1979, and has served in many government, cabinet, and international posts.

Lilly Rivlin, a seventh-generation Jerusalemite, is a filmmaker and writer. She has been involved in Israeli-Palestinian dialogue since 1967 and was an early proponent of Middle East peace. Most recently she has conducted sociodrama workshops, using the story of Sarah and Hagar to focus on reducing stereotypes and enabling conflict resolution from a feminist perspective. She has many film credits, as producer, director, writer, and researcher, including *Miriam's Daughters Now, The Tribe,* and *Pillars of Fire.* She has written and published widely on issues related to women and the Middle East. Her photographic book entitled *When Will the Fighting Stop? A Child's View of Jerusalem,* was published in 1991.

Hanna Beate Schoepp-Schilling was the first director general for the Department for Women's Affairs in the Federal Ministry of Youth, Family, Women, and Health, West Germany. She is currently the director of American Friends Service Committee Interkulturelle Begegnungen e.V. She also serves on the United Nations' Committee on the Elimination of Discrimination against Women. Dr. Schoepp-Schilling, an activist in the German and international women's movements, has lectured and published extensively on women's issues.

Hege Skjeie is a researcher at the Institute for Social Research in Oslo, Norway. Her current research is on national political leadership, focusing in particular on cabinet government. She has published on Nordic equal opportunity legislation and policies, trade union politics, and women's participation in national political elites. Among her articles in English are "The Rhetoric of Difference: On Women's Inclusion into Political Elites" in *Politics and Society* (1991), "The Uneven Advance of Norwegian Women" in *New Left Review* (1991), and "Ending the Male Political Hegemony: The Norwegian Experience" in *Gender and Party Politics,* Joni Lovenduski and Pippa Norris, eds. (1993).

Lisa Stearns, a U.S. citizen, left Columbia University in February 1990 to teach law at Peking University. Since September 1993, she has been a full-time consultant to the Ford Foundation, Beijing, on programming for the 1995 UN Fourth World Conference on Women.

Valentina Stoev is a journalist and writer whose work has been published in Bulgaria, Great Britain, Hungary, Italy, Russia, and the United States. She is the author of *From the Horse's Mouth,* life stories of young women workers, and was the researcher and interviewer for the film *Voices from a Forgotten Land,* a documentary for Belgian television about women in Bulgaria during the changes. Stoev was a cofounder of the Women's Studies Center at New Bulgarian University and is active in the Bulgarian Women's Union.

Marilyn Waring is a lecturer in the Department of Social Policy and Social Work at the Albany Campus of Massey University, Auckland, New Zealand, a national and international consultant, and a farmer. Her expertise in women's rights, politics, economics, and public administration has been employed by many organizations, including the United Nations Development Program (UNDP), the UN Food and Agriculture Organization, and the New Zealand Ministry of Women's Affairs. She is the author of numerous articles, papers, and books, including the best-selling *Counting for Nothing (If Women Counted)*. She is a co-chair of the Women's Environment and Development Organization (WEDO) and a contributor to and member of the international advisory board of *Ms.* magazine. Marilyn Waring was a member of the New Zealand Parliament from 1975 to 1984.

Wu Qing is a people's deputy to the Haidian District People's Congress and the Municipal People's Congress, Beijing. She is associate professor of English and American studies at the Beijing Foreign Studies University. She is also an adviser to the Global Fund for Women and numerous women's NGOs in China. Wu Qing lectures widely in North America, Europe, and Asia on issues relating to women in China, and has published several books on teaching English. She has been honored as a Fulbright Scholar, spent a year as a visiting scholar at MIT, and received many awards for her outstanding work as an educator.

PERMISSION
ACKNOWLEDGMENTS

Permission to reprint the following pieces is gratefully acknowledged:

Bella Abzug, "Martin, What Should I Do Now?", is reprinted by permssion of *Ms.* magazine, ©1990.

Rabab Hadi, "The Feminist behind the Spokeswoman," is reprinted by permssion of *Ms.* magazine, ©1992.

Emiko Kaya, "Mitsui Mariko: Feminist Assemblywoman," is an excerpt from "Mitsui Mariko: An Avowed Feminist Assemblywoman," in *Japanese Women: New Feminist Perspectives on the Past, Present, and Future,* Kumiko Fukimura-Fanselow and Atsuko Kameda, eds. (New York: The Feminist Press at CUNY, 1995). Reprinted by permission of the author and editors.

Rigoberta Menchú, "Guatemala: A Story of Tragedy and Promise," is reprinted by permission from *Guatemalan Women Speak,* by Margaret Hooks (Washington, D.C.: Ecumenical Program on Central America and the Caribbean [EPICA], 1991)

Maria de Lourdes Pintasilgo, "Portugal: Daring to Be Different," ©1994 by Robin Morgan, is from *Sisterhood Is Global: The International Women's Movement Anthology,* Robin Morgan, ed. Reprinted by permission of Edite Kroll Literary Agency.

Hege Skjeie, "From Movement to Government: Women's Political Integration in Norway," is adapted from the article by Hege Skjeie published in the September 1995 issue of *The UNESCO Courier,* Paris, France.

The Feminist Press at The City University of New York offers alternatives in education and in literature. Founded in 1970, this nonprofit, tax-exempt educational and publishing organization works to eliminate stereotypes in books and schools and to provide literature with a broad vision of human potential. The publishing program includes reprints of important works by women, feminist biographies of women, multicultural anthologies, a cross-cultural memoir series, and nonsexist children's books. Curricular materials, bibliographies, directories, and a quarterly journal provide information and support for students and teachers of women's studies. Through publications and projects, The Feminist Press contributes to the rediscovery of the history of women and the emergence of a more humane society.

New and Forthcoming Books

Always a Sister: The Feminism of Lillian D. Wald. A biography by Doris Groshen Daniels. $12.95 paper.

The Answer/La Respuesta (Including a Selection of Poems), by Sor Juana Inés de la Cruz. Critical edition and translation by Electa Arenal and Amanda Powell. $12.95 paper, $35.00 cloth.

Australia for Women: Travel and Culture, edited by Susan Hawthorne and Renate Klein. $17.95 paper.

Black and White Sat Down Together: The Reminiscences of an NAACP Founder, by Mary White Ovington. Edited and with a foreword by Ralph E.Luker. Afterword by Carolyn E. Wedin. $19.95 cloth.

Changing Lives: Life Stories of Asian Pioneers in Women's Studies, edited by the Committee on Women's Studies in Asia. Foreword by Florence Howe. Introduction by Malavika Karlekar and Barbara Lazarus. $10.95 paper, $29.95 cloth.

The Castle of Pictures and Other Stories: A Grandmother's Tales, Volume One, by George Sand. Edited and translated by Holly Erskine Hirko. Illustrated by Mary Warshaw. $9.95 paper, $23.95 cloth.

Challenging Racism and Sexism: Alternatives to Genetic Explanations (Genes and Gender VII). Edited by Ethel Tobach and Betty Rosoff. $14.95 paper, $35.00 cloth.

China for Women: Travel and Culture. $17.95 paper.

The Dragon and the Doctor, by Barbara Danish. $5.95 paper.

Japanese Women: New Feminist Perspectives on the Past, Present, and Future, edited by Kumiko Fujimura-Fanselow and Atsuko Kameda. $16.95 paper, $45.00 cloth.

Music and Women, by Sophie Drinker. Afterword by Ruth A. Solie. $16.95 paper, $45.00 cloth.

No Sweetness Here, by Ama Ata Aidoo. Afterword by Ketu Katrak. $10.95 paper, $29.00 cloth.

Seeds 2: Supporting Women's Work around the World, edited by Ann Leonard. Introduction by Martha Chen. Afterwords by Mayra Buvinic, Misrak Elias, Rounaq Jahan, Caroline Moser, and Kathleen Staudt. $12.95 paper, $35.00 cloth.

The Slate of Life: More Contemporary Stories by Women Writers of India, edited by Kali for Women. Introduction by Chandra Talpade Mohanty and Satya P. Mohanty. $12.95 paper, $35.00 cloth.

Solution Three, by Naomi Mitchison. Afterword by Susan Squier. $10.95 paper, $29.95 cloth.

Songs My Mother Taught Me: Stories, Plays, and Memoir, by Wakako Yamauchi. Edited and with an introduction by Garrett Hongo. Afterword by Valerie Miner. $14.95 paper, $35.00 cloth.

Streets: A Memoir of the Lower East Side. By Bella Spewack. Introduction by Ruth Limmer. Afterword by Lois Elias. $19.95 cloth.

Women of Color and the Multicultural Curriculum: Transforming the College Classroom, edited by Liza Fiol-Matta and Mariam K. Chamberlain. $18.95 paper, $35.00 cloth.

Prices subject to change. Individuals: Send check or money order (in U.S. dollars drawn on a U.S. bank) to The Feminist Press at The City University of New York, 311 East 94th Street, New York, NY 10128. Please include $4.00 postage and handling for the first book, $1.00 for each additional. For VISA/MasterCard orders call (212) 360-5794. Bookstores, libraries, wholesalers: Feminist Press titles are distributed to the trade by Consortium Book Sales and Distribution, (800) 283-3572.